THE
WHALEBOAT

A STUDY
OF DESIGN, CONSTRUCTION AND USE FROM
1850 TO 2014

by Willits D. Ansel

with Walter Ansel and Evelyn Ansel

Table of Contents

Mystic Seaport
75 Greenmanville Ave.
Mystic, CT 06355
www.mysticseaport.org

ISBN: 978-0-939511-38-9

First edition set in Baskerville and designed by
Behri P. Knauth and Benda Huffman
Additions to the third edition designed by
Trish LaPointe, tslapointedesign.com
Printed by GHP Media, ghpmedia.com

Publication of the first edition made possible with
funds from the Daniel W. Dietrich Foundation, Inc.
Publication of the third edition made possible by
the generosity of Peter Kellogg

Library of Congress Cataloging-in-Publication Data

Ansel, Willits Dyer,
    The whaleboat : a study of design, construction,
    and use from 1850 to 2014 / by Willits D. Ansel
    with Walter Ansel and Evelyn Ansel. – 3rd ed.--
    Mystic, CT : Mystic Seaport, c2014.
    p. : ill ; cm.

    Includes bibliography and index.
    ISBN 978-0-939511-38-9

    1. Whaleboats. I. Ansel, Walter. II. Ansel,
    Evelyn. III. Title.

GVM465 .A57 2014

Foreword

When I arrived at Mystic Seaport on April Fool's Day, 1969, to take charge of its watercraft collection as shipyard supervisor, the half-dozen decaying whaleboats lying in the grass where the Henry B. duPont Preservation Shipyard is now located were one of the first things I felt required attention. They needed either to live or to die with dignity. Very soon we'd taken care of them—with two or three placed inside as part of the Museum's permanent collection and others being donated to sister whaling institutions. We cut up the last one that was beyond redemption after cannibalizing what could be recycled.

The message from that experience was that Mystic Seaport had just run out of whaleboats for display aboard the *Charles W. Morgan* or to use for in-the-water demonstrations.

Will Ansel ended up solving the problem. Will showed up one day in response to an advertisement I'd placed for shipwrights. He was looking for a part-time job doing what he loved to do (i.e., build boats) in order to augment his primary livelihood of teaching. I hired him on the spot, and soon, working alone, he vigorously began attacking various projects that he and I thought needed doing. Within a year or two, part-time became full-time for Will.

Will produced amazingly fast results in creating new exhibits, building new replica boats, or restoring hurting old ones. I was amazed at his thoroughness and speed, and now, after more than four decades of knowing him, I continue to admire how much he can accomplish in an hour, a day, or a month. With his skill in turning out authentic replicas and restorations, coupled with his ability to research, sketch, and write, Will Ansel became Mystic Seaport's first true scholar-shipwight.

By the time Will retired from Mystic Seaport in 1989, he'd built some thirty historic replicas, including ten dories for the *L.A. Dunton*, two 38-foot seine boats for youngsters to row, and over a half dozen whaleboats. His first were of the Leonard model; then, after he and the Museum's naval architect, Bob Allyn, measured the Beetle whaleboat at The Mariners' Museum and Bob drew its plans, Will built three or four of that type. For a time, whaleboats became his life at Mystic Seaport because, in addition to building them, he went on to produce this book—perhaps the most comprehensive ever written on the subject. First published in 1978, it went through a second edition with few changes. Now, with renewed interest because of the *Charles W. Morgan*'s restoration, Will's book has emerged again, this time with input from his son Walt and from Walt's daughter Evelyn (Evie), both of whom carry on the scholar-shipwright role that Will Ansel initiated more than 40 years earlier. It's an amazing three-generation effort!

Walt, like his father Will before him, has had more than one stint at Mystic Seaport, beginning as a volunteer in the 1970s, and later as a skilled shipwright helping or leading restorations of such craft as *Roann, Sabino, Nellie,* and *Annie,* and helping to build the schooner *Amistad.* As I write this introduction, he's a key member of the crew that's restoring the *Morgan.*

Back in 2002, Walt persuaded his father Will to come back "just one more time" and share with him a whaleboat-building experience so that, by working together, and with Mark Starr shooting video, another new boat would emerge and the process would be permanently recorded. A decade later, in 2012, with this firsthand knowledge under his belt, Walt played coach to the nine different shops that were each building a new whaleboat for the *Charles W. Morgan*'s thirty-eighth voyage. Beyond that, because whaleboats will continue to be needed from time to time, the information within this book—and the full-scale drawings and the CD that the Museum has produced to accompany it—will find even more use in the years ahead.

Evie is the third generation of Ansels to become hooked on historic watercraft, and on whaleboats in particular. Christening (at age 13) the 2002 boat that her father and grandfather built got her started thinking about whaleboats. She went on to work at the Museum's Boathouse, where she taught rowing, and upon graduating from Brown University she worked for a year-and-a-half helping restore the *Morgan*. She's now in Sweden working to preserve the historic warship *Vasa*.

*****

Like a modern jetliner, the wooden whaleboat is a marvelous blend of form and function. She's just as long as the mother ship could accommodate when three of them were hoisted one behind the other. Length is a distinct advantage, since the longer the boat, the faster its speed under oars. Being narrow at the waterline makes for a fast boat as well, and this feature—together with generous beam at the rails to accommodate the longest possible oars—makes a whaleboat unusually swift. She's double-ended for seaworthiness, and when the wind serves and the mast is raised and the sail set, the oarsmen can save their strength for wrestling a whale later on.

Besides having a perfect form, whaleboats had to be light enough to hoist on davits, yet strong enough to occasionally fetch up against the whaler's hull in a heavy sea without damage. They were specially planked so as not to dry out while hoisted; otherwise, they'd leak in use. The combination of seam battens and plank laps achieved this, and resulted in boats that were smooth-skinned at the water plane for silent running—vital when within a whale's earshot.

These features and more made the whaleboat a highly sophisticated hunting implement of the nineteenth century, and one that, thanks to this book, can be understood and authentically replicated in the twenty-first.

Maynard Bray
Brooklin, Maine

Acknowledgments for the 1978 Edition

Many People have given their time, counsel, and encouragement in the course of this study. First, I thank former Shipyard Supervisor Maynard Bray and Curator J. Revell Carr at Mystic Seaport for their support. They gave me the rare opportunity to research the construction of whaleboats, and to have a hand in building two boats to text them and, finally, to write about them. It is an unusual museum, I believe, that would sponsor such a project.

The resources of Mystic Seaport's G. W. Blunt White Library were at my disposal for research, and the staff showed a great understanding as my papers expanded and spread from desk to desk. The late Marion V. Brewington, while director of the Kendall Whaling Museum, opened his museum to me, allowed me to measure the whaleboat in the collection, lent photographs and sailmaker's notebooks, and kindly gave me his time. Richard Kugler of the New Bedford Whaling Museum had the *Lagoda*'s boats lowered for measuring, and allowed me to examine the equipment in their model of a boatbuilder's shop and measure their Arctic and Azorean whaleboats. Mr. Kugler also made available whaleboat plans and bills for outfitting. He did a great service in giving the manuscript a careful, expert reading; his knowledge of terminology was particularly valuable. The thoughtful comments and notes of another reader, Erik A. R. Ronnberg, Jr., modelmaker and former assistant curator at the New Bedford Whaling Museum, also were a great help, as were his encouragement, insight, and advice in directing me to sources. John Gardner of Mystic Seaport also read the manuscript and gave me the benefit of his wide knowledge and seasoned judgment.

I am very grateful to the directors of the other museums whose boats I examined and measured.

Whaleboat crew drilling at Mystic Seaport. Photograph by Claire White, Mystic Seaport

Often the process required some shifting of boats and removal of gear, or opening up a building at odd hours. My thanks to William D. Wilkinson of the Mariners' Museum; Edouard A. Stackpole, historian of the Nantucket Whaling Museum; Dr. David Egan of the Cold Spring Harbor Whaling Museum; Everett T. Rattray of the East Hampton Town Marine Museum; and the staff of the Sag Harbor Whaling Museum.

The correspondence of Commander G. E. G. Mc-Kee of the National Maritime Museum in Greenwich, England, was of great help in referring me to English sources and in providing me with information on British Royal Navy whaleboats. R. Tual of the Musèe de la Marine in Paris is thanked for a photograph and description of French whaleboats. Captain David G. O'May of Tasmania provided me with photographs of a model of a whaleboat from there, and John R. Bockstoce gave valuable firsthand knowledge of the whaleboats still in use in Alaska. Herman W. Kitchen of New York gave me a showing of films of Azorean boats, and Peter Tripp of Stonington, Connecticut, lent me photographs of boats at Madeira and the Azores. John McVitty, also of Stonington, Connecticut, showed films and gave me the use of his notes, photographs, and measurements of whaleboats from Bequia. The administrator of Tristan da Cunha, J. I. H. Fleming, circulated my queries among the coxwains of the longboats of that island and even went on the Tristan radio to seek information.

I am particularly grateful to Leo Telesmanick of South Dartmouth, Massachusetts, for advice on whaleboat construction. Twice he came to Mystic Seaport for a day and worked beside us. John Bauman, grandson of Charles Beetle, provided photographs, gave his time, and lent tracings of molds used to make the Beetle boats. Harold Beetle, son of Charles, lent many photographs and one of his father's manuscripts.

George H. Hodgdon of East Boothbay, Maine, lent the William Hand whaleboat plans, and from these three boats were built at Mystic Seaport. I thank Thomas Adams of the John Carter Brown Library at Brown University for showing me sailmakers' plans. Robert Allyn, N.A., made the plans of the Mariners' Museum's Beetle whaleboat, and checked and redrew my rough drawings of lines that appear in the appendix.

Willits D. Ansel

Acknowledgments for the 2014 Edition

With the re-issue of *The Whaleboat*, Evelyn and I would like to recognize and thank folks who have supported and helped us in this venture. Thank you to Willits, who has obviously given his blessings and countless hours of advice and council, even to relatives!

At Mystic Seaport, we thank Steve White and Matthew Stackpole, whose unstinting support of the National Whaleboat Project and the *Charles W. Morgan* restoration has inspired us all. And thanks to the stalwart duPont Preservation Shipyard crew who let us work on the book when we should have been caulking or spiling to get the *Morgan* ready: Dana Hewson, Quentin Snediker, and Rob Whalen.

We thank our ever-capable editors Maynard Bray, Bill Sauerbrey, and Andy German; also our producer Mary Anne Stets and designer Trish LaPointe. And thank you to Carol Ansel for patient technical support.

Finally, we give our sincere thanks to all the builders of the ten beautiful new whaleboats for the *Morgan*'s thirty-eighth voyage—she will be a complete ship when she sails.

Walter Ansel

Introduction

The term "whaleboat" properly describes boats used for hunting whales, although it has also been applied to other boats having some similar features, generally sharp ends. Whaleboats were used by the thousands aboard American whaleships in the middle of the nineteenth century and, in lesser numbers, aboard the vessels of other nations and at shore stations around the world. The whaleboat was a double-ended, light, open boat with a length at that time of between twenty-seven and thirty-one feet and a beam of slightly more than one-fifth the length. It was pulled with oars and sailed. It was a fine sea boat, not only well adapted to its function but also handsome. Though there were variations in size, lines, and construction, the general characteristics were well defined.

The whaleboat was once the most widespread of all small craft. In the late 1800s it was known in the Pacific in such widely separated places as Easter Island, Tasmania, the Bonin Islands, and the Aleutians. In the Atlantic, it appeared in the north off Greenland, in the Azores, the Grenadines, and south to Tristan da Cunha and still farther south to Antarctica. In the Indian Ocean it was seen in the Mozambique Channel, Kerguelen Island, and Cocos. It was used in the Arctic Ocean at Herschell Island on one side and Spitzbergen on the other. Whaleboats were seen in the most remote places in the sea.

The last voyage of a whaleship that carried whaleboats was in the 1920s. At a few far-scattered places the boats continued to be used for shore whaling, as at Tonga and Norfolk Island in the Pacific and at Bequia and the Portuguese Islands in the Atlantic. Two whaleboats are still maintained at Bequia, and whaling continues on Pico and Madeira. In 1969 there was whaling at Fiji.

Towing the whaleship was sometimes a task for whaleboats. These boats from the schooner ERA *were also used as shelters for the crew when the ship wintered in Hudson Bay. A framework with canvas cover was built over each boat.*

1

Elsewhere on remote islands the type survived for carrying cargo and passengers.

In the United States, where the whaleboat was carried to its final stage of development and where the boats were built by the thousands, very few remain outside of museums, although an undetermined number survive in Alaska.

Much has been written in praise of whaleboats:

Their shape "ensures great swiftness as well as qualities of an excellent seaboat."[1]

The boats were dry and rode "as gracefully as an albatross . . . for lightness and form, for carrying capacity compared with its weight and sea-going qualities, for speed and facility of movement at the word of command, for the placing of men at the best advantage in the exercise of their power, by the nicest adaptation of the varying length of the oar to its position in the boat, and lastly, for a simplicity of construction which renders repairs practicable on board ships, the whaleboat is simply as perfect as the combined skill" of generations of boatbuilders could make it.[2]

As surf boats, whaleboats were "without rival, better than a lifeboat which is a compromise because it has to carry a larger number of people . . . The whaleboat was the best seaboat that man could devise with no limits to size, weight, or model."[3] A whaleboat type, locally called a longboat, was adapted on Tristan da Cunha around 1886, after fifteen men were lost in a lifeboat. The longboat coxswains consider their light, canvas-covered boats fine surf boats.[4]

Howard Chapelle cites the whaleboat's reputation for good performance under oars and sail under all conditions.[5] Others noted their maneuverability and speed and, last but not least, the cheapness of their construction.

Such praise was deserved. However, the whaleboat was the product of compromises, too, and was excelled in some functions by specialized boats. There were faster pulling boats, such as certain ones used in nineteenth-century smuggling in southern England, and certainly some lifesaving boats were safer in surf or a breaking sea. In terms of all-around performance, however, the whaleboat rated very high.

The structural design of the whaleboat was well suited to its function. Whaleboats were very lightly, though strongly built. Lightness was necessary because they had to be hoisted aboard the whaleship or launched and beached in the case of shore whaling. A twenty-eight foot boat weighed about 1,000 pounds without men or equipment. The boat had to be strong because of the racking strains of being towed by the whale or being lowered and raised in the davits in all weather. This successful combination of lightness and strength was a noteworthy feature. The boats lowered and attacked whales in the open sea, and often the pursuit and killing lasted hours. Another achievement of the builders was a design that was extremely seaworthy but still easily driven without the exhaustion of the crew.

Around whaling ports the production of whaleboats was a minor industry. In some shops they were built with incredible speed, with standard parts and assembly line techniques. The design itself was suited to fast construction: plank lines were easy, stem and stern timbers were bent on the same form, and frames were bent to the same curvature. Speed of building was a matter of economics.

Simplicity and utility in rigging and fitting out were other characteristics. Though there was considerable variety, rigs were invariably stripped to basics. One sail plan and rig for a gaff main and jib with a total of 340 square feet of sail had no blocks and only one sheave in the entire rig. Simplicity is another lesson of the whaleboat.

While the boats were specialized for the capture of whales, not all whaling was carried on under the same conditions; hence boats varied in hull design and rig to meet the differing conditions. Arctic boats in the bowhead fishery were generally different from those in the sperm fishery. Boats used in shore whaling were often longer than those carried aboard ship. Almost all reasonable sailing rigs were used. Sail areas ranged from the diminutive sprit-sail of the shore whalers of Long Island in the 1890s to the seemingly overcanvassed boats found in the Azores today. Variety in types of rigs included sloops with gaff, leg-of-mutton, sprit, and lug sails. Some used in naval service were ketch-rigged. Whaleboat rigs reflect many experiments and adaptations to a variety of conditions.

The emphasis in design was always on whaling, but the boats were successfully put to many other uses as well. Whalemen used them like any other ship's boat for carrying liberty parties, provisioning, and towing water casks out to the ship. A certain Captain Bodfish once watered his vessel by pulling two whaleboats up a river into fresh water, swamping one, and towing it down and out to the ship with the other boat. There he filled his tanks from the swamped boat. The boats could tow the whaleship out of harbor and, if disaster befell the ship, serve as lifeboats. Among the longest and most harrowing voyages were those of the *Essex*'s boats, two of which sailed over two thousand miles after their ship was stove in by a whale. The greatest rescue was that of the crews of the ice-beset ships in 1871: 1,200 people were saved without loss of life. Some sailors used whaleboats as a means of deserting their ship, a case in literature being Melville's *Omoo*.

Others besides men in whaling used the boats. Traders south of the Line carried them for landing through the surf. Whaleboats built by Charles Beetle of New Bedford were ordered by Perry, Greeley, and MacMillan for Arctic exploration, and one lone voyager, a Captain Crapo, chose a modified whaleboat for an early trans-Atlantic crossing. In the early years of this century, when whaling was dying, Charles Beetle sold reconditioned New Bedford whaleboats to merchantmen for use as lifeboats, and also built smaller whaleboat-like boats for lifeboats.

Why did the whaleboat not survive? Reginald Hegarty's reasons are these:

> Although for their size and usefulness, whaleboats were the lightest, weakest, and cheapest to build, they nevertheless were the most efficient ever built. They were well-suited for their work or there would have been many radical changes through the years. These boats seemed to have attained their degree of perfection very early in the history of New England whaling since they remained practically unchanged for generations. While they were perfect for whaling, they were almost useless for anything else—too large for rowboats and, although fitted with centerboards, which came into general use about 1850, they were poor sailers close-hauled.
>
> One must remember that the whaleboat, like the whaleship, was constructed for a specific purpose. . .[6]

Undoubtedly, whaleboat influence is reflected in surviving boats of some remote islands, particularly where the boat must pass through surf and be beached, but these boats will have their unique characteristics. The Pitcairn Islander's long boat has some features in common with the whaleboat, but

December   *1855*

9th Sunday. At 6 A.M. raised whales and lowered
₊36°51′ without success — at 9 A.M. lowered the quarter
W 10°53′ boats again for a right whale. And Mr Ben

and the boat you get but little encourag
from the other whalemen! Keep your weather
eye open for a fighter my boy—then
blaze away your popping things

ABOVE: *Going on under oars. The approach is head
to head. Depending on wind and sea conditions,
course and speed of the whales, their distance
and direction; the mate in charge of the boat will
use sails, oars, or paddles and will go on head to
head or range up the whale's quarter. In the Weir
drawings, head to head approaches are under oars
and quarter attacks under sail and paddle. Sketch
from Robert Weir's Journal, 1855.*

LEFT: *An approach on the whale's quarter, a
blind sector in his vision, under sail and
paddles. The boatsteerer's knee is jammed
in the clumsy cleat and he is about to dart
the first of his live irons. The second
iron is ready in the harpoon crotch. Robert
Weir's Journal.*

May- 1856

Going on to a whale.   Sperm whales

25th Sunday - Saw a school of sperm whales last

57   December

25th Friday - 1 p.m. Mr Whale secure alongside; saw

ABOVE: A drawing from the journal of Robert Weir, 1856. The whaleboat is approaching from behind with spritsail set. Undisturbed whales moved at speeds of three to four knots. The sail appears to be near luffing and the wind is light; oars are peaked and the men are paddling for a quiet approach. The boatsteerer is poised in the bow and the mate or boatheader is at the steering oar. This kind of sailing on whales was a fairly new technique in 1856.

LEFT: Sailing on the whale from astern. The boatsteerer is darting the second iron. The first iron is fast, darted an instant before; the whale is raising his flukes under the boat. The drawing illustrates the confusion in a boat at such moments. Robert Weir's Journal.

5

it is considerably longer because of the need for greater cargo capacity. The native of Tristan da Cunha makes his boat of canvas, and the Eskimo, who still has original whaleboats, prefers his skin boat.* The boats in Bequia, though they have the standard whaleboat fittings, are far different in lines and hull construction. The whaleboat used as a work boat on Cocos Island in the Indian Ocean retains many whaleboat features but has developed its own peculiar characteristics. The Azorean boat is the closest foreign survivor, though it, too, has significant differences.

The whaleboat disappeared first in the country that did so much to develop it**It became extinct for practical reasons connected with a changing technology. The reasons for the boats' success in their day, however, merit review. Their success resulted from observing principles and practices in design and construction that have continuing importance. It is the purpose of this study to describe these principles as they relate to function. Though there are references and comparisons with foreign and earlier whaleboats, the focus is on the American whaleboat of the late nineteenth and early twentieth century. I have included a brief survey of earlier development of the whaleboat in Chapter I.

* The Alaskan Eskimo's umiak is lighter, has greater capacity, is more seaworthy in the chop found in the open water between ice flows, is more easily repaired and, overturned on shore, is more suitable as a shelter. The whaleboat's only advantage is that it is faster under sail. Information supplied in 1973 by J. R. Bockstoce, who has used both whaleboats and umiaks.

** The name "whaleboat" was sometimes applied to surf boats, as in Marblehead where the Massachusetts Humane Society surf boat was so-called. Today the U.S. Navy's twenty-six-foot double-ended, engine-powered boat carried aboard many ships is called a whaleboat, though it has evolved far from the ancestral type and is now fiberglass.

Such background was made particularly necessary by the death of Charles Batchelder, who had long been gathering material for a comprehensive work on the earlier history of the boats.

In collecting information for this study, written sources were used and boats in a number of museums were examined and their lines taken off. Practical experience came from the building of whaleboats of two designs and the testing of these boats in the waters around Mystic, Connecticut.

1. Charles M. Scammon, *The Marine Mammals of the Northwestern Coast of North American and the American Whale Fishery*, rev. ed. (Riverside: Manessier Publishing Co., 1969), p. 224.

2. William Davis, *Nimrods of the Sea*, rev. ed. (North Quincy: The Christopher Publishing House, 1972), pp. 157-58.

3. Clifford W. Ashley, *The Yankee Whaler*, (Garden City: Halcyon House, 1942), p. 59.

4. Notes on the Tristan da Cunha boats were provided by the island's administrator, J. I. H. Fleming, in 1973.

5. Howard I. Chapelle, *The National Watercraft Collection*, (Washington, D.C., Government Printing Office, 1960), p. 262.

6. Reginald B. Hegarty, *Birth of a Whaleship*, (New Bedford: Free Public Library of New Bedford, 1954), pp. 135-36.

Chapter I

DEVELOPMENT OF THE WHALEBOAT TO 1870

The whaleboat is old. It evolved gradually until by the 1870s it had become a craft highly adapted to its primary task of hunting whales. This much is generally agreed upon, but there are questions about its remote origins and the sources and importance of the influences that affected its development.

Some believe that Americans or New Englanders were primarily responsible for the boat's development. The term "New Bedford whaleboat" implies a boat unique to that whaling center. While Americans and particularly the builders of the New Bedford area made many contributions to the boats of the 1870s, Europeans long ago had whaleboats with many of the features found in the ultimate boat of the nineteenth century. In its use the boat was not restricted to men of any single country, and in its development builders of a number of countries appear to have made contributions over a long period of time.

The origins of the whaleboat,* according to British writers, are Norse.[1] The ninth century Norwegians were the first Europeans to have a record of whaling, and some boats of the Shetlands and Norway still bear a marked resemblance to the whaleboat. Basques or Viscayans were whaling off Greenland and Iceland in the fifteenth century and, if they had not developed a whaleboat independently, they would have had opportunities to borrow the boats of the Norwegians. A seal dated 1335 of Fuenterrabia, a town in the Basque region of Spain, depicts a whaling scene. Four men are

* Smythe, in writing of the sixern, the six-oared boat of the Shetlands, points out they were "not unlike the Dundee whaler." The Norwegian Brevik Skiff and Arenda yawl also have strong resemblance to whaleboats. These boats were nineteenth-century descendants of early Norse vessels. Chatterton states that the design of whaleboats can be traced to early Viking craft.

The Seal (ca. 1335) of the town of Fuenterrabia in the Basque region of Spain. The whaleboat is lapstrake, double-ended, with a steering oar on the port side. Note the drogue on the whale line. Courtesy of Service Photographique des Archives Nationales de France.

shown in a double-ended, lapstrake boat with strong sheer and raking ends. One man is at the steering oar and another has thrown the harpoon from the bow, while two men pull at the oars.

The Basques taught whaling to the Dutch and English, and later to the Germans. Writings of the early 1600s describe techniques of whaling and equipment used which changed little in the following centuries. The whale was harpooned from the boat. The line, of 300 fathoms, was the same length as that used in New Bedford whaleboats three centuries later. It was played from the boat; if the whale took all the line, the end was passed to another boat, which bent on its line. When the whale tired, the boat was pulled up alongside and the whale was lanced. The boat's crew was six men: "harpeneir," "steersman," and four oarsmen. The titles were to change, but the crew is the same number carried in the New Bedford whaleboats. In the New Bedford boat the "boatsteerer" darted the harpoon or iron, and then went aft to steer the boat, while the mate, the senior man in the boat, killed the whale. The mate was sometimes known as the "boatheader." Hakluyt, writing of whaling in 1575, says that there should be five "pinnases" on each ship. Purchas in 1613 refers to the boats as "shallops." He notes that during the lancing, the whale "friskes and strikes with his tayle so forcibly, that many times when he hitteth a shallop hee splitteth her in pieces."[2]

By 1630, each whaleship carried at least three boats, and some carried six or seven. There is little information about the boats themselves, but with the methods so developed and with the large number of boats carried, it is reasonable to assume the boats were a special type rather than ordinary ship's boats fitted out for whale hunting.

The drawings of the boats in whaling scenes of

the 1600s tend to be either fanciful or stylized and are of little help in presenting realistic pictures. An engraving of 1711 shows the Dutch boats used off Greenland: they appear to be double-ended and steered with an oar. The bows are painted white, a practice that continued into the 1800s. Six men man the boat. A British illustration of a scene in the 1720s clearly shows single-banked oars and a steering oar. The boats are double-ended and of lapstrake construction. Bow and stern have great flare, making ends that are fine at the waterline and full at the rail. They have "bollards"—the "loggerhead" of later American boats—and a Dutch description speaks of the necessity of wetting the line, something no writer on whaling for the next two centuries fails to mention. He speaks of the extra line in the bow—the "voorganger" of about five fathoms—which connected the harpoon to the whale line. Such a length of line is still found coiled in the warp boxes of Azorean whaleboats today to give slack when the iron is darted.

Whaling by Europeans in America, except for an early Dutch attempt on Delaware Bay, began before the middle of the seventeenth century with the trying out of blubber from dead whales washed ashore on Long Island and the beaches of New England. Shore whaling followed. The English colonists used Indian harpooners as the English earlier had used Basques. The boats used in American shore whaling were probably small and light. Henry Hall, writing of them in 1882, says they were shallops "built after the fashion of ships' boats, but sharper"—in short, the shallop was lengthened and made narrower. He believed that by 1700 the boat had "reached nearly the form it keeps today." By the time of the Revolutionary War, he writes, it was a large double-ender, famous for its speed, lightness, and capacity. Hall provides

a cut of the profile of a whaleboat of 1789 that shows a double-ended boat quite similar to a boat of one hundred years later except for a skeg and greater freeboard. He makes no mention of any possible influence of European whaleboats on American boats.[3]

In 1725, Paul Dudley described the boats used in Nantucket for shore whaling. They were made of cedar planks, "clapboards," and were so light two men could carry one.[4] The boats were twenty feet long and carried six men: a harpooner, four oarsmen, and the steersman.* The boats "run very swift and by reason of their lightness can be brought on and off (the whale) and so kept out of danger."

The legend has persisted that New Bedford whaleboats evolved from or were strongly influenced by American Indian canoes. This was perhaps based on these common features: lightness in construction, double-ended hulls, flat floors, and little flare in the sections, the sides having a uniform curve without the flatness of ships' boats of the eighteenth century. Also Indians were shore whaling and porpoise-hunting in ocean canoes when the colonists arrived; this experience led to their being employed later as harpooners. It is known that Englishmen, beginning with George Weymouth in 1603, were impressed with the speed of bark canoes seen in Penobscot Bay, and while the English colonists adapted the dugout as a means of transportation in the Chesapeake, both the French and English used the bark canoes in the fur trade in the Northwest.

* This statement, and others, about the lightness of the boats led to the weighing of a twenty-eight foot boat in 1960. It weighed about 1,000 pounds. The boat described by Dudley, though only twenty feet long, must have been of very light construction.

9

It is possible that the colonists, who were familiar with double-ended boats in Europe, and probably those used in whaling, may have been inspired to build their boats with thin planking and light "basket construction" after seeing the canoes perform, but proving such influence is very difficult. With respect to another native craft, the Eskimo umiak, Chapelle warns against seeing whaleboat influence and vice versa:

> Despite the resemblance of this type of umiak to the whaleboat, it is highly doubtful that its model was influenced by the white man's boat. In fact, it might just as well be claimed that since the whaleboat appears to have been first employed in the early Greenland whale fishery, the latter had been influenced by the umiaks found in that area. However, one might also point to the fact that the model of an early European whaleboat is much like that of a Viking boat, from which will be seen the danger in accepting chance similarities in form or detail as evidence of relationship, particularly when it is not impossible that the similarities in use and their requirements have produced similar boat types. . . .[5]

The question of influence, either of Indian canoes upon American whaleboats, or European whaleboats on American, or even American whaleboats on European, later becomes speculative, particularly because so little is known at this time about the early American boats.*

* One view holds that the whaleboat, as a distinct type of boat for a specific service, was a unique American development of 200 years. It is my opinion that while Americans pioneered sperm whaling and there were some differences in the techniques and equipment, including boats, of that fishery compared to the earlier Greenland whaling, the similarities are more impressive than the differences.

There are references to American whaleboats in reports on the colonial wars against the French in Canada—perhaps some still lie on the lake bottoms with the bateaux found on Lake Champlain by divers. In the American Revolution they were used for raids along the shores of Long Island Sound:

> The whaleboats were sharp at each end, the sheathing often not over half an inch thick, and so light as to be easily carried on men's shoulders either to be hid in the bushes or relaunched in the South Bay. Some were thirty-two feet long, and impelled by from eight to twenty oars, and would shoot ahead of an ordinary boat with great velocity, and leave their pursuers far behind.[6]

These were reported to carry fifteen or sixteen men with equipment, which is far more than could be crammed into a whaleboat of ordinary dimensions. The term may then have been used in a broad sense for any light, double-ended, open boat resembling the boat used for whaling.

The record of English whaleboats is more complete. An engraving published in 1754 in London shows boats with fine ends and sharply raking bows and sterns which resemble the boats of a century later. The first actual lines were drawn by Fredrik Henrik Chapman. He shows a Greenland whaleboat or "pinace" of the 1760s, twenty-four feet six inches long and five feet three inches in beam. She is double-ended and the keel has a strong rocker. The entrance is fuller than the run; the midships sections are quite similar to boats of the late nineteenth century. The construction of stem, stern post, keel, and knees appears very heavy; steamed members in whaleboat construction came later. The boat has a box in the bow, thwarts for six oarsmen, and cuddy boards aft. No bow chocks are visible.

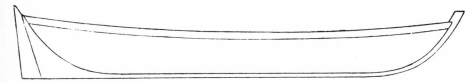

American whaleboat (1789). Note skeg with rudder. Except for boats for the naval service, skegs were not found on whaleboats in the nineteenth century. From Henry Hall, REPORT ON THE SHIPBUILDING INDUSTRY OF THE UNITED STATES, *1882.*

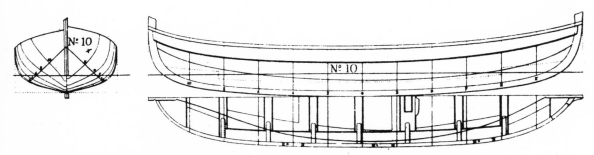

Greenland pinnace for the whale fishery (ca. 1760). In plan view it has straighter sides and fuller ends than American boats of a century later. Length, 24' 6'', beam 5' 3''. Plate L. ARCHITECTURA NAVALIS MERCATORIA *by Fredrik Henrik Chapman.*

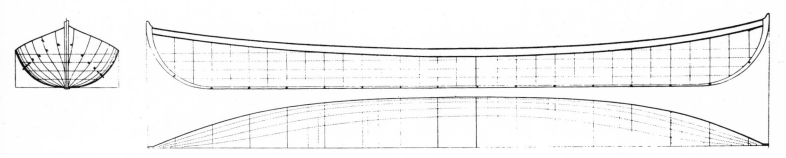

English whaleboat (ca. 1800). The lines show a long, narrow, slack-bilged boat. Length 32' 9''; beam 5' 6''. From David Steel, NAVAL ARCHITECTURE, *1805 ed.*

American whaleboat (1835). The boatheader leans across the thigh board as he lances the whale. The boatsteerer aft at the steering oar and the men at the pulling oars maneuver to keep the boat in position. They are ready to stern with the oars to avoid the whale in its flurry. The boats are the older lapstrake model. Aquatint by William Page from sketch by C. B. Hulsart, courtesy of Kendall Whaling Museum.

British whaleboats in Greenland (ca. 1781). The boats resemble the boat in the plans by Fredrik Henrik Chapman. Etching by Robert Dodd, courtesy of Kendall Whaling Museum.

The next set of lines of a whaleboat was published by David Steele in 1805. This thirty-two foot nine inch boat is quite different from Chapman's, showing a boat with a beam of only five feet six inches and very slack bilges. The depth is only eighteen and a half inches. The keel has no rocker, in contrast to Chapman's lines. She must have been fast under oars, but does not appear to have been a good boat for rough waters.[7]

Some British boats of this period had transom sterns. An engraving in W. Scoresby (1820) shows a boat with a small transom, and boats from Scotland continued to be built with this feature. The transom in some whaleboats is worth noting, as the double-ended hull is often considered the salient feature of the whaleboat.

Scoresby provides the best description of the Greenland boats used by the English. They were fast under oars, maneuverable, light, safe, and good sea boats. They carried six or seven men and seven or eight hundred pounds of gear. "Firboards" one-half to three-quarters of an inch thick, were used for planking. He writes that they were carvel-built for ease of repairs, though many illustrations appear to show lapstrake boats. Length of the boats was twenty-three feet to twenty-eight feet and beam five feet three inches to five feet nine inches. Greatest beam was forward of the center. Bow and stern were sharp in profile and the stern had greater rake. The keel had a deeper portion in the middle to act as a pivot in turning. Scoresby also notes that boats and techniques in the Greenland fishery were much the same as among the whale fishermen of various other nationalities.

Information about American whaleboats from the 1830s on comes through illustrations, descriptions, bills for outfitting, and models. From the illustrations, the boats used in sperm whaling in the 1830s and 1840s were light, shallow, lapstrake, double-ended boats with strong sheer and raking ends. Forward they had bow chocks, warp box, and thigh board with clumsy cleat. There were five thwarts for the men pulling the long, single-banked oars, three on the starboard and two on the port side. Aft was the cuddy board and loggerhead, which tended to rake aft in earlier boats. The steering oar was on the port side of the stern post. Judging from illustrations, there was general similarity between whaleboats used by English, French, and Americans except for the transom stern in some English boats. There are no accurate plans or lines of American boats until those of William Hand, drawn in the 1890s.

No descriptions or illustrations prior to 1825 give evidence of sails being used on whaleboats. The first sails appear in illustrations of scenes in sperm whaling by Americans. Rudders, centerboards, hinged mast steps, and a variety of rigs were quickly developed, and with the use of sails came new techniques in attacking whales.*

Modifications in construction and hull form were made between 1830 and 1860, with many of the innovations first appearing in American whaleboats. Batten seams, closer frame spacing, and the use of steamed frames, thwart knees, and stem and stern posts were new methods of construction. The boats became beamier to make them stiffer under sail, and on the average, they were longer. Sheer was reduced, forward sections be-

came fuller, and in some the turn of the bilge became harder.

By the 1870s the whaleboat as used aboard whaleships had reached its final development. In the forty years left to traditional whaling the sailing rig changed in style, but there were no substantial modifications in the boats, their fittings, or equipment.*

* The whaleboat has continued to develop in the hands of the shore whalers of the Azores and Madeira, but is now quite different in lines and construction from its ancestor, the New Bedford boat.

1. Herbert Warrington Smythe, *Mast and Sail in Europe and Asia* (New York: E. P. Dutton & Co., 1906), pp. 113-14.

Edward Keble Chatterton, *Whalers and Whaling* (London: T.F. Unwin, Ltd., 1925), p. 39.

2. Samuel B. D. Purchas, *Hakluytus Post Humus or Purchas His Pilgrimes* (Glasgow: James MacLehose & Son, 1907), vol. 8, p. 27.

3. Henry Hall, *Report on the Shipbuilding Industry of the United States,* 1882, 10th Census, vol. 8, p. 23.

4. The Hon. Paul Dudley, Chief Justice of Massachusetts, *An Essay upon the Natural History of Whales.* Transactions, Philosophical Society of London, vol. 3, 1725.

5. Edwin Tappan Adney and Howard I. Chapelle, *The Bark Canoes and Skin Boats of North America.* (Washington: Government Printing Office, 1964), pp. 187-88.

6. Henry Onderdonk, Jr., *Revolutionary Incidents of Queens County,* 1846, p. 250.

7. David Steel, *Elements and Practices of Naval Architecture,* (London: C. Whittingham, 1805), plate 31.

* The early Spitzbergen and Greenland whaling was carried on in near ice, and oars were the safest and most practical. Sperm whaling developed later in open water: sails were first used in that fishery. American whalers continued to use sails when their whaling took them into the Arctic.

Chapter II

PERFORMANCE
AND USE

Function rigorously determined design in the whaleboat of 1870. The boats aboard whaleships were unnamed, unadorned, and considered expendable.* It is true that the captains and mates each had their boats and the mates sometimes had a say in the choice of a builder. Boatsteerers were responsible for the readiness and maintenance of their boat, and mates for the training of the crew, in which they took pride, but their interest in the boat tended to be practical. Whaleboats were utilitarian craft; nothing about lines, rig, construction, or fittings was for show or without purpose. To understand their design, one must examine the use to which they were put.

On sighting a whale and on the order of the captain to lower, the boat's crew—mate in charge, boatsteerer, and four oarsmen—ran to the davits, lifted the line tubs into the boat, put in the plug, threw off the gripes and gig tackle, raised the boat enough to swing in the cranes that supported the keel, and then lowered. Mate and boatsteerer went down in the boat, the former in the stern, the latter in the bow; the men came down after it was waterborne, scrambling down the chains and over the channels. Davit tackles were cast off as oars were shipped and the boat shoved off. One English writer said that two boats could be pulling away from the side of the ship one minute after sighting a whale.[1]

Lowering in rough seas was routine. Joseph Conrad in *Last Essays* describes meeting a whaleship in the wastes of the Southern Ocean on Christmas Day, 1879. A keg full of newspapers was thrown overboard as a present.

---

* The boats of the Bark *Esquimaux* (c. 1840) were exceptions. Her log has a drawing of a whaleboat with the name *Osprey* on the quarter. Boats used in shore whaling lasted longer, were named, and were often painted up.

What appears to be a crack racing crew. Fairhaven, Massachusetts, in the background. Courtesy of Kendall Whaling Museum.

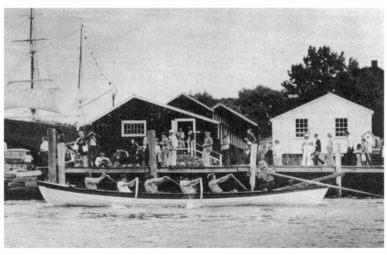

Whaleboat races at Mystic Seaport. Photograph by Claire L. White, Mystic Seaport.

16

I never saw anything so ready and so smart as the way that whaler, rolling desperately all the time, lowered one of her boats. The Southern Ocean went on tossing the two ships like a juggler his gilt balls, and the microscopic white speck of the boat seemed to come into the game instantly, as if shot out from a catapult on the enormous and lonely stage. That Yankee whaler lost not a moment in picking up her Christmas present from the English wool clipper.[2]

Once under way, the oars were immediately "lined"—that is, the whale line or warp was led out of the larger after tub, back around the loggerhead, forward over the oars, through the bow chocks, under the pin, back to the box for several coils of four or five fathoms (the "stray line"), and then to the "live" irons in the crotch on the starboard side.

Away from the side of the ship, the boat might raise the mast.* Going on the whale under sail was the preferred way, particularly if the whale was to leeward and the boat could run down on it. Oars were used if the whale was to windward, and paddles, because of their silence, in light airs and if the speed under sail dropped below three knots. Sometimes sails and paddles were used together.

An undisturbed sperm whale moves along at three to four knots. The approach must be made as quietly as possible to avoid "gallying" or frightening it. "Sailing on" became increasingly the rule after 1850. In 1880, Henry Hall noted that whales

* If a sea was running, it was no easy matter to raise a mast which might be twenty-four feet tall, four and one-half inches in diameter for most of its length, and with shrouds and halyards, weigh eighty pounds. A crew at Mystic Seaport practiced raising and lowering a whaleboat's mast. The sea was calm and the wind light during our drills; the operation won respect for the men who used to do it in blowing weather.

had become shy and were easily gallied by oars; sailing on therefore was more successful.[3] A whaling captain in the bowhead Arctic fishery wrote later that anyone not going on under sail if wind permitted did not know his business.[4] A gallied whale moves at eight to ten knots and was rarely approached successfully under oars.

If the wind did not permit, the crew pulled toward the whales. A trained crew in smooth water could pull five miles the first hour and four the second. Pulling to windward, they could make four knots; a green crew not over three.[5] These figures were verified in trials on the Mystic River in a loaded whaleboat in 1973. In one sprint over a quarter-mile course, a Mystic Seaport boat made six and one-half knots. The boats are fast and easily driven under oars; they are also very quick to accelerate. The writer observed a boat lying dead in the water with the oars ready; on the order to pull, the boat got up to speed rapidly. The long oars are limber as the men put their backs into the stroke. The boats pull easily; as part of a green crew, I once pulled some four miles in one with little effort or fatigue.

Extravagant claims were sometimes made for the speed of the boats and the endurance of the crews. One author states that a whaleboat could make "ten miles an hour in dead chase of a whale by oars alone."[6] This would have been driving the boat at considerably greater than hull speed. Another author, Robert Ferguson, quotes a mate as saying it was nothing for a crew to pull twenty miles to windward in a rough sea with "never a whimper out of them."[7] There probably was no whimpering but it must have exhausted the toughest crew. At another point in the book Ferguson describes the men's condition and feelings after whales were raised early in the morning and the boats pulled all day to windward without getting close enough to strike. They returned to the ship, he said, after six, tired and hungry.

Five men pulled the oars of the standard whaleboat carried by an American whaleship. The boatsteerer pulled with the four regular oarsmen. The mate handled the steering oar in the stern: sometimes, to give an extra bit of power and to control the stroke, he put his hand on the stroke oar and pushed with each stroke. I have seen motion pictures of an Azorean boat with the men pulling hard. The mate is not only pushing with his right hand on the stroke oar, but he is sculling the steering oar as well with his left hand. To scull an oar perhaps twenty-two feet long with one hand takes a big man.

The steering oar had several advantages over the rudder, which was only used when the boat was under sail. The moving boat could be turned faster because of the great leverage of the oar, and it could be used in a seaway when a rudder could be out of water. A boat without way on could be turned by sweeping the stern around with the oar. The oar had other uses, too: it could be used for sculling through narrow leads through ice floes, around docks where there was no room to use the oars, or for very quiet approaches on whales. It was invariably used in working around the whale when it was lanced.

Under sail, as noted by Brown,[8] the boats with the larger rigs of the late nineteenth century could make seven to eight knots in smooth water with a fresh breeze well aft of the quarter. Some, Brown said, even claimed ten knots, but four to six knots was a good average for a boat beating and running over a period of time on a number of headings. These figures appear reasonable in the light of tests made with whaleboats at Mystic in 1973. The boats were more weatherly than expected and were fast in light airs.

17

TOP FAR LEFT: Lowering from the WANDERER. *Normally mate and boatsteerer went down in the boat and the other four members of the crew got in after it was waterborne.Courtesy of Kendall Whaling Museum.*

BOTTOM FAR LEFT: Boat from the JOHN R. MANTA *raising her mast. Courtesy of Kendall Whaling Museum.*

BOTTOM CENTER LEFT: The mast has just been raised. Shrouds are being taken up with the lanyards; halyards are being straightened out and the mainsail is about to be raised. Note the tiller has been shipped. Courtesy of Kendall Whaling Museum.

BOTTOM CENTER RIGHT: Boat from the DAISY *raising sail. Robert Cushman Murphy Collection at Mystic Seaport.*

BOTTOM RIGHT: Boat with reefed mainsail. The mate at the tiller tends the single main sheet. Courtesy of Kendall Whaling Museum.

TOP LEFT: Boat from the DAISY *pulling away from the side of the ship. Spars are stowed inside the boat, the normal place when the boat is in the davits. A boat away from the ship with its mast lowered stows the mast out of the way by jamming the heel under the aftermost thwart and allowing mast and boom to project over the starboard quarter. Robert Cushman Murphy Collection at Mystic Seaport.*

The boat tested had a gaff main and a small jib, for a total of about 340 square feet of sail. Its waterline length was about twenty-six feet, and with her long run and low wetted surface, she should have been fast. She was sensitive to weight shifts and trim, as is to be expected in a light vessel: the 900 pounds or so of live ballast was actively used. She proved tender initially and stiff when heeled, sailing with the lee rail level with the water, occasionally taking in small amounts. The boat accelerated rapidly with her length and light weight, but sometimes lost headway in coming about, requiring the backing of the jib. However, this was not always necessary and the observation that a "whaleboat because of its length and comparative flatness of its keel and the slight purchase of the rudder, will not come about easily under sail" is a bit strong.[9]

It has often been observed that a looser boat is fast, and the same has been said of whaleboats. Captain Bodfish wrote of a boat which had been strained through negligent hoisting when half-full of water. Thereafter, she worked a great deal under sail, and proved very fast. Captain Bodfish gave his the same treatment, and claimed they did not leak despite this rough handling.

The techniques of approach under sail and oar varied with the type of whale. In going on the bowhead under sail, the danger is mainly from the flukes, so the boat is layed about or paddles are used to keep her off when darting. Approaching a right whale, the boats sailed directly at it, and since the whale settled very rapidly when hit, they sometimes sailed over it without touching.

Going on under sail took able handling. Captain George Comer, whaling in Hudson Bay around 1900, describes in his journal a boat that jibed and capsized at the instant of darting.[10] Captain Bodfish also wrote of losing whales through poor handling of sails. Boats were sometimes sailed up to the point of collision with sperm whales, but usually the boat ranged up on the whale's starboard quarter to give the boatsteerer, who was normally right-handed, an easier dart. The boat then sheered off, sometimes using oars or paddles to clear the flukes. If the boat had a jib, it was generally taken in before darting to clear the forward part of the boat.

The boatsteerer darted his first iron and, if time permitted, his second, which was attached to the whale line with a short warp. If the second iron could not be darted, he threw it overboard to prevent its flailing around in the boat as the line was taken out. He then attended to the lowering of the mast as the whale sounded.

Lowering the mast and later maneuvering around the whale for lancing were supreme tests of a crew's training. Captain Earle of the *Charles W. Morgan* described the steps in lowering the sail and mast of a gaff-rigged whaleboat:

1. Halyards were let go by the boatsteerer after throwing warp over the side from the box.
2. The boat's crew, remaining seated, caught the sail and tied it.
3. Bow oarsman cast off shrouds and wound them around the mast.
4. Boatsteerer lifted mast while the men steadied it.
5. Mate and men aft caught the mast while it was lowered, its heel in the hinged tabernacle.[11]

The mast was finally passed aft, its heel was jammed under the after thwart, and it was rested on and lashed to a fitting on the cuddy board. The end was allowed to hang over the starboard quarter. All this was done "quicker than it takes in the telling," as the boat pitched and rolled, line ran out, the whale sounded, and the boat picked up speed as the line was snubbed.

Another description of lowering the mast with a spritsail, apparently after the boatsteerer and mate had changed ends, has the bow oarsman furling the sail around the mast, placing the sprit up against the mast and lashing the whole with two half hitches. The mast was then unshipped, with the men aft catching it. In this instance the mast was small, only thirteen feet tall, used in a boat whaling from shore, and it was stepped in a hole in the second thwart.[12]

A description of striking the large mast of an Azorean boat concludes by saying: "The speed with which the heavy mast and huge sails are lowered, rolled, and lashed together is incredible."[13] The mast of one whaleboat I measured, small by Azorean standards, was twenty-four feet six inches tall and five and three-quarter inches in diameter most of its length. The boom was almost twenty-six feet long.

The technique of attacking the whale when under oars was different from going on under sail. The sperm whale is approached from directions out of his limited field of vision, generally from on his quarter or, less frequently, head on. In the latter case, the boat turns sharply just before striking. On order the boatsteerer peaks his oar, stands, seizes the iron from the crotch, and darts it.* Im-

* Melville makes the point that many whales were lost because the harpooner, pulling his heart out to the last, was expected to leap up, turn around, instantly take stock of the situation, and heave the harpoon. It took more strength and judgment than most men could muster, Melville thought. Charles Beetle wrote of one young, recently promoted harpooner who, standing and turning to face the whale for the first time, fainted dead away.

mediately after darting, the oars were used for backing off or sterning. Sterning was an exercise in which the crew had received much drilling. It was claimed a boat moving forward under oars at its highest speed could be stopped in one boat's length.[14] This was tried and, to our surprise, found possible by a crew at Mystic Seaport.

In attacking the bowhead under oars, the boat came up alongside, the harpoon was darted, and at the same time the mate swung the stern out at right angles with the steering oar and ordered stern all to clear the flukes. After gaining sternway, the men peaked their oars, and the line, now running out as the whale sounded, ran down through a channel formed by the peaked oars. Mate and boatsteerer then changed places.

Changing ends by the mate and the boatsteerer was the universal practice except until recently in the Azores. Presumably it was done when the line was not running out and during a lull in the towing. That it seemed unnecessarily dangerous was remarked upon by several writers. One, W. J. Dakin, persisted in asking an old whaleman why, and the impatient answer was that harpooning a whale and killing it were two different jobs. Killing took special skill and was the duty and prerogative of the more experienced mate. Perhaps it was a matter of prestige that the senior man dispatched the whale.

A whale that is harpooned may tow a boat at twenty knots for short sprints. He may tow the boat for hours, until beyond sight of the whaleship. If towed to windward, the bow pounds into head seas and sends spray bursting up in sheets. If it is rough, likely as not the boat will be half-swamped. The boatsteerer, foot jammed in a brace in the stern sheets, must struggle to control the boat with the steering oar, while the man who pulls the after

TOP LEFT: Going on the whale with paddles. Paddles were quieter but much slower than oars. They were used when there was not enough wind for an approach under sail. The steering oar was used when the boat was under oars or paddles. Courtesy of Kendall Whaling Museum. TOP RIGHT: Going on the whale under oars. The boatsteerer has peaked his oar and is ready to dart the iron. Courtesy of Kendall Whaling Museum. BOTTOM LEFT: The boatsteerer has gone aft and taken the steering oar. The boat is probably being maneuvered around the whale as the mate in the bow lances. The line is slack in the after part of the boat; forward, the bow oarsman tends the line, keeping the boat alongside the whale. Courtesy of Kendall Whaling Museum. BOTTOM RIGHT: A boat from the DAISY *with dead whale. Whaleboats often towed the whale to the whaleship. Robert Cushman Murphy Collection at Mystic Seaport.*

oar tends the line at the loggerhead and the others bail. If the whale sounds, he threatens to pull the bow under and the men move aft so the boat can settle evenly. Sometimes the boat ships water over the gunwale amidships. The racking of towing and sounding puts great strains on the ends of the boat, sometimes starting the fastenings.

As the whale tired, the men faced forward and hauled in the line, which the after oarsman coiled down in the stern sheets. It was coiled carefully, since the whale might yet make several runs taking line back out. As the boat was pulled up to the whale, the line was taken out of the bow chocks and brought back to one of the large cleats on each gunwale near the thigh board. This, called "bowing on," allowed the boat to be brought up alongside for lancing. The bow oarsman tended the line, heaving the boat in close as the mate, leg braced in the clumsy cleat, thrust the lance.

Often considerable maneuvering and work with the line, oars, and steering oar was done alongside the whale during the lancing. The steering oar and the veering action of the line around the bow cleat kept the boat in position if the whale was moving; if the whale was not moving, the steering oar was used to sweep the stern around, or the oars were pulled or sterned together, or backed on one side while the other pulled ahead to turn the boat and put the mate in the most advantageous postion. In the "flurry," all sterned to avoid the whale's death throes.

After the killing, the whale had to be brought alongside the whaleship. If possible the ship worked toward the whale. Sometimes other boats could assist in towing, which could last hours and put still more strain on boats and crew. Towing whales head first was the method usually, but not invariably used.

Whaling from shore is basically the same operation as whaling from a whaleship. The boats are launched from the open beach or from a ramp, usually with plenty of help from interested bystanders.* If permanent ramps are available, larger boats such as the thirty-eight foot Azorean boat may be launched, with skids placed under the keels. The boats put out on the sighting of whales from shore, although in Australia, boats sometimes went out on patrol and pulled along the coast ten miles or more on the lookout for whales. The Azoreans are now towed by power boats* to the vicinity of the whales, and the approach is then made under sail, oars, or paddle. The power boats may assist in the killing and generally help in towing the whale to the factory.

Wherever shore whaling was carried on, the boats relied more on oars or, more recently, on a tow by a power boat rather than sail, although local weather was the determining factor. Centerboards were often omitted and the rig reduced, though the larger rig of the Azoreans is an exception. In Bequia centerboards are used.

The performance of the boats was directly related to the condition and state of training of the crews, and undoubtedly the high reputation of whaleboats was partly the result of efficient crews showing the boats to their best advantage. In the whaleships, green crews were drilled on the voyage

* An old photo shows the launching of a boat from the beach on Long Island, with eleven men helping. This was a small boat between twenty-seven feet and twenty-eight feet long. A ramp makes launching far easier. The author with another man, using planks, rollers, and a block and tackle, easily hauled a whaleboat up on a beach, cleaned the bottom, and put it back in. The boat was thirty feet long and had ballast equal to the weight of gear carried. Another time four men rolled one over on the beach to clean and paint the bottom.

Crew from Mystic Seaport raising mast. Photograph by the author.

Crew from Mystic Seaport drilling. Photograph by Les Olin.

out. Boats were lowered and raised, the mast set, and sail made until the men worked quickly and safely. There was much exercise with the oars, drilling the men for speed in pulling and quick response to sterning or twisting the boat by pulling three oars and sterning two. They drilled in the silent use of paddles. A spar was sometimes towed and the boats made runs on it to simulate going on a whale. A by-product of their efficiency with the oars in attacking whales showed in the excellent landings the crews made alongside vessels or docks in port.

Landing through surf also came naturally after the training at sea. The mates encouraged competition between boats, and the morale and aggressiveness of a crew—a function of proficiency—had a good deal to do with the number of whales taken. Despite all the training, there was still danger, sometimes panic, and plenty of opportunity for foul-ups in the excitement of the chase.*

Attempts were made at Mystic Seaport in the summer of 1973 to duplicate the action in a whaleboat in drills. Approaches were made on a slow-moving launch under oars, paddles, sail, and sail and paddles together. When within darting distance, the whale line was thrown to the launch, where it was secured, and the launch speeded up. The crew practiced sterning and then peaking the oars, handling the boat under tow, lowering the mast under tow, letting line run from the tub, snubbing the line at the loggerhead, pulling up on the launch and recoiling the line, letting the line run out from the coils in the stern sheets, and bowing on.

Lowering the mast under tow and with the line

* Recording his interviews with whaling captains, Brown mentions that green crew members sometimes jumped overboard at the moment the harpoon was darted.

24

Crew testing a whaleboat built at Mystic Seaport. Main-sail is reefed. Note bend in spars.
Photograph by Maynard Bray, Mystic Seaport.

Crew from Mystic Seaport drilling. The crew, under tow by a launch, is pulling up on the whale-line. Photograph by author.

running out was not difficult or dangerous under the conditions that prevailed. Sailing approaches were made running down on the launch and sailing on it close-hauled. The jib was taken in first, followed by the main after making fast. The main could be got down in about five seconds; releasing the shrouds and lowering the mast required another five. Furling the sails, passing the spars aft, and lashing them down took ten to fifteen seconds. The whole could be done in less than a minute.

Mistakes were made at first. In one run close-hauled in a stiff wind the shrouds were released on the weather side before the sail was all the way down. The heel of the mast jumped out of the step, in which it was none too well seated, and knocked the side out of the trough. The mast became jammed and could not be lowered. On another approach the whale line was "lined" on the wrong side—the starboard side of the mast—making it

impossible to lower the mast over the starboard quarter without dropping it on the line. Tending the line and taking turns of the running line around the loggerhead took practice. It became clear why nippers were safer than gloves, which could be caught and pull a hand into the running turns. The crew was mindful to avoid the line running out as they lowered the mast, but found they could still work in reasonable safety.

It was found that the boat was controlled easily with the steering oar when under tow. Hauling up on the launch as it slowed to two or three knots was easy for the crew. The line was coiled in the stern sheets as it came in and was allowed to run out as the launch made another run. This was done a number of times and the line ran without kinks. The whaleboat was brought up alongside the launch and bowed on at the end of each practice run.

DUTIES OF A WHALEBOAT'S CREW

MATE OR BOATHEADER	Officer in charge of the boat. He steers the boat while approaching the whale. After the whale is harpooned and the boat is "fast" to the whale with the whale line, the mate goes forward and does the lancing or killing of the whale.
BOATSTEERER	Pulls the forward oar, called the harpooner's oar, until close enough to dart the harpoon. After darting, he exchanges places with the mate and steers the boat.
BOWMAN	Pulls the second oar. Assists the boatsteerer in stepping and lowering the mast. He pulls in on the whale line and tends it while the mate is lancing. He is the most experienced foremast hand in the boat.
MIDSHIP OARSMAN	Pulls midship oar.
TUB OARSMAN	Pulls tub oar. Wets the whale line as whale sounds to prevent its burning from friction.
AFTER OARSMAN	Pulls the stroke oar. He coils the line as it is brought aboard while the boat is being pulled up on the whale. He helps catch and secure the mast after it is lowered. He also bails the boat. The after oarsman works under the boatsteerer in maintaining the whaleboat. He is generally the lightest man in the boat.

All oarsmen heave in on the whale line, bail, and move aft to trim the boat as ordered while the boat is under tow.

The point should be made that the first exercises were done slowly for the sake of safety and subsequent ones were controlled. Conditions of sea and wind were calm on the three days the crew drilled. In cold weather with a sea running and with a strong wind, all these operations would have been far more difficult.

In a further test of performance, one boat was measured and entered in a race against modern boats around Fishers Island, New York. Under the formula used, her rating was high, mainly because of the long waterline length. She was placed in a class with about a dozen smaller sloops of three different designs. The whaleboat was third over the starting line and maintained this position for most of the first leg of the course, which was a spinnaker reach for the sloops. The wind became very light, and the others pulled ahead. The next leg was to windward and the whaleboat was left far behind. With the tide at the Race off Fishers Island about to turn to a strong ebb, the crew of the whaleboat dropped out of the race and took to the oars. The conclusion was that whaleboats cannot compete to windward against yachts of modern design, particularly in light air. Off the wind, they hold their own very well.

In September, 1973, one of the Seaport's whaleboats sailed from Mystic to Newport, Rhode Island, a distance of about forty miles. Along the Rhode Island shore, the boat beat into a swell of about five feet. Progress was slow to windward under the small jib and reefed main. Halfway along the shore, the rudder pintals broke and thereafter the steering oar was used. The observation of the person in charge of the boat was that whaleboats were poor to windward if there was much swell or chop. The boat was wet and there was some pounding, though at no time were there doubts about its safety. When the sail was not reefed, the loose-footed main was not flat enough to be very effective to windward. The boat was slow in coming about and markedly so with the steering oar. Under sail the rudder brought her through the wind faster.

The voyage took two days. The crew of six spent the night sleeping beside their beached boat at Point Judith, and in the morning proceeded in the direction of Newport, pulling most of the distance until a southwest wind came up and took them in.

Another aspect of the performance of whaleboats is how the boats used the men. A crew of six was jammed into a small boat filled with a great amount of gear. Often the men had to spend hours of exhausting labor in the boat, fully exposed to the elements. Probably as tiring as the physical effort was the tension of the hunt. Whaleboats were not easy on their crews.

The boats were crowded. About 900 pounds of gear, which by its nature was difficult to stow, went into them. This equipment had to be in a special place, often awkward from the point of view of comfort. Down the center of the boat was the potentially dangerous whale line, and aft were the coils that had to be kept free and unobstructed. On two occasions crews from Mystic Seaport spent a full day in the boat. Their only equipment was oars and sails, yet the boat was found to be cluttered. When the mast was lowered, though it was passed aft and hung over the stern in the approved manner, it was in the way of the after oar. Oars were in the way when under sail. Yet this boat had no line tubs, live and spare harpoons, lances, drogues, paddles, lantern kegs and the other pieces of gear found in a fully equipped boat.

Men in a whaleboat are exposed to the weather, for there is little shelter in these open, shallow boats when they are loaded with gear. In the trials at Mystic, one trip was made on a raw day in March; after a few hours, several of the crew members had gravitated to the bilges as we sailed along. They lay under the thwarts in the bottom of the boat trying to find a little shelter. They could not have done this in a fully equipped whaleboat because there is too much gear and likely as not their weight would have been needed on the weather side if there had been more wind. Part of the pulling done that day was just to keep warm. The crews of yore were out in the boats in Arctic weather and certainly the clothing supplied by the ship's slop chest was inferior to modern foul weather gear.* A whaleboat did not offer much protection for its crew.

In a calm sea, the boats are easily pulled. Any boat is hard on the crew if it is being pulled to weather and there is a sea running. Under sail the whaleboats require attention and effort. The rig is very simple, and the absence of mechanical advantages in sheaves and blocks has to be met with manpower alone. There were plenty of men in the boat, and therefore the main sheet was a single line from a bridle on the boom to the hands of a man. He might take a turn around a cleat, but the sheet could not be belayed. The lack of washboards along the sides and the relative tenderness of the boats meant a boat could ship water quickly. The crew had to be attentive. The boats depended heavily on live ballast, which put demands on the men. Even the privileges of rank added little to the comfort of the mate. He had no real place to sit as he steered, and the tiller pointed up at an angle that

---

* The Mystic boats also had plenty of coffee and sandwiches; the oldtimers had to make do with thirty pounds of biscuits and water.

suggests it was meant for a man standing. As a matter of fact, the mate was supposed to be on his feet looking for whales.

Though the men might become exhausted and suffer from exposure, whaleboats could save men's lives, as they proved many times. They were fine seaboats and men survived terrible voyages in them; in the end, the boats served their crews well.

> The whaleman's boat must be light, for it has to be quickly lowered, and it must be able to sail and carry sail, because arms are things that tire and oars are things that make a noise; it must be strong, for it has to bear the roughest usage. All these good qualities the true whaleboat possesses.[15]

1. W. Scoresby, *An Account of the Arctic Regions, with a History and Description of the Northern Whale-Fishery* (Edinburgh, 1820). p. 236.

2. Joseph Conrad, "Christmas Day at Sea" in *Last Essays* (Garden City: Doubleday, Page & Co., 1926), p. 33.

3. Henry Hall, *Report on the Shipbuilding Industry of the U.S.*, 1882, 10th Census, vol. 8, p. 23.

4. Hartson H. Bodfish and Jos. C. Allyn, *Chasing the Bowhead* (Cambridge: Harvard University Press, 1936), p. 145.

5. George Brown Goode, ed. *The Fisheries and Fishery Industries of the United States,* (Washington: Government Printing Office, 1887), Section V, p. 242.

6. William Davis, *Nimrods of the Sea* (North Quincy, The Christopher Publishing House, 1972), p. 158.

7. Robert Ferguson, *Harpooner* (Philadelphia: University of Pennsylvania Press, 1936), p. 181.

8. James Templeman Brown, *The Fisheries and Fishery Industries of the United States* (Washington: Government Printing Office, 1887), p. 242.

9. William John Hopkins, *She Blows! And Sparm at That* (Boston: Houghton Mifflin Co., 1922), p. 35.

10. Capt. George Comer, Journals of the *Era,* G. W. Blunt White Library, Mystic, Connecticut.

11. Capt. J.A.M. Earle, "Fighting Sperm Whales," in *Yachting,* February, 1927, p. 32.

12. Everett Joshua Edwards, *Whale Off* (New York: Coward-McCann, Inc., 1956), p. 57.

13. Trevor Housby, *The Hand of God* (New York: Abelard-Schuman, 1971), p. 19.

14. Reginald B. Hegarty, *The Rope's End* (Boston: Houghton Mifflin, 1965), p. 54.

15. *Rudder,* II, no. 3 (March, 1900) p. 123.

Chapter III

LINES OF THE WHALEBOAT

It is worth observing that functional things often have beauty. The use to which the whaleboat was put demanded a design that was seaworthy, light, maneuverable, pulled easily, sailed reasonably well, had the capacity to carry considerable gear, and could be handled from davits or launched from a beach. Charles Beetle, the New Bedford builder, used the words "sweet curves" to describe the lines of a whaleboat. "Lightly-borne," "sweet-sheered," "buoyant-looking" are other appreciative phrases that have been applied to it.[1]

L. Francis Herreshoff had the whaleboat in mind when he described characteristics that make for seaworthiness. He would have the boat double-ended, long, narrow, with considerable sheer. Freeboard may be low amidships, he wrote, if the ends are high, as the ends have a self-righting effect when each is in a sea. The double-ended boat will not be pooped and the narrow stern will not force the bow under as will a wider stern.[2] These features made the American whaleboats of the 1870s outstanding seaboats.

In a letter to the editor of the *New Bedford Standard-Times* August 30, 1930, Beetle emphasized the differences between boats. "Whaleboats vary in shape according to the different shops in which they were built," he wrote. Some rowed well and some did not. As sailing on the whale became more the rule after 1880, some builders "gave up trying to keep the lines of a good rowing boat." Also, the boats built for the southern sperm fishery were much easier to pull, he wrote, than those built for the later Arctic whaling. The former often "showed considerable speed."

The lines of the boats changed with time, and the builders followed no standard set of lines. Their size varied with conditions and employment but, as

Henry Hall wrote, "the model is substantially the same wherever in America the whaleboat is built."[3] The general characteristics of the lines of American boats as they developed toward the end of the nineteenth century were:

1. Length generally twenty-eight to thirty feet; beam six feet two inches to six feet seven inches; depth twenty-five to twenty-seven inches; sheer twelve to sixteen inches.
2. Double-ended with spoon bow and stern having the same profile.
3. Midship sections with little deadrise, hard bilge, and little or no flare to the sides above the turn of the bilge.
4. Fine entrance and long run. Entrance somewhat fuller than the run.
5. Greatest beam in the center. Looking down on the boat, sides have a fair curve from bow to stern. There is no flatness in the waist.
6. Rocker in keel and no deadwood.
7. Fairly strong sheer.
8. Light displacement and shallow draft.
9. Equipped with sails, centerboards, and rudders.

The length of the boats depended upon a number of conditions. If carried aboard ship, it could not be much over thirty feet—longer boats were difficult to handle on the davits and could not be brought inboard in heavy weather. Longer boats also took up too much space and were strained when hoisted by the lifting eyes in the ends. The spacing and positioning of davits aboard most barks and ships were for boats no longer than thirty-one feet, and it was less than this for whaling schooners. Experimental boats thirty-eight feet long with nine oars were built for the sulphur-bottom whale off Spitzbergen by George Rogers of New London, but they were not a success. Boats of thirty-six feet with seven oars were made for whaling in Delgado Bay in the 1840s, where it was too shallow for the whaleships to penetrate and the men might spend several days in the boats, but they proved too heavy and unwieldy and the experiment was given up. Another model longer than the standard was exhibited at the International Exhibition in Philadelphia in 1876: a thirty-five foot boat built by Williams, Haven, & Company.

The length of the boats had gradually increased from about twenty feet in the mid 1700s to twenty-five feet by 1800. In 1825, James Beetle was making twenty-seven and twenty-eight foot boats, though smaller ships were still carrying the twenty-five foot size. From the 1860s on, twenty-eight and twenty-nine feet were the usual lengths in the sperm fishery, and thirty to thirty-one feet in the Arctic fishery. Smaller schooners still carried the twenty-eight foot boat.[4]

The smaller boats were preferred in sperm whaling because of their greater maneuverability; the sperm whale, it was said, was dangerous at both ends. The bowhead was found in the Arctic, and because of the severe weather conditions and the need for some protection from exposure, and because the men sometimes spent longer periods in the boats, larger boats were used. The wales of the Arctic boats were built up an extra two inches with a cap to give slightly more freeboard.

Boats used in shore whaling were generally longer than those used from whaleships. Greater length gave more room inside for men and gear, and an extra thwart and oarsman could be added, which meant greater speed under oars. Weight was little affected by the added length. The larger boats could be launched from permanent launching sites and there were generally extra hands about to help. Contemporary Azorean boats are six-oared, with lengths from thirty to thirty-nine feet. The boats used in the past in New Zealand shore whaling carried seven or eight men. Competition was keen among the companies of shore whalers and emphasis was on getting to the whale first: hence maneuverability was sacrificed for speed. The long Azorean boats appear unhandy when maneuvering during the lancing of the whale. In two films of whaling in the Azores, the whale is alongside the boat rather than off the bow, and in another case the whale has doubled back and is passing close aboard under the stern. Since the Azoreans use neither chock pins nor kicking straps, the men must be particularly careful of the line sweeping aft.

When boats in shore whaling were to be launched from open beaches over sand, smaller ones were used because of the difficulty in launching. Two boats from Long Island used in shore whaling around the turn of the century were twenty-seven and one-half feet, and Brown describes a boat used in shore whaling from Provincetown, Massachusetts, that was twenty-eight feet.

Perhaps the longest of all whaleboats was one built by James Beetle in 1882 to be used in the Azores for carrying passengers and cargo between the islands: she was fifty-two feet long with a beam of nine feet. She was towed to New York and placed aboard a ship for the Western Islands.

Whaleboats are narrow, making an easily driven hull. American boats had a beam of slightly more than one-fifth the length. The greatest beam was in the center of the boat, the width increasing from the bow in a uniform curve to the point of greatest beam and then continuing to curve inward to the stern. British boats were narrower, with straighter sides; the extreme beam was carried for a greater distance along the sides, and the ends were fuller.

Whaleboats of the ARTHUR V. S. WOODRUFF. *The boat across the stern on the tail feathers is carried as a spare. Courtesy of Kendall Whaling Museum.*

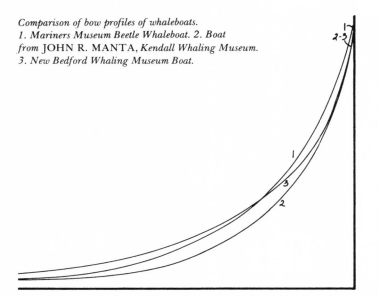

Comparison of bow profiles of whaleboats.
1. Mariners Museum Beetle Whaleboat. 2. Boat
from JOHN R. MANTA, *Kendall Whaling Museum.*
3. New Bedford Whaling Museum Boat.

Comparison of bow and stern profiles of a boat
from the JOHN R. MANTA. *The boat is at the Ken-*
dall Whaling Museum. It shows evidence of repairs; it
is probable that the stern post was replaced.

American oars were of varying length, in part because of the curvature of the sides. British oars, on the other hand, were shorter and of uniform length. Earlier British boats had the greatest beam forward of the center, with sides tapering gradually inward from that point aft, giving something of a codhead effect.

The beam of Azorean boats is proportionately less than that of American boats. A boat of thirty-eight feet may have a beam of six feet eight inches, which produces a very slim hull. This, with slack bilges, makes a tender boat. It is said an Azorean boat, with its heavy mast and large sail, would capsize in still air without its crew aboard to act as ballast.[5] By contrast, the boats used today at Bequia have a proportionately greater beam than was found in the earlier American boats.

Double-ended boats were the rule for whaleboats of all nations, except for the Scots in the nineteenth century. In addition to its seaworthy features, the double-ended design permitted sterning and agile maneuvering around the whale. Also the long run made for easier pulling boats. The Scottish whalers preferred a boat with a transom. Basil Lubbock in *The Arctic Whalers* has photographs of such "Peterhead" whaleboats. They appear to be cut off about at the cuddy board. There is hollow in the run, making an hourglass stern, and a lifting ring is placed low on the outside of the plumb stern.

The spoon bow and stern give a fair sweep from keel to head. In many boats it was a beautiful line, following naturally from the fineness of the ends. The bows and sterns of different builders had different profiles. In the William Hand plans of a whaleboat, the greatest curvature is midway between the scarf joint attaching stem or stern to the

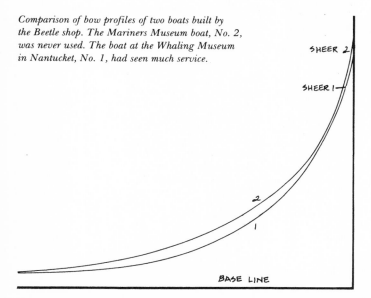

Comparison of bow profiles of two boats built by the Beetle shop. The Mariners Museum boat, No. 2, was never used. The boat at the Whaling Museum in Nantucket, No. 1, had seen much service.

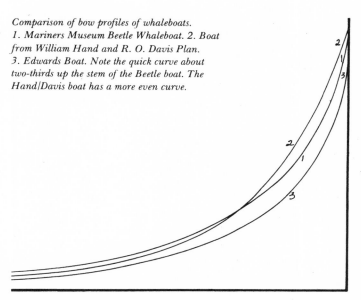

Comparison of bow profiles of whaleboats. 1. Mariners Museum Beetle Whaleboat. 2. Boat from William Hand and R. O. Davis Plan. 3. Edwards Boat. Note the quick curve about two-thirds up the stem of the Beetle boat. The Hand/Davis boat has a more even curve.

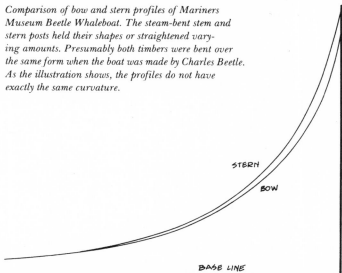

Comparison of bow and stern profiles of Mariners Museum Beetle Whaleboat. The steam-bent stem and stern posts held their shapes or straightened varying amounts. Presumably both timbers were bent over the same form when the boat was made by Charles Beetle. As the illustration shows, the profiles do not have exactly the same curvature.

keel and head.* Beetle boats characteristically had a quicker curve higher up the stem, and the Delano boats aboard the half-scale model of the whaleship *Lagoda* have a curve further down. The latter two had greater curvature with the face at the top tending toward the vertical. Other boats had a uniform curvature from scarf to head, forming the arc of a circle.

Bow and stern timbers in American boats were bent on the same form and therefore should have the same curve, but of the original boats measured and those built at Mystic Seaport, curvature of bow seldom matched. The oak straightened or held its curve in varying degree.

* There is a question about what these plans represent. The lines may have been taken from a Leonard-built whaleboat and the construction details from the boat exhibited in the New Bedford Whaling Museum.

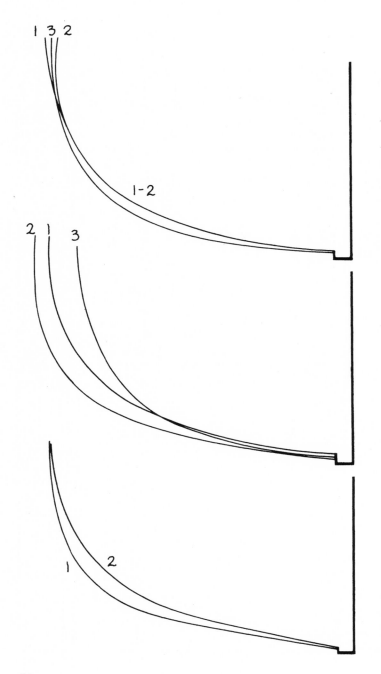

*THE THREE DRAWINGS COMPARE THE MIDSHIP
SECTIONS OF WHALEBOATS.*

1. Mariners Museum Beetle Boat. 2. Boat from JOHN R.
MANTA, *Kendall Whaling Museum. 3. New Bedford Whaling
Museum Boat. Note the* MANTA's *boat and the Mariners
Museum boat have very similar sections except that at
the rail the latter has more flare. The boat at the
New Bedford Museum, which is the largest of the three,
has somewhat less dead rise and more freeboard. The
Mariners Museum boat has greater flare to the sides
and more sheer than many boats built after 1900.*

*1. Mariners Museum Beetle Boat. 2. Leonard Boat, Hand and
Davis Plan. 3. Edwards Boat. A comparison of midships sections.
The Edwards boat is the smallest, 27' 5''; the Mariners
Museum boat is 28' 5''; and the Leonard
boat is just under 30'. The Edwards boat is
comparatively narrower and bilges are slacker. The
Leonard boat, compared to the others, has greater
freeboard, less sheer and a harder turn at the bilge.*

*1. Nantucket Whaling Museum Boat. 2. Mariners Museum
Boat. Note: Builders sometimes varied the spacing
between molds, used shims, or adjusted molds to make
boats with different lines. Note the Nantucket boat
has less dead rise and sides are more plumb at the
sheer.*

34

Little deadrise and hard bilges made American boats stiff, with shallow draft and considerable carrying capacity for men and gear. The flatness along with a rockered keel also allowed a hull that could be quickly turned. British boats tended to have more deadrise and slacker bilges, according to Ashley;[6] this is markedly the case with Azorean boats.

Sides above the turn of the bilge vary even in boats from the same builder. James Beetle writes that he began making the sides nearly plumb in the midsections at the rail in the 1850s. I had the opportunity to examine tracings of molds used in the Beetle shop for many years. Each mold had two positions, made by the top of the mold being movable and fixed with pegs. The molds were adjusted to the amount of flare desired and the size of the boat.*

Two boats with the Beetle brand are now in museums. One was unused and the other, older boat was rather roughly used before becoming a museum exhibit. The newer boat has more flare to the sides; the older has the double, inner and outer wales, which might tend to pull in the sides. In some cases the variation was probably intentional and in other cases not. In older, loose boats, depending upon how supported, hog or sag might effect the flare of the sides.**

* The tracings were made around 1933 and were lent by John Bauman, of South Dartmouth, Massachusetts, grandson of Charles Beetle. J. C. Beetle, brother of Charles, who left New Bedford to build boats in California, may have taken tracings of the molds with him; Charles Beetle remarked on the family resemblance between his brother's boats and his own.

** This was demonstrated by Erik Ronnberg, Jr., former assistant curator at the New Bedford Whaling Museum. He took a model whaleboat he was making and bent the ends down. Overhang was increased, sheer was flattened, flare was decreased, and rocker disappeared to be replaced by hog. Pushing stem and stern together produced the effect of sagging.

The lines of the William Hand plans show nearly plumb sides at the rail in the midsections, and the sides are dead plumb in the boat at the Kendall Whaling Museum. Taking it further, a model of a whaleboat type used on Cocos Island actually has tumble home in the midsections. But the opposite case is found in a small whaleboat built for shore whaling on Long Island: it has considerable flare, as do the modern Azorean boats.

There are advantages in both flared and plumb sides. Flared sides give greater buoyancy and stiffness when heeled, which would be needed in a boat used in surf. Plumb sides are stronger structurally; a boat being hoisted and perhaps slammed against the side of a whaleship would suffer less damage to the rail, which is structurally weak. The force of the blow is distributed to a lower level where thwarts and seat risers strengthen the sides at the lower edge of the sheer strake. Also, there is a practical limit to the beam of a boat carried on davits; reduced flare increases capacity for a given beam.

The whaleboat has a rather narrow entrance and a long run, for making an easily driven hull. The bows are fuller to give greater buoyancy forward when the whale sounded, or when being towed into a head sea. The fullness also made a somewhat dryer boat. The after sections are slacker; those toward the stern form almost a straight line from keel to sheer and a few show hollow. In some boats, the forward and after sections are quite similar, producing one of the most balanced hulls.[7] There are advantages in construction to the fine ends; plank lines are straight and the boat is easy to plank.

James Beetle wrote that he was the first to make boats with fuller forward sections: he began adding shims to his molds forward. Later the practice became general in American boats, but the greatest

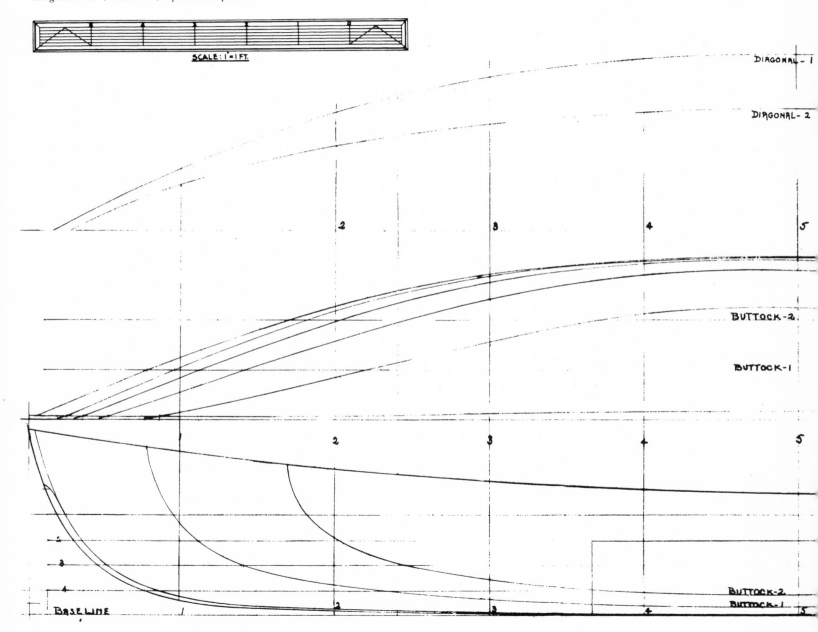

Lines of whaleboat taken off by William H. Hand in 1900.
Length 29' 10'', beam 6'6'', depth amidships 29''.

SCALE: 1" = 1 FT.

DIAGONAL - 1

DIAGONAL - 2

BUTTOCK - 2

BUTTOCK - 1

BUTTOCK - 2
BUTTOCK - 1

BASELINE

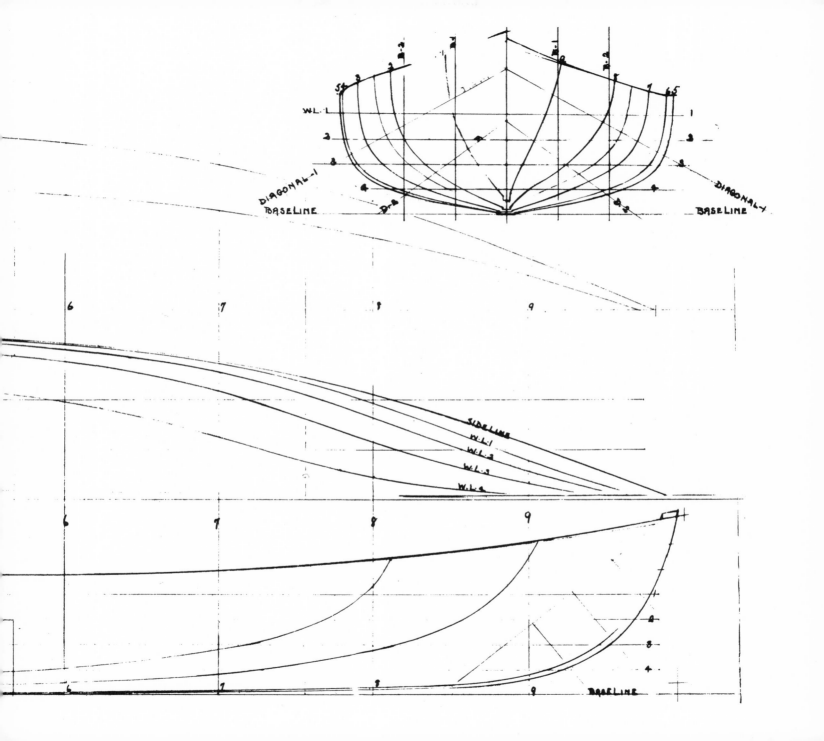

Boat built at Mystic Seaport hauled ashore and turned over for painting. The lines, taken off by William Hand, possibly are of a Leonard whaleboat. Photography by author.

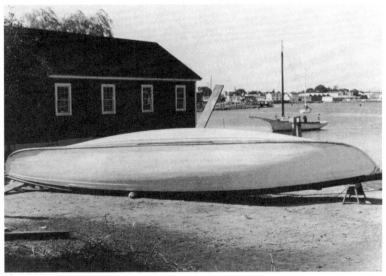

Mystic Seaport whaleboat. Note narrowness of hull, fine entrance and long run. Photograph by author.

beam was still kept in the center. Apparently the British had long been making their boats fuller forward to give buoyancy when the whale sounded. Scoresby, writing in 1820, mentions this feature and provides some proportions. The main breadth of the larger six- and five-oared boats was three-sevenths of the distance aft of the stem. In their small, four-oared boats, twenty-three to twenty-four feet long with five foot three inch beam, the greatest beam was one-third the distance aft. The result was a boat that was still sharp in the ends compared to other boats of the times, but with a bow markedly fuller than the stern. Azorean boats today have extremely sharp entrance and long runs with hollow sections aft.*

American whaleboats were built with a rocker to the keel of about two and one-half inches over a distance of twenty-two feet and no deadwood. The keel projects only about one-half inch below the garboard. The rockered keel and the absence of deadwood made for greater maneuverability. The whaleboats used on Bequia and some later American boats equipped with engines were exceptions. Bequian boats have deadwood in the area of the forefoot, a deeper keel and deadwood aft.**

The sheer of whaleboats is fairly strong. It was said the higher ends threw waves off in rough seas and made greater stability in heavy weather. Sheer was greater in earlier boats.*** In later boats it ranged from twelve inches to sixteen inches, with

* Henry Hall writes of hollow lines forward and aft. None I measured had hollow sections forward; he may have been referring to waterlines.

** U. S. Navy whaleboats and gig whaleboats of 1900 had deadwood aft. The whaleboats at Keeling, Cocos Island, have a substantial, deep, straight keel, according to a model.

*** Henry Hall in 1800 wrote that the sheer was about sixteen inches.

the lowest point slightly aft of middle of the boat. A boat at the Sag Harbor Whaling Museum, said to be old, has great sheer, seventeen and one-half inches, with the lowest point forward of the center. It has been extensively rebuilt, however, which perhaps changed the sheer line. The boats built from William Hand's plans have a tendency to show powderhorn in the bows at certain angles; this does not appear in the Beetle boats, the sheer of which tucks up at the ends.

It was desirable to have the whale line at a level as it passed from bow chocks to loggerhead so that the men could heave on it with all their strength as the boat was pulled up to the whale for lancing. The men sat on thwarts or stood facing forward with feet braced on the thwart ahead. The amount of sheer set the height of the line. The efficiency of the oars was also affected by the sheer line. In the replicas built from the Hand plans, it was found that the harpooner's oar, the farthest forward, was the most difficult to pull effectively because of the height of the sheer and the narrowness of the hull in the bow. Possibly the tucked-up sheer forward in the Beetle boats was designed to avoid this.

Sheer amidships affected the amount of water shipped when heeling under sail and when the boat settled in the water as the whale sounded. Thus, several considerations determined the sheer of the whaleboat.

Whaleboats were extremely light for their size and drew little water. Little deadrise and light construction meant very shallow draft.* Lightness was an advantage in raising and lowering the boats on davits. It also meant a boat that was faster, less tir-

* The draft is not shallow enough for the Eskimo, however, who finds his umiak superior to the whaleboat in traveling in the strip of water between the shore and the ice in summer. The umiak, sometimes towed by dogs on shore, carries twice as much without grounding.

ing to pull, quick to accelerate and to stop dead in the water and go astern. These features were necessary in pursuing and maneuvering around the whale. Launching and beaching a light boat with little draft was also easier.

Earlier statements had the boats unbelievably light. James Templeman Brown quoted 500 to 550 pounds for a boat by Reeves and Kelly of New London, and 1,528 pounds for a full equipped boat presented to the National Museum. The last figure, despite its precision, is hard to accept. William E. Schievill weighed an empty, dry twenty-eight foot boat on the *Charles W. Morgan* in 1960 and found it weighed 1,000 pounds, plus or minus ten pounds.[7] Charles Beetle said his boats weighed 1,200 pounds and, in 1900, *Rudder* put the weight at 1,050. I weighed the equipment piece by piece in a boat that was a museum exhibit and believe 900 pounds for equipment is reasonably accurate. An equipped boat, therefore, weighed about 2,000 pounds without its crew. This is heavier than the earlier claims, but is still very light for a twenty-eight foot boat.

With respect to trim, the center of weight of the loaded whaleboat was slightly aft. The line tubs, between the third and fourth, and fourth and fifth thwarts, were the heaviest weights. The weight aft was an advantage when the whale sounded and pulled the bow under. Also performance under oars was probably improved by this trim as there was less tendency to gripe with the wind aft. It was found in sailing the boats at Mystic Seaport that they came about more easily and were more responsive to the helm if ballast was shifted aft to trim the boats down by the stern.

Efforts were made to improve the sailing qualities of the boats through the nineteenth century. Henry Hall writes that the beam was increased to "make the boats bear up under a press of canvass." From the 1860s on, the boats on the whaleships increasingly used centerboards. James Beetle in a letter to Brown writes that he made the first whaleboat with a centerboard in 1841. It was not a success and he continued to experiment. A bill for boats dated 1855 for the bark *Mermaid* lists a centerboard boat. Ashley writes that the first centerboard was used in 1857 and that they were generally adopted in the 1870s. The boards in the early boats tended to be small; later five feet in length was fairly standard.* Depth was about fifteen inches. The center of the slot was located slightly forward of the center of the boat. The board was raised and lowered by a rod twenty-two inches long, meaning that when the board was fully down, the draft of the whaleboat was increased by about three feet.

Boats in shore whaling often were not equipped with centerboards. Of the boats in the Azores, some from the island of Pico have boards, but most do not. The boats used in shore whaling in Australia did not have them nor did the two boats examined for shore whaling off Long Island. Provincetown, Cape Cod, whaleboats came both with and without boards. It was sometimes said the boards could be jammed by stones during launching and beaching; however, this problem would seem to be avoidable if the boats were being launched from prepared ramps. Local conditions determined the degree to which sailing was done in shore whaling and centerboards were used accordingly.

The rudder was unshipped and swung up on the port side with two lines. One, the tripping line, secured with a knot through a hole high on the rudder, lifted the pintles out of the gudgeons when pulled. This line passed through a fairlead on the starboard side of the stern timber, or through a hole bored through the extreme after end of the lion's tongue aft of the loggerhead.

Rudders, used only when the boats were under sail, varied in design, some projecting forward and following the curve of the stern, making a more balanced rudder; others turning downwards and being more spadelike. Some rudders were shallow and others projected below the line of the keel.

1. *Rudder*, Vol. 11, no. 3, (March, 1900), p. 123.

2. L. Francis Herreshoff, *The Common Sense of Yacht Design* (New York: Rudder Publishing Co., 1946), p. 11.

3. Henry Hall, *Report on the Shipbuilding Industry of the United States,* 10th Census, Vol. 8, 1882, p. 250.

4. James T. Brown, *The Fisheries and Fishery Industry of the United States* (Washington: Government Printing Office, 1887), p. 241.

5. Bernard Venables, *Baleia! Baleia!* (New York, Alfred Knopf, 1969), p. 82.

6. Clifford W. Ashley, *The Yankee Whaler* (Garden City: Halcyon House, 1942), p. 62.

7. The whaleboat is used as an example of a nearly perfectly balanced boat, according to a theory known as the metacentric shelf theory. See Juan Baader, *The Sailing Yacht* (New York: W. W. Norton & Co., 1965), p. 60.

8. Wm. E. Schievill, "The Weight of a Whaleboat," *The American Neptune* (January, 1960), p. 63.

* Henry Hall writes in 1880 that boards were eight feet long. This figure is difficult to accept.

Chapter IV

HULL STRUCTURE

Whaleboat at St. Lawrence Island, Alaska, 1973. Note the clumsy cleat is centered, indicating a left-handed mate or boatsteerer. The boat has Arctic features of rails on top of the gunwales and a strengthening shelf, under the thwart. In recent years all whaleboats in the Arctic have had outboard motor wells. Courtesy of the photographer, John Bockstoce. **Copyrighted.**

The whaleboat builder achieved strength and lightness at minimum cost. In the boat's basket construction, strength depended on light members placed to balance and lock each other to make the whole strong, rather than gaining strength through individually strong pieces. For example, though the frames are light, they are notched over laps and battens to make a strong, elastic structure. If not damaged in some accident, most boats stood the abuse for about one voyage, though Charles Beetle writes of boats that lasted three. He speaks with pride of one boat built for the mate of the *Morning Star*. At the end of a three-year voyage it was credited with having taken some thirty whales yielding 1,500 barrels of oil. After minor repairs, it could still be used on two more voyages.

Whaleboats were built cheaply and quickly. It was expected that they would be used hard, become racked and battered, and be disposed of before rot or rusting fastenings destroyed them.*

Whaleboats were built of cedar, spruce, pine, and oak. Cedar went into planking and ceiling, the cuddy board, and the box. Cedar was light, easily worked, rot resistant, responded to steaming, and was tough and "leathery" when wet. It was also

---

* Some boats lasted many years. One from the wreck of the whaleship *Balaena* was still in use occasionally at St. Lawrence Island, Alaska, in 1973. Boats along the coast of Alaska seem particularly long-lived, probably because galvanized fastenings are slow to deteriorate in a colder climate.

Enough boats survived their first voyages for Charles Beetle to have a side business repairing used boats for use as spares. In general, boats used in shore whaling lasted considerably longer than those aboard ships. This was the case with boats in the Azores, Bequia, Australia, Provincetown, or East Hampton, New York—where they were often owned by the men who used and maintained them, and therefore received greater care.

39

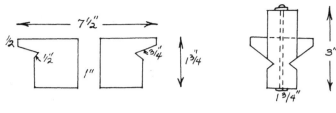

Keel at c.b. case   Stem and keel scarf

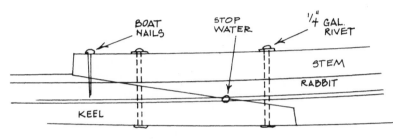

Scarf joint – stem to keel

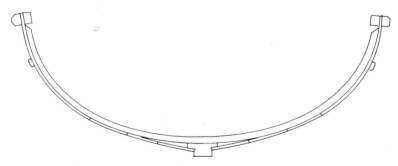

MODERN AZOREAN BOAT (1973). Note conventional carvel planking. Frame is one timber wale to wale.

available locally at low cost.* Spruce, because it was light and strong, was used for seat risers, thwarts, and thigh board. Pine was sometimes used for ceiling and thwarts. White oak, and sometimes yellow bark or grey oak, were used for strength members. Oak is strong, may be steamed and bent, is fairly rot resistant, and holds fastenings well. Fastenings were of black iron until galvanized fastenings became available in the middle of the nineteenth century, according to Charles Beetle.**

Whaleboats were built heavy above and light below. Above were the relatively heavy oak wales, thwart knees, rubbing strips, and guards. Below, the keel was light and there were no floors. The heavy construction at the rail was to save the boat from being damaged against the side of the whaleship during raising and lowering.

A whaleboat's keel is a relatively light, flexible, single piece of oak, six inches to ten inches wide, and one and three-quarter to two and one-quarter inches thick. It is a plank keel with a rabbet cut along on the bottom edges. Laid flat, it has little strength, and the keels of old boats tended to sag between keel blocks except where the centerboard case provided stiffening. In service, to prevent sagging between the cranes, the line tubs were removed from the boats.

Stem and stern timbers were steamed and bent to the same curve. Although light and strong when

* Cedar was used in "boat boards" for whaleboats in Nantucket in the 1700s. Azoreans until recently imported cedar for their whaleboats, though they also used a local wood, a type of Cryptomeria, and wood imported from Scandinavia.

** Boats were also made with composition or copper fastenings, according to Henry Hall. Charles Beetle made two copper-fastened boats for the port authorities at Bermuda, but his other whaleboats used clenched, galvanized nails. Most Azorean boats today are copper fastened.

new, they often cracked in older boats. Natural crooks for stem and stern timbers were used in American boats until the 1820s, when a builder, William Cranston, began using steamed stem and stern posts. The bent stems were quick and cheap to make and were stockpiled in the shops. Photographs of whaleboats taken in 1933 in New Zealand show them with natural crook stems, and the boats today on Bequia use crooks.

Planking in early boats, according to most sources, was lapstrake, though the British were building carvel-planked boats in the 1820s. James Beetle made the first combination carvel-planked and lapstrake, or "smooth" boat, with batten seams in 1833. The batten-seam boats were more expensive to build because they used more fastenings and took more time. In building whaleboats at Mystic Seaport, we estimated the batten-seam construction increased the time of planking by one-third. The boats with smooth bottoms were quieter, it was said, and gallied fewer whales. Perhaps a more important consideration was that smooth boats were more easily repaired. They came into general use in the 1850s, though clinker boats were still listed (without the price, however) in "The Whalemen's Shipping List" until 1861.

James Beetle described the adoption of batten-seam construction. It had been the practice to nail battens behind checks or shakes in the thin, cedar planking until it occurred to Beetle to put battens behind all the seams in a carvel-planked hull to make it stronger and tighter.[2]

The general practice in American boats was to plank the hull with a combination of eight lapstrake and batten-seam carvel planks. The garboard was lapped by the plank above it and the sheer strake lapped the plank below it, which in

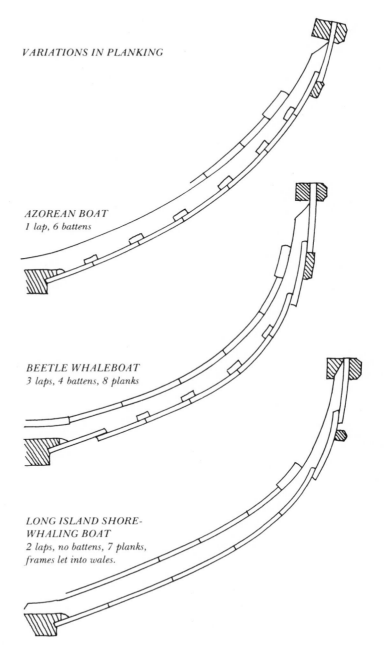

VARIATIONS IN PLANKING

AZOREAN BOAT
1 lap, 6 battens

BEETLE WHALEBOAT
3 laps, 4 battens, 8 planks

LONG ISLAND SHORE-
WHALING BOAT
*2 laps, no battens, 7 planks,
frames let into wales.*

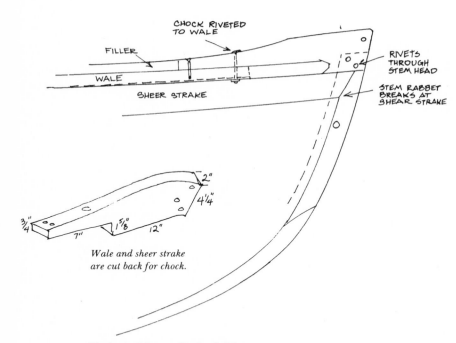

CHOCK RIVETED TO WALE

FILLER

WALE

SHEER STRAKE

RIVETS THROUGH STEM HEAD

STEM RABBET BREAKS AT SHEAR STRAKE

2"

4¼"

¾"

7"

1⅛"

5⅞"

12"

Wale and sheer strake are cut back for chock.

Single-chock bow on Beetle whaleboats

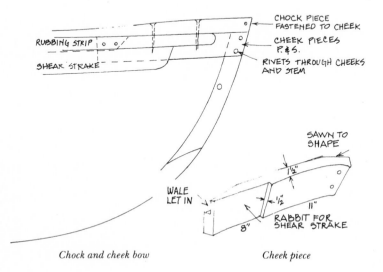

CHOCK PIECE FASTENED TO CHEEK

RUBBING STRIP

CHEEK PIECES P. & S.

SHEAR STRAKE

RIVETS THROUGH CHEEKS AND STEM

SAWN TO SHAPE

1½"

WALE LET IN

1½"

11"

RABBIT FOR SHEAR STRAKE

8"

Chock and cheek bow

Cheek piece

turn lapped the strake below it.* Planks between were carvel with batten-seams.

Both batten-seam and lapstrake construction are strong and flexible. The former is perhaps stronger, not only because the edges are together, but because each plank is fastened to and has the backing of the batten. Both methods make a tight boat little affected by drying, a necessity with a boat which is in and out of the water. The batten-seam boats had one strand of wicking rolled in the seams, making them very tight.

Boats in use on Long Island around 1900 had no laps on the garboard and, surprisingly for a boat built for beaching, no battens. In these boats, which had nine planks to a side, the planking was a fraction over one-half inch.** Azorean boats often have only the sheer strake lapping and some modern boats are built with neither laps nor battens. The boats at Bequia are carvel-planked throughout with three-quarter inch planking; boats in Tasmania were sometimes built without laps, and those in New Zealand were completely lapstrake. An entirely different method of diagonal planking is found on a half model, dated 1883, in a museum in Dundee, Scotland.

The oak frames of the whaleboat were steam bent, sided three-quarter inch and molded one and three-quarter inches at the heel and one and one-

* Ashley writes that the upper of the two topside planks was not a true lap; it resulted from a thicker plank which was used for a stiffer gunwale. Though the sheer strake was sometimes nine-sixteenths inch, all the boats I have seen have the sheer strake lapping the plank below it.

The garboard was lapped by the plank above it, it was said, so the men would have at least something to hold on to if the boat capsized.

** These boats were used off the beaches for at least twenty years; despite their seeming frailness, one was in excellent condition.

quarter inches at the top. The sections of a whaleboat are similar enough so that all the frames may be bent to the same curve. Thus, a number of frames could be steamed, bent over a form or trap, and stayed and stored until use.

W. Scoresby, writing in 1820, tells of the recent adaption of bent frames in British whaleboats. He reports that the oak was boiled or steamed, and that the frames produced were stronger and lighter than the earlier ones sawn from natural crooks.

Frame spacing varied. Earlier boats placed frames at equal distances of about twelve inches on centers; Hall wrote that they ranged from nine to eighteen inches. In the 1860s James Beetle began increasing the number of frames between thwarts from three to five to make a stronger, longer lasting boat. Toward the end of the century, Leonard and Beetle boats had the frames spaced eleven inches at the bows and stern and in the way of thwarts. Spacing between thwarts was seven inches, making between sixty-two and seventy-two frames in all. Other builders spaced frames eight to twelve inches apart.

Two boats, the Edwards and Dominy boats, apparently made by the same builder, that were in use on Long Island around 1900 have even frame spacing, twelve inches on centers. Azorean boats and Australian boats from Twofold Bay also had even spacing. In the case of boats built at Provincetown, Massachusetts, which were somewhat more expensive than stock boats built elsewhere, boats with centerboards have fifty-eight timbers and those without forty-eight.[3]

Although the framing was very strong, it was still flexible because of the practice of notching over laps and battens, which locked the structure together. The planks were fastened through laps and at each side of a seam through battens. At the heel, the frame lapped across the keel and was nailed to it, which gave adequate strength without the use of floor timbers.*

The general practice was for the top of the frame to stop under the wale, relying on the seat knees to brace the wale. This makes for speedy construction but it is weak, and it was common for seat knees to break and for the sheer plank under the wales to split. The two boats used in shore whaling on Long Island had the frames let into notches in the wales. The tops of the frames showed at the sheer. This made for strong construction.**

The wales were of oak and were heavy compared to other strength members. Most boats had a single wale, one and three-quarters inches square or one and five-eighths by one and seven-eighths inches, running along the sheer on the inside of the sheer strake from the bow chocks, to which they were fastened, to the stern timber. The wales were important structurally as they stiffened the rail; these were made up of two or three pieces scarfed and riveted together. Some later boats had added strength in an inner wale lying against the inside face of the seat knees, which gave a heavy appearance to the rail. Gaps between the two wales were filled with filler pieces. These double wales were deemed a Portugese feature in New Bedford, though Beetle built some boats with them, and whaleboats in Tasmania also had them. Azorean boats today lack them.

* Henry Hall speaks of an oak keelson fastened on top of the heels of the frames, but I did not find this construction in any of the original constructions of boats I examined or in any plans.

** Because of the lack of battens and the frames notched into the wales, it would have been easy to have built these boats upside down, framing them before planking. See Chapter VII for the usual contruction methods.

At the bow were the chocks through which the whale line passed. These were strongly made to stand the strains as the whale towed the boat, sounded, and turned. The design of the chocks followed two general patterns. In 1833 James Beetle began to make a solid chock; thereafter, the Beetle boats had a chock made of a single piece on each side, the two being riveted to each other through the stem and also riveted to the wales. The Azorean boats today use a modification of this. Leonard and other builders used a block sawn to shape that filled a space between the wales and the sheer strake, the latter being cut back. The after end of the piece lapped and was fastened to the wale, which was beveled to fair into it. A rabbet was cut for the end of the strake. At the forward end the pieces were through-fastened with rivets. Chocks were then fastened on top of these lower pieces and to the wales. They were sawn to shape, flaring outwards at the stem and running aft, tapering, to the thigh board.

There were five thwarts in the standard American boat. Earlier British and modern Azorean boats commonly had six, and in the past seven- and eight-oared boats were built for shore whaling or as experimental boats. The thwarts rested on risings, the top of the thwart being nine to eleven inches below the sheer. Spacing between thwarts, although striving to be uniform, usually varied. In one boat, thwarts were thirty-five to thirty-seven inches apart. Others spaced thwarts anywhere from thirty-four to thirty-eight inches apart. The first, or harpooner's thwart, was six or seven feet aft of the bow.

Thwarts were made of spruce or pine, seven to eight inches wide. Together with their knees on top, they played an important part in tying the boat together athwartships and in taking the force of blows against the sides; old boats with broken thwarts are found with their hulls spread apart. Two thwarts rested on top of the centerboard case, which provided mutual bracing. Other thwarts, being only one inch thick and five to six feet long, were springy. Presumably no stanchions were placed under because they would be in the way of gear stowed in the bottom of the boat. However, some modern Azorean boats have stanchions but no centerboards. Where the oarsman sat, a pad of dunnage was nailed on the thwart so the man did not have to sit on the seat knee on the thwart.

The seat risers, also called risings or stringers—three-quarters to seven-eighths of an inch thick and three and one-quarter to four inches deep—were generally of spruce, though oak was sometimes used. The latter, though tougher and more rot resistant, is heavier. In some boats the risers ran from the stem to the stern; in others from the first to the last frame. Their sheer varied: some followed the sheer of the boat itself and others were flatter. The riser was fastened to each frame and gave longitudinal stiffness to the hull.

The boat at the New Bedford Whaling Museum, built for use in the Arctic, had added strength through a shelf, four by one and one-eighth inches, sawn to the shape of the curve of the hull and laid against the riser. It was riveted through the frames and planking at intervals of about one foot. Azorean boats have similar shelves running under the first, second, and third thwarts; these are riveted through the hull and give strengthening to the mast partner and tabernacle.

Standing knees were fastened on top of the thwarts; these stiffened the thwarts and braced the wales. In the stock boats of the late nineteenth century the knees were steam bent. James Beetle wrote that he tried the first steamed knee in 1830 when natural crooks were growing scarce, after hearing of boats built in France with them. A whaleboat at the Sag Harbor Whaling Musuem appears to have had natural crook knees originally. Henry Hall writes of the use of cedar knees in American boats, and an Australian whaleboat, said to be an old one when photographed in the early 1930s, appears to have natural crooks.[4] Modern Azorean boats sometimes use cast metal knees, but steamed knees are cheap and fast to produce, and they are easy to fit with a filler piece between them and the planking.

The knees were bent 90° on a radius of about six inches. To prevent breaking, they were cut with a kerf. Made of oak, they were sided one inch and molded one and one-eighth inch to one and one-half inches at the top, and three-quarter to seven-eighths of an inch at the inboard end.

The number of knees to a thwart varied, though each thwart had at least one set. Generally the second and fifth thwart had two standing knees placed on the forward and after edges of the thwart; the others had a single standing knee in the middle of the thwart. The leg of the knee on the thwart extended inboard about two feet; the vertical leg went up to the rail. It was fastened with rivets through the wale, sheer strake, and rubbing strip at the top, and at the throat through the planking, filler piece, and guard under the sheer strake. Clench nails fastened it to the thwart. The knees were important to the strength of the sheer. In older boats they were often found to have failed, though presumably they were adequate for the short life of most of the boats. They cracked because of the tight bend and the one-quarter inch rivet hole through the throat.

Whaleboats were generally ceiled from the risers down to the center line and from the first frames forward to the last frame aft. Ceiling added

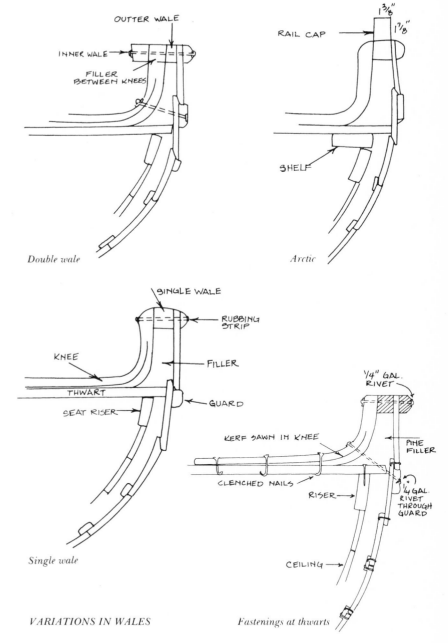

Double wale

Arctic

VARIATIONS IN WALES

Single wale

Fastenings at thwarts

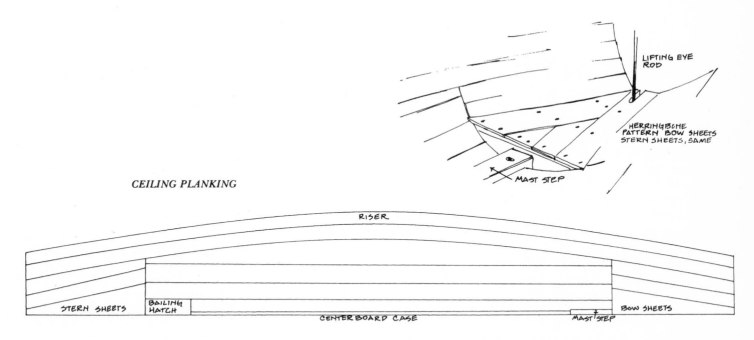

CEILING PLANKING

strength to the hull; the ceiling planking was fastened to each frame and, after swelling, the seams became very tight. The ceiling covered the frames and with no projecting frames, the boat was easier to move about in, while gear could be more easily stowed. Ceiling also distributed weight, such as heavy line tubs, and prevented walking directly on the planking. A further advantage was the protection it gave the planking from drying and direct sunlight when the boats were in the davits.*

The pattern of the ceiling in the stock boats was fairly standard. The first plank under the riser was of uniform width for its entire length. Below it was a shaped plank tapered at both ends and extending from the bow sheets to the stern sheets. Under it

* Several models of whaleboats show open ceiling with gaps between the planking. The drawing in Goode shows a boat with no ceiling below the riser for a space of about one foot. The bilges have ceiling.

the planks could be fitted with their edges almost straight. In the area of the bow and stern sheets shorter pieces filled in. In the Edwards and Dominy boats, which were somewhat smaller and less deep than standard, the planks immediately below the risers were tapered. The material in the ceiling was generally one-half inch cedar scrap pieces from the side planking, or sometimes pine.

At the bow and stern, the bow and stern sheets formed short platforms. The forward one provided footing for the men who harpooned and lanced the whale, the one aft a platform for the helmsman. The length of these varied, the forward one being from three feet long, and the stern sheets generally about five and one-half feet. Both were built about eight inches above the keel, lying level with the waterline and supported by beams underneath on eleven or twelve inch centers which were notched over and nailed to the frames. The planks were three-quarters of an inch thick and five to six inches wide, laid herringbone fashion. Several models in museums show this planking laid fore and aft.

The foredeck was made up of a box in the bow and a plank called the thigh board laid athwartships on the gunwale. The latter was notched to form the clumsy cleat for the harpooner's leg. Made of spruce or pine, one and one-half inches thick and seven and one-half to nine inches wide, it was rabbeted at the ends to let down on the wales, to which it was strongly fastened with boat nails. Thus the thigh board formed a strong tie athwartships on the gunwale.

The box, in which four or five fathoms of line were coiled, was lightly made of one-half inch cedar laid athwartships on top of the lap of the second strake and, in the bows, on short nailing strips. A plank of the same thickness was nailed fore and aft on the under side and ran up to the stem. The after end of the box was vertically staved and nailed to the forward edge of the thigh board.

The cuddy board in the stern was four to five feet long, made of cedar planks laid athwartships on the gunwale. In the Beetle whaleboats the two inboard planks were one and one-half inches thick, rabbeted on the underside to let down on the wales. This put them level with the rest of the planking, which was three-quarter inch, and made a stronger athwartships tie. An entirely different design is found in boats from Tasmania, in which the cuddy board is built with a strong crown.

The strains of towing were taken by the loggerhead stepped through the cuddy board. It was strongly braced by the lion's tongue or loggerhead strip, a curved oak plank laid fore and aft to starboard of the centerline of the cuddy board. The loggerhead pierced the lion's tongue, which was three-quarters of an inch thick and clench-nailed to the planking of the cuddy board. The design of the lion's tongue varied with the builders. Beetle branded his name on the lion's tongue aft of the loggerhead.

The loggerhead was a bitt of oak or hickory, four or five inches in diameter and projecting eight or nine inches above the tongue. Braced at the top by the lion's tongue, it was stepped below in the side of the ceiling. The loggerhead had a staff with square cross section to keep it from rotating, while beneath the cuddy board a key prevented it from lifting. The whale line was snubbed around this post; older loggerheads show deep grooves from the line. The loggerhead was raked aft in older boats, but tended to be more plumb in later ones. The one on the Long Island Dominy boat was angled strongly to starboard, The loggerhead is to starboard of the center line to give room on the port side of the whale line for the boatsteerer handling the steering oar, which, in whaleboats, was always mounted on the port side.

The loggerhead of some British boats was in the bow, which would eliminate the dangerous whale line running down the center of the boat. Americans preferred the loggerhead aft because it was easier to tend the line when it was running out, and easier to haul it in when pulling up to the whale. It was also claimed that there was less strain on the boat since the tension of the towing line was applied aft.*

The steering oar was rigged in several ways. It had to be strong, for the boatsteerer exerted great

* British boats sometimes had two posts, called bollards, in the bow. These, in line on the centerline, are seen in sketches of W. G. Burn Murdoch. William J. Hopkins, *She Blows! And Sparm at That* (Boston: Houghton Mifflin Co., 1922), pp. 40-41.

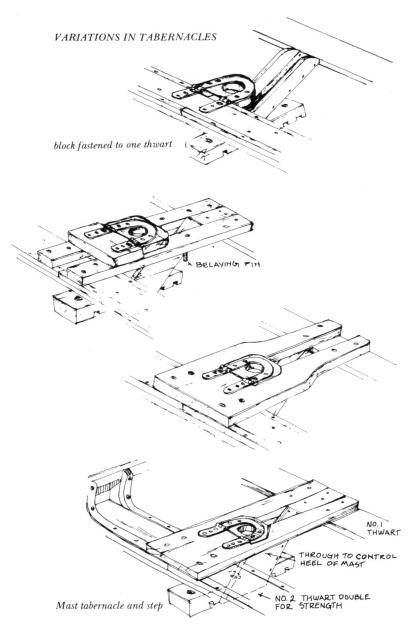

VARIATIONS IN TABERNACLES

block fastened to one thwart

A BELAYING PIN

NO. 1 THWART

THROUGH TO CONTROL HEEL OF MAST

NO. 2 THWART DOUBLE FOR STRENGTH

Mast tabernacle and step

leverage in swinging the stern around with the long oar when maneuvering close to the whale. For normal steering with way on, little pressure on the oar was necessary to turn the boat. A preferred way of rigging it in the later boats was with an outrigger across the after end of the cuddy board which projected from the port side. This acted as a rest, with the oar passing through a becket on the stern timber. Another later method used an iron oarlock on a brace. Earlier boats sometimes used a grommet through a hole in the gunwale or an oarlock in the wale. To prevent wear on the oar and to make the rig silent, steering oar braces were thrummed and oarlocks served with marline. If the becket rig was used, the bight holding the oar was tightened by a lanyard fastened to a cleat on the lion's tongue.

The sides of the boats were protected with chafing or rubbing strips and guards. These were necessary to minimize damage when the boats were hoisted aboard or lowered from the ships. The rubbing strip was along the outside of the sheer at the rail, and the guards were under the lap below the sheer strake. Sometimes a second guard was put under the second lap. Such precautions were necessary when lowering, as there was danger of the lap hanging up and catching on the ship's side. Boats used in shore whaling had less conspicuous guards. Some boats built for the Arctic had guards on the bottom for protection while being dragged over ice.

The rubbing strips, with chamfered or sometimes rounded edges, ran from the bow chocks to the stern. The strips were of oak, one and one-half to two inches wide and five-eighths to seven-eighths of an inch thick. The guards ranged in thickness from one-half to three-quarters of an inch and in width from one and one-half to three and one-half inches. The latter tapered in some boats to follow the plank lines. Guards did not run full length, but usually started five to six feet from the bow and ended seven or eight feet from the stern.

The mast partners and tabernacle were designed in various ways, varying from a simple hole in the thwart to hinged blocks through which the mast was stepped.* The latter was generally in use in later days when the rig became larger and going on under sail was general practice. In this case, a massive, strong tabernacle was necessary if it was not to carry away as the mast was lowered. The heel of the mast was kept under control in a trough that ran at an angle from the step on the keel up to the forward thwart. The Edwards boat used in shore whaling had a small rig, and her mast was stepped in the old way through a hole in the second thwart.

The partners that held the hinged step sometimes spanned the first and second thwarts, the latter being double thickness for strength. Partners were oak, one and one-half or one and three-quarters inches thick, about fourteen inches wide and four feet long. A five inch slot allowed the heel of the mast to pass through as the mast was tumbled. The hinged block with the hole for the mast was recessed into the plank; the hinge itself was a heavy bronze casting held by rivets, or a cheaper iron strap secured to the thwart with eyes.

The centerboard trunk was simply and rather lightly constructed. It was braced by the two thwarts that rested on it, but there were no bed logs and the case sides were only seven-eighths or one inch pine or cedar fastened from below with nails driven up through the keel. The ends of the ledges formed tennons letting into the centerboard slot. The trunk was cheap and fast to build and proba-

* James Beetle applied for a patent on the hinged mast step.

Centerboard case

bly leaked before the boat had been in service very long, but there were plenty of men in the boat to bail. It is likely that far more water came over the sides than leaked through the case.

The centerboard itself was generally made of two seven-eighths inch thick oak planks. Some were cleated at the ends as well as being fastened with drifts. A five-sixteenth or three-eighths of an inch rod was used for raising and lowering the board which was weighted with ten pounds of lead.*

Summing up, the construction of the whaleboats, as with the lines, was adapted to the use to which the boats were put. Strength is found where there is greatest stress. Scantlings are light. The design was suitable for quick, cheap construction. The methods of building and the materials used produced a tough, elastic, tight boat, fast and quiet in the water and, if for use aboard whaleships, built for a limited time of service. Boats built for shore whaling were generally built with greater care, were maintained better, were not so hardly used, and consequently lasted longer.

* James Beetle's first experimental centerboard trunks were off center, to the side of the keel. All in use later used the slot in the keel. The early boards were small.

1. Scoresby emphasizes that British whaleboats were always "carvel-built" because they are repaired more easily, with planking of one-half to three-quarters inch "firboards." W. Scoresby, *An Account of the Arctic Regions, with a History and Description of the Northern Whale Fishery* (Edinburgh: Archibald Constable and Co., 1894), p. 222.

2. James Beetle letter in *The American Neptune,* vol. 30, no. 4 (October, 1943), p. 352.

3. James Templeman Brown, *The Whale Fishery and its Appliances* (Washington: Government Printing Office), 1883, p. 241.

4. William John Dakin, *Whalemen Adventurers* (Sydney: Sirus Books, 1963), photographs following p. 80.

Chapter V

FITTINGS AND EQUIPMENT

The fittings and equipment aboard whaleboats, no matter what their time or place, show a remarkable lack of variation and change. Hulls and sail plans are more varied. Thus the whaleboat of Bequia today, whose hull and sail have many of the features of other local boat types, has the same cleats and fittings as a boat used in the sperm fisheries of a century ago. Sometimes different materials were used to make fittings, such as bone cleats replacing wood, but the placement and design of fittings remain basically the same.

There was the same conservative approach to equipment. A comparison between a contemporary Azorean boat and an American whaleboat of 1883 shows that they were fitted out almost identically. The Azoreans are, in some respects, even less progressive, for they abandonded explosive devices—whalecraft in the whaleman's parlance—such as darting guns and bomb lances and put sole reliance on hand harpoons and lances.*

New whaleboats procured by the ship's agent and delivered by the builder, were usually bare of fittings and equipment. Sometimes the boat was covered only by a coat of priming paint. If ordered, builders would do some fitting out. For example, the *Mermaid*'s boats were fitted out at a cost of three dollars each in 1885. Generally they were equipped and readied at sea, a process which according to one account took three weeks, painting them inside and out, and equipping them.[1] On some whaleships the cotton drill sails were made on board by the mates and boatsteerers. Spruce poles were carried for spars and fitted by the carpenter. The

---

* The Azoreans have made other concessions to progress, however. They now use a hemp whale line with nylon core, radios, molded plywood whaleboats, and power boats for a tow.

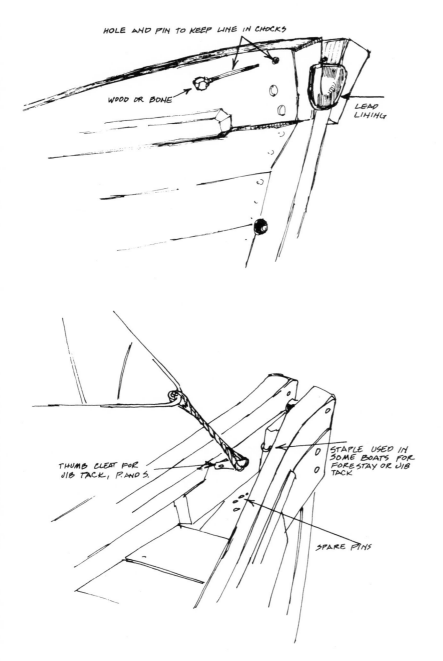

HOLE AND PIN TO KEEP LINE IN CHOCKS

WOOD OR BONE

LEAD LINING

THUMB CLEAT FOR JIB TACK, P. AND S.

STAPLE USED IN SOME BOATS FOR FORESTAY OR JIB TACK

SPARE PINS

cooper made and overhauled the line tubs, piggins, boat buckets, and lantern kegs; irons were set up and the boats were loaded with all necessary gear.

One writer, exaggerating somewhat, wrote: "There were numberless little beckets and cleats to be nailed and fastened in numberless little out-of-the-way nooks and crevices about the bow and stern."[2] None of these fittings was without purpose. Most were roughly but strongly made and fastened, and there was no unnecessary decoration on the boats used aboard ship.

In the bows of the whaleboats were the chocks. The builders protected the stem head and the line from chafe with a lining of lead, brass, lignum vitae or whalebone, or a roller placed between the chocks. Without this, "in one season's successful whaling the boat would be cut right down through to the water's edge" by the whale line.[3]

Above the roller or lining in athwartships holes was the chock pin to keep the line in the chock. These were made weak, according to Hopkins, so that "if there is an obstruction or kink in the line, the pin breaks instead of carrying the boat under."[4] Scammon, on the other hand, writes that they were made of tough wood or whalebone.[5] In some museums bamboo pins are found in the boats. The heads of the pins were sometimes carved with a twelve-sided knob at the end, with extra pins stuck in holes in a triangular-or diamond-shaped pattern in the planking of the warp box at the forward end. In tests at the Seaport it was found difficult to break a thin pine pin when preparing to bow on. If the pin was designed to break, as claimed by Hopkins, it would have to be very weak indeed.

On the chock to port a slot about one inch deep was cut at an angle across the top. Lances bent in killing the whale were straightened in this slot. A mallet attached by a lanyard under the thigh board was also used for pounding the bent lances straight. The lance shafts were made of soft iron and were often bent when the mate, churning the lance with all his strength, struck bone.

In the bow on the inside of the chocks on each side were small, wooden thumb cleats; an eye at the tack of the jib was slipped over one of these. The jib was set flying, having no forestay. As the whale was approached, the boatsteerer quickly took in the jib to give himself a clear field, slipped the eye off the cleat, released the halyard from the belaying pin in the mast partners, and pulled down the sail. The jib was then stuffed out of the way under the warp box. Some boats without jibs had forestays that went to a stout staple in the inside stem face.

A sheath of canvas or leather was tacked on the staving forming the after end of the warp box, holding a knife to cut the line in an emergency. Spare pins for the toggle irons were held in a strap nailed to the staving. A hatchet was attached by a lanyard and stowed behind the riser under the thigh-board. This also was used for cutting a running line.

In later boats there was a becket of manila line called a kicking strap on top of the thigh board. The whale line passed under it as it ran from loggerhead to chocks. The ends of the kicking strap were passed through holes and knotted under the thigh board. The purpose of the strap was to prevent the line from sweeping aft and endangering the crew if the whale changed course and the line jumped out of the chock. On the starboard side of the clumsy cleat was a small hole through which some hanks of rope yarn were threaded. These were used for lightly securing the harpoons lying ready for use in the crotch.

The boats were lifted by eyes forward and aft. The rod, or hoisting strap of the forward eye

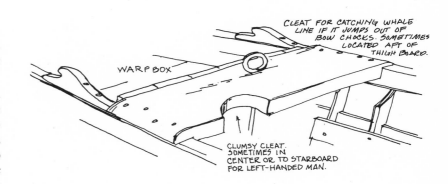

CLEAT FOR CATCHING WHALE LINE IF IT JUMPS OUT OF BOW CHOCKS. SOMETIMES LOCATED AFT OF THIGH BOARD.

WARP BOX

CLUMSY CLEAT. SOMETIMES IN CENTER OR TO STARBOARD FOR LEFT-HANDED MAN.

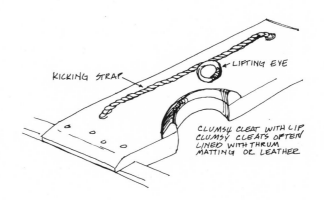

KICKING STRAP

LIFTING EYE

CLUMSY CLEAT WITH LIP CLUMSY CLEATS OFTEN LINED WITH THRUM MATTING OR LEATHER

passed through the clumsy cleat, and the one aft through the cuddy board. Earlier boats had the eyes farther toward the ends. The rods were five-eights to three-quarters of an inch in diameter. The forged eye had an inside diameter of about one and one-half inches. The rod passed through the stem and stern close to the scarf joining those members to the keel. The end of the rod was headed up over a rove or washer. The distance between the eyes on the Beetle boat at the Mariners Museum is twenty-one feet eight inches; between the eyes of the boat in the William Hand plan, twenty-two feet ten inches. The lifting eyes were put to severe strain, particularly when a half-swamped boat was raised by the bow to drain it.

On either bow, immediately in front of or directly behind the thigh board on the wales, were two large thumb cleats called bow cleats. These stood some three inches high and were about eight inches long, and were strongly fastened to the wales with boat nails. They had two functions: to catch the whale line if it jumped out of the chocks and there was no kicking strap to hold it; and, to facilitate hauling up on the whale for lancing. The line was brought back to the bow cleat and pulled in by the bow oarsman, bringing the boat up alongside the whale. This was known as "bowing on" the whale.

On the starboard side aft of the thigh board was the crotch for the two live harpoons, made like a fork with three tines. The poles rested in the crotches, the "first" slightly higher. The harpoon tended diagonally forward and lay between the bow chocks. The crotch was usually a stick of wood with two saw cuts wedged open. Some, however, were forged and resembled a double oarlock.

On the ceiling below the thigh board on the starboard side there was sometimes the shoulder gun

that fired bomb lances. A small case with lances might be stowed in the box, or the lances might be kept in a canvas bag under the box. A case of wood or canvas for holding the heads of the spare harpoons was sometimes mounted on the port side of the forward thwart.

When harpooning or lancing the whales, both the boatsteerer and the mate braced their thighs in the clumsy cleat. The notch was usually to port, this being most convenient for right-handed men, but it was sometimes in the middle, and a boat from the *Manta* shows one notch to port and one to starboard. The cut was usually semicircular; some, however, showed a curve hooking to right or left. Several boats used in shore whaling increased the bearing surface with a lip along the edge of the notch, and it was common practice to pad the notch with thrumming or leather.

Pins or cleats for belaying the halyards were on the thwart or partners; the pins were made to project only below to prevent injuries to a man thrown against them or falling on them.

Pads for the oarlock sockets were fastened to the wales, and placed twelve inches to thirteen inches aft of the thwart. In some boats they were beveled and chamfered to give a finished appearance. Up until the 1850s, thole pins were used in whaleboats; they were then replaced with forged rowlocks. The tub rowlock was double with a higher and lower position—the higher one kept the oar clear of the tub. Earlier, a wooden extension with a crotch cut in the top was used rather than the double rowlock. The rowlocks were served with marline or leather and the wale between the pins was thrummed to quiet the oars.

Peak cleats were nailed to the ceiling at each rowing position. These were beveled to eliminate unnecessary projections and a hole was bored in the center to receive the end of the oar when peaked. The cleats were placed to give the peaked oar an angle that would keep it out of the water as the boat rolled when under tow. Both the tub and the harpooner's peak cleat were placed higher than the others on the frames above the riser so the oar would clear the tub and the mast, if it was left in the mast hinge after lowering.

Not all boats were equipped with such cleats. Charles Beetle wrote of one captain who would not have them in his boats, claiming the oars thumped the sides when peaking and gallied the whales.

Opposite the masts on the gunwales were the strops and thimbles for securing the shrouds. There were several ways to rig these. One method was to bore a hole down through the wale, pass a line through and splice an eye both above and below the wale. A thimble was placed in the eye above for the shroud lanyard. The eye below the wale was seized to a hole in the riser. A simpler method was a grommet passing under the wale through a hole in the sheer strake. The grommet had a thimble seized into it above the gunwale. In later boats, an eyebolt in the wale was used. Some whaleboats with small rigs dispensed with the shrouds altogether. On the inside of the wales, port and starboard, and generally just aft of the third thwart, was a cleat for the jib sheet.

In the stern a curved foot brace was fastened on the port side for the boatsteerer. One end was let in the ceiling planking and nailed to a frame, and the other was let in the planking of the stern sheets. The boatsteerer and mate gained leverage while using the steering oar by jamming a foot under the brace. Above it were the standing cleats nailed to the risers, port and starboard. These, shaped somewhat like small half models about eighteen inches long, provided footing for the mate, raising

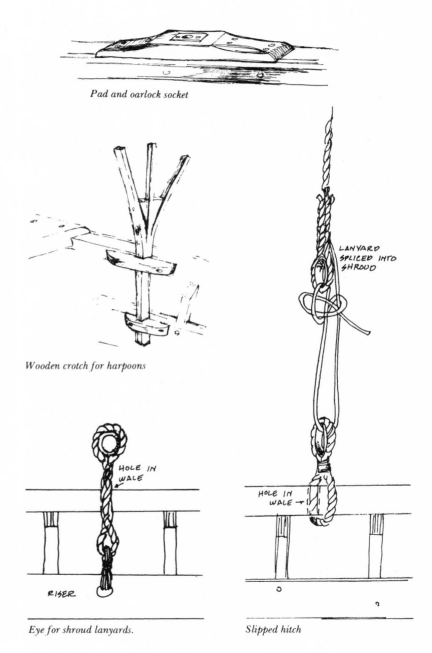

Pad and oarlock socket

Wooden crotch for harpoons

Eye for shroud lanyards.

Slipped hitch

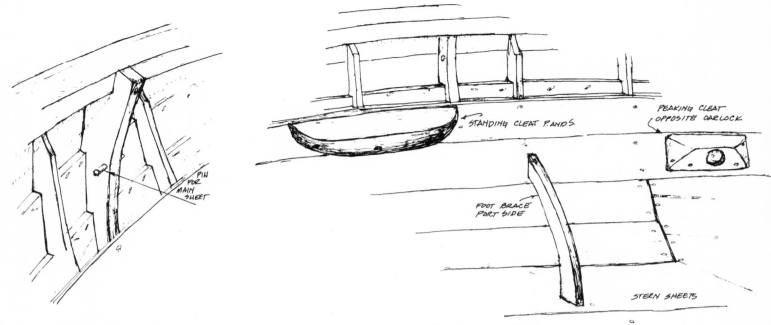

Chocking piece on quarter.

Stern sheets (port side aft).

his height of eye about one and a half feet as he looked for whale.*

Under the wales in the quarters were short timbers which the plans of William Hand identified as "chocking pieces". These were notched over the laps and placed rather like sister frames. Their function is not clear. Some boats had pins in them for the sheets, but this would not be the main purpose for pieces so stoutly made, and not all boats had the pins. It is probable that the original purpose was to provide stiffening to the wale between the after thwart and the cuddy board.**On the inside of the wales forward of the cuddy board were

* Visibility was a problem in whaleboats. In *Moby Dick,* the short mate stood on the shoulders of the boatsteerer to see over the tops of the waves.

** Charles Batchelder, Erick A. R. Ronneberg, Jr., and I speculated about the function of the pieces one day while look-

the cleats for the main sheet—sometimes made as jam cleats.

The cuddy board had a number of fittings added aboard ship. The builder delivered the boat with lion's tongue, loggerhead, steering oar brace, and rest for the mast when lowered. There remained to be added cleats for adjusting the steering oar becket, cleats for the pennants for unshipping the rudder, holes and fairleads for the pennants, the knife sheath underneath, a mounting for the boat com-

ing at a boat, and Mr. Batchelder summed up our thoughts in a letter: "These stiffening timbers helped to keep the gunwale strake from splitting in the comparatively long space between knees on the after thwart and the cuddy boards. The stiffening timbers were places to resist the pull of the gripes when hauled tight and the weight of the whole boat when it might have been turned up on the cranes in very rough weather."

That Azorean boats have the pieces does not destroy the argument that the gunwale between cuddy board and aftermost thwart needed stiffening.

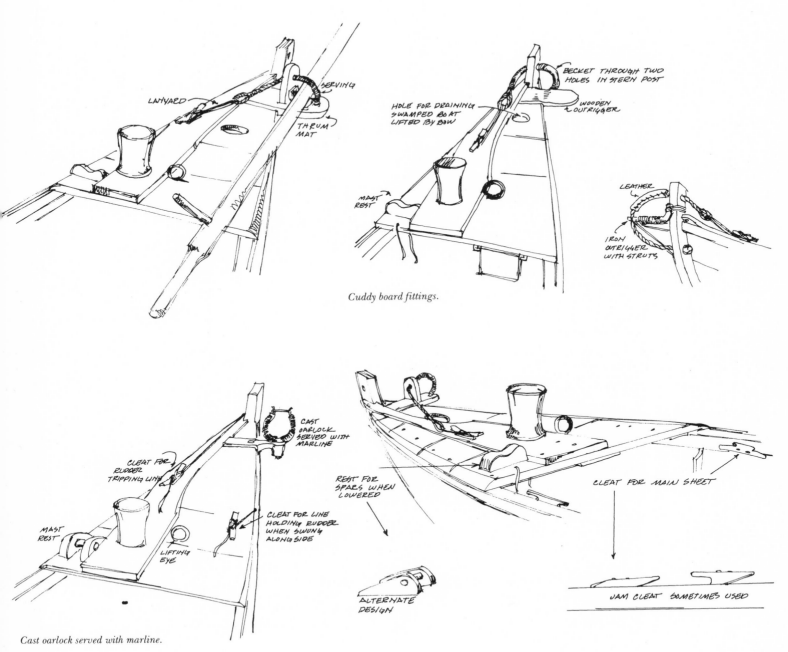

LANYARD   SERVING

THRUM MAT

BECKET THROUGH TWO HOLES IN STERN POST

HOLE FOR DRAINING SWAMPED BOAT LIFTED BY BOW

WOODEN OUTRIGGER

MAST REST

LEATHER

IRON OUTRIGGER WITH STRUTS

Cuddy board fittings.

CAST OARLOCK SERVED WITH MARLINE

CLEAT FOR RUDDER TRIPPING LINE

CLEAT FOR LINE HOLDING RUDDER WHEN SWUNG ALONGSIDE

MAST REST

LIFTING EYE

REST FOR SPARS WHEN LOWERED

ALTERNATE DESIGN

CLEAT FOR MAIN SHEET

JAM CLEAT SOMETIMES USED

Cast oarlock served with marline.

57

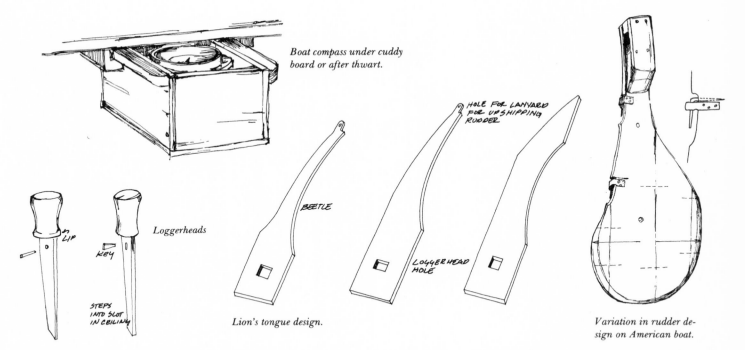

Boat compass under cuddy board or after thwart.

LIP

KEY

Loggerheads

STEPS INTO SLOT IN CEILING

BEETLE

Lion's tongue design.

LOGGERHEAD HOLE

HOLE FOR LANYARD FOR UP-SHIPPING RUDDER

Variation in rudder design on American boat.

pass, and perhaps a protective canvas flap nailed under the forward edge of the cuddy board.

The rigging of the steering oar varied in design. Generally a strop with a wall knot at one end and an eye splice at the other passed through holes in the stern timber or an outrigger. The strop was served where it held the oar. A lanyard from the eye to the cleat adjusted the tension of the strop.

The rudder was unshipped and swung up on the port side with two lines. One, the tripping line, secured with a knot through a hole high on the rudder, lifted the pintles out of the gudgeons when pulled. This line passed through a fairlead on the starboard side of the stern timber, or through a hole bored through the extreme after end of the lion's tongue. It was secured to a cleat on the lion's tongue aft of the loggerhead.

The other line, which swung the rudder up, was attached lower on the blade. This line led up through a hole bored at an angle under the rubbing strip, emerging on top of the cuddy boards from where it ran to a cleat. Sometimes a fairlead was worked in. The mate could unship the rudder and swing it alongside with a jerk on the one line and a pull on the other after the iron was fast to the whale and the steering oar was put to use. The latter, when not used for steering, was slid forward and the handle slipped through a leather strap or grommet and thimble on the wale. The after end of the oar rested on the brace.

The boat compass was mounted on slides under the cuddy boards on the port side or under the aftermost thwart.

Whaleboat oars were the longest of any in general use. The oars of a five-oared American boat ranged from fourteen to eighteen feet in length.

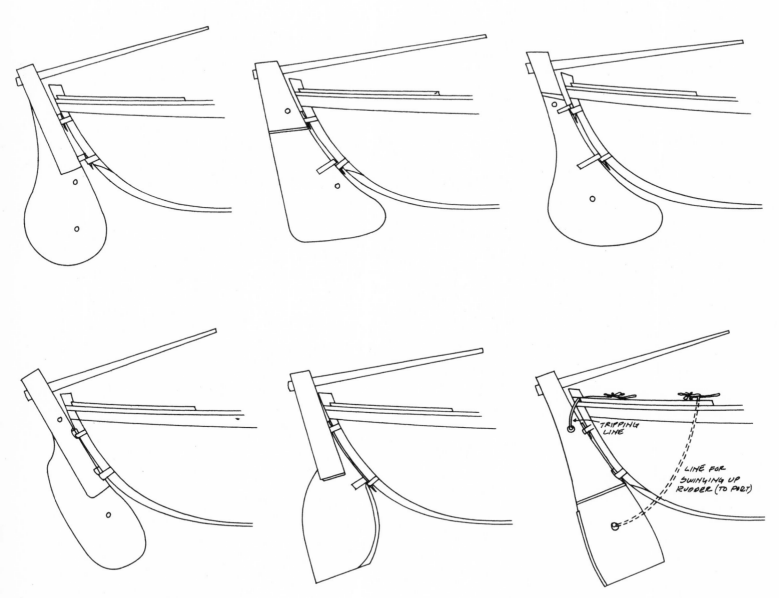

TRIPPING LINE

LINE FOR SWINGING UP RUDDER (TO PORT)

VARIATION IN RUDDER DESIGN

59

The harpooner's oar, the midship oar, and the after oar pulled on the starboard side. The midship oar was the longest pulling oar in the boat, while the other two, equal in length, were the shortest. The bow and tub oars were the same length and pulled on the port side; in length, they were between the midship oar and the two at the ends. This arrangement of oars of unequal length was necessary because of the curvature of the sides. Also, it left the boat reasonably well balanced when the boatsteerer peaked his oar in preparation for darting the iron.

The oars on British boats were sometimes shorter than American ones. Scoresby writes they were fourteen to sixteen feet, and all the same length. Azorean boats, which were longer, had six oars: those at the ends were sixteen feet, numbers two and five seventeen feet, and three and four eighteen feet.

Ashley writes that oars were seventeen feet, seventeen feet six inches, and eighteen feet; fifteen feet, sixteen feet, and seventeen feet; and sixteen feet, seventeen feet and eighteen feet.[6] The steering oar ranged from twenty feet to twenty-three feet. Brown lists sixteen, seventeen, and eighteen feet with the steering oar length twenty-two feet.[7] Davis has lengths of fourteen feet, sixteen feet, and eighteen feet, with a steering oar twenty-two feet long.[8]

The pulling oars had blades about six inches wide and five to five and one-half feet long. The loom next to the handle was three inches in diameter, tapering to two and one-quarter near the blade. The handle was about one and one-half inches in diameter and nine to ten inches long. The steering oar blade was seven inches wide and about six and one-half feet long. The diameter of the loom next to the handle was three and three-sixteenths inches and tapered to two and one-half inches. The handle was about one foot long and tapered from one and seven-eighths inches to one and eleven-sixteenths inches. About one and one-half inches from the end, and in the same plane as the blade, was a peg about six inches long for the left hand of the boatsteerer.

In trials at Mystic Seaport it was observed that the long ash oars flexed considerably as the crew laid into them. Occasionally oars were counterbalanced with sheets of lead wrapped around the loom near the handle, or the handle was bored and filled with lead. Narrow bands of paint at the ends of the blades, and circles or Roman numerals on the blades served to identify the oars so the men could quickly seize their own when manning the boat. The same bands marked oars in the Azores as well as halfway around the world in whaleboats pulled by New Zealand Maoris.

The five paddles were generally roughly hacked out of a plank or made of two pieces forming a handle and a blade. The former, about five feet long, had a narrower blade and resembled paddles used by islanders in the South Pacific.

In American boats the whale line was held in two tubs after the centerboard came into use. A large tub with two-thirds to three-quarters of the line was in the space between the fourth and fifth thwarts. The smaller tub was to starboard of the centerboard between the third and fourth thwarts. The amount of line varied in different periods; 225 fathoms in the large tub and 75 in the smaller, for a total of 300 fathoms, was fairly standard in American boats in the sperm fisheries in the 1880s. British boats carried a total of 220 fathoms in two tubs, according to Chatterton.[9] Azoreans today have 100 fathoms to 120 fathoms each in two tubs, making a total of 200 fathoms to 240 fathoms.

OAR LENGTHS OF BOATS IN VARIOUS MUSEUMS

	Harpooner	Bow	Midship	Tub	After	Steering
Off brig *Daisy*, Cold Spring Harbor Whaling Museum	14 ft.	16 ft.	18 ft.	16 ft.	14 ft.	23 ft.
Nantucket Whaling Museum	12 ft. 8 in.	14 ft. 6 in.	15 ft. 1 in.	14 ft. 6 in.	12 ft. 7 in.	19 ft. 7 in.
New Bedford Whaling Museum	15 ft.	16 ft.	17 ft.	16 ft.	15 ft.	18 ft. 2 in.
Beetle boat at Mariners Museum	15 ft.	16 ft.	17 ft.	16 ft.	15 ft.	21 ft. 4 in.

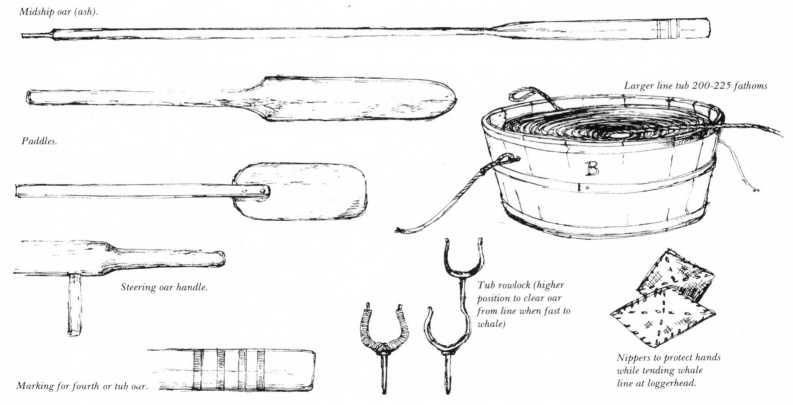

Midship oar (ash).

Paddles.

Steering oar handle.

Marking for fourth or tub oar.

Tub rowlock (higher position to clear oar from line when fast to whale)

Larger line tub 200-225 fathoms

Nippers to protect hands while tending whale line at loggerhead.

STOPPERS

Water keg

S B

MARKING FOR
STARBOARD
BOAT

LIST OF EQUIPMENT ABOARD
AN AMERICAN WHALEBOAT

6 oars, 5 for pulling and 1 for steering

6 paddles

2 tubs for whale line

1 bucket for wetting whale line

1 wooden keg for fresh water

1 piggin for bailing

1 lantern keg for lantern, tinder box, matches, candles, pipes, tobacco, hard bread, etc.

1 drug or drag to be attached to the whale line

Several waifs or flags

Several pairs of canvas nippers for handling the whale line

1 boat hatchet

1 fog horn

2 knives

1 bomb gun or darting gun

Bag of bomb lances

5 or 6 harpoons

3 hand lances

1 boat spade for cutting hole in lips of whale to reeve towing line

Spars, rigging, and sails

300 fathoms of whale line

Bucket for wetting whale line.

Piggin for bailing.

Waif, 10' (pointed to be stuck upright in dead whale).

Boat hook, 7'

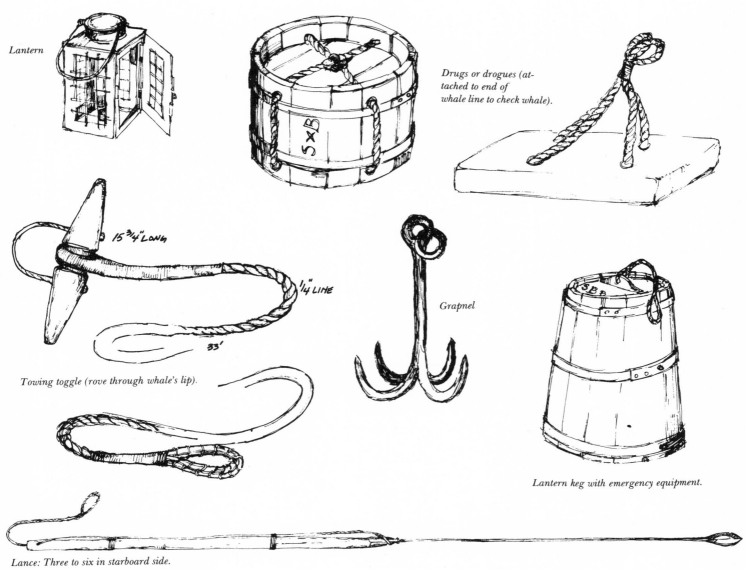

Lantern

Drugs or drogues (attached to end of whale line to check whale).

15 ¾" LONG

¼" LINE

33'

Towing toggle (rove through whale's lip).

Grapnel

Lantern keg with emergency equipment.

Lance: Three to six in starboard side.

Toggle iron, two live irons attached to whale line, two to four spares.

The line used earlier in American boats was lightly tarred, three-strand American hemp, of sixteen or seventeen yarns each, and two-thirds to seven-eighths of an inch in diameter. Later, manila was substituted because of its greater strength. According to Ashley, this was a special long-fiber slack-laid line with a breaking strength of about three tons.[10] The circumference was two inches and the line was three-strand, with thirteen threads to a strand. The Azoreans later went back to a good grade of Italian hemp, and recently have been using a manila line with a nylon center, which is said to be thinner, more flexible, and stronger.[11]

The line was the responsibility of the boatsteerer. To work out kinks and twists, he hung it from aloft and then coiled it in Flemish coils in the line tubs.[12] The Azoreans today flake out the line on the launching ramps before coiling. Once in the tub, the line was covered with a canvas cover.

Some tubs were made for their purpose; others apparently were cut-down barrels. The bottom was perforated and cut with grooves for draining, and a notch was cut in the top edge so the tail could be hung over the side. Short lines were secured on opposite sides of the tubs to lash them to the thwarts so that they could not slide around in the bottom of the boat as she rolled. The smaller tub, placed to the side of the centerboard trunk was sometimes made elliptical.[13] The line in the smaller tub weighed about 120 pounds if it contained 75 fathoms of manila; the 225 fathoms of manila in the larger tub weighed about 230 pounds.

The irons or harpoons were stowed in two places. The live irons were kept in the crotch in the starboard bow, with two or three spares forward to port on top of the thwarts below the wales. Lances, sometimes as many as half a dozen, lay in racks to starboard, with latches or pins to keep them in place. Both spare harpoons and lances were kept well forward. Shoulder gun and bombs, if carried, were also in the bow for the mate to use in killing the whale. The boat spade, which was sometimes used in attempts to disable the whale by cutting the tendons to the flukes, was also stowed forward.

Drug, grapnel, waifs, pokes, water keg, piggin, paddles, and boat hook were stowed under thwarts in the waists. Behind the fifth thwart was the boat bucket, and aft under the cuddy board were the lantern keg and compass. The former held matches, lantern, candles, bread, and sometimes tobacco. There were a few other smaller items such as canvas and copper tacks for emergency repairs, canvas nippers or cloths for protecting the hands from burns as the line ran out, and a canvas-wrapped bottle of oil. Counting spars, something like 900 pounds of gear went into a whaleboat.

The whaleboat put limits on the type of and the amount of equipment that could be carried. The boat's size was limited and it was loaded to the utmost. The gear had to be stowed with great care, with a particular eye to its being well secured so it did not come adrift in the small, tossing boat. At the same time, it had to be near at hand where it could be used quickly when needed. Some pieces had to be kept clear: for instance, nothing could be in the way of the whale line. The proper stowage of gear was vital to the effective and safe operation of the boat.

Some experiments were made with more complicated types of equipment. Heavier swivel guns were used in larger British whaleboats and boats in California Bay whaling. Usually the bow had to be reinforced for these guns; they were not widely used in American whaleboats operated from ships. The English also used winches for whale lines, which required a larger boat with special reinforcement, adding more weight. The size and weight limitations of whaleboats were not the only factors, but they did help account for the continued reliance on light, handy equipment.*

---

* It is interesting to speculate on why primitive equipment continued to be used. The simpler equipment was more reliable and took less training, although teamwork, training, and familiarity with the boat and gear were essentials in using the boats effectively. Cheapness and reliability of the simple equipment were probably most important. Salt water makes many mechanical things inoperable, and there was always plenty of manpower in the boats.

Simple inertia, devotion to the traditional way, or ignorance may also have been reasons for eschewing improvements. In some places and in some periods it undoubtedly was. On the other hand, considerable Yankee ingenuity was expended in the nineteenth century in devising new ways to kill whales, although in the end the means remained much the same.

Perhaps there was a dash of the sporting instinct or bravado in the whalemen that made them spurn improvements. It has been suggested that the Azoreans have some of this feeling, and Americans were not immune to it. "Whaling for victory" was the term, not intended as a compliment, in New Bedford, and it was said the boys shore whaling on Long Island were careful to get whale blood all over themselves to prove that they had been in at the kill.

1. Herbert Lincoln Aldrich, *Arctic Alaska and Siberia or Eight Months with the Arctic Whalemen* (New Bedford: Reynolds Printing, 1937), p. 3.

2. Charles Nordhof, *Whaling and Fishing* (New York: Dodd, Mead and Co., 1895), p. 112.

3. W. Scoresby, *An Account of the Arctic Regions with a History and Description of the Northern Whale-Fishery* (Edinburgh: Archibald Constable and Co., 1820), p. 246.

4. Wm. J. Hopkins, *She Blows! And Sparm at That* (Boston: Houghton Mifflin Company, 1922), p. 39.

5. Charles Melville Scammon, *The Marine Mammals of the North-Western Coast of North America and the American Whale Fishery* (New York: G. P. Putnam's Sons, 1874), p. 224.

6. Clifford W. Ashley, *The Yankee Whaler* (Garden City: Halcyon House, 1942), p. 62.

7. James Templeman Brown, *The Fisheries and Fishery Industries of the United States* (Washington: Government Printing Office), 1887, p. 240.

8. William Davis, *Nimrods of the Sea* (North Quincy: The Christopher Publishing House, 1972), p. 159.

9. E. Keble Chatterton, *Whalers and Whaling* (London: T. Fisher Unwin, 1925), p. 72.

10. Ashley, *op. cit.,* p. 94

11. Trevor Housby, *The Hand of God* (New York: Abelard-Schuman, 1971), p. 22.

12. Ashley, *op. cit.,* p. 516

13. Brown, *op. cit.,* p. 32.

14. Brown, *op. cit.,* p. 240. There were other odds and ends of gear which Brown does not list such as short warps, bottles with oil for the lantern, oarlocks, chock pins, pins for toggle irons, harpoon sheaths, boat compass, harpoon crotch, lance warps, lance sheaths, tub covers, boathook, grapnel.

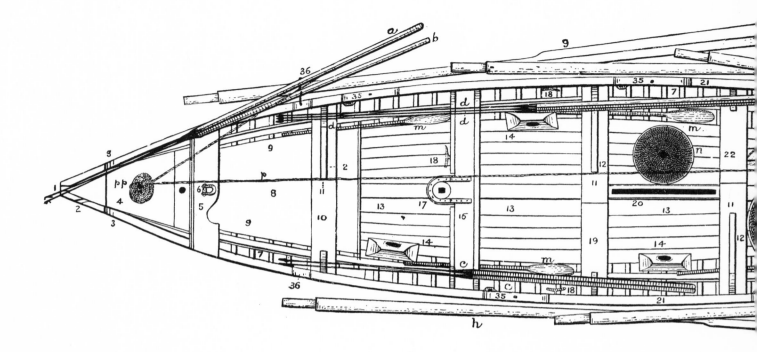

DECK VIEW OF WHALE BOAT READY FOR THE CHASE

1, Bow-chocks through which tow-line runs when fast to a whale. 2, Lance straightener; a slot in gunwale for straightening bent irons. 3,3, Top or false chocks, nailed on gunwales. 4, Box of boat. 5, Clumsy-cleat or thigh thwart used by boatsteerer to steady himself during the capture. 6, Shackle or iron strap, for hoisting and lowering the boat to and from the ship. 7,7,7, Timbers of boat. 8, Platform (forward) upon which boatsteerer and officer stand when striking and working a whale. 9,9, Risings, or top board of ceiling, on which the thwarts are placed and nailed. 10, Harpooner thwart. 11,11,11,11, Knees on all thwarts. 12,12,12,12 Dunnage for all thwarts; the main thwart (16) is dunnage all the way across. 13,13,13, Boat ceiling (inside planking): the bottom of boat. 14,14,14,14, Peak cleats; wooden cleats for

the reception of the handles of the oars when apeak; used when fast to a whale, when the oarsmen are resting, &c. 15, Peak cleat for tub-oar. 16, Bow-thwart; a seat for the bow oarsman. 17, Mast-hinge and strap, showing mast-hinge block. 18,18,18, Sail-cleats. 19, Mid-ship thwart for mid-ship oarsman. 20, Center-board, box and well. 21, Gunwales. 22, Tub-thwart for tub oarsman. 23, After thwart. 24, Well for bailing boat. 25, Plus for letting water out of boat when on the cranes. 26, Platform (aft) on which officer and boat-steerer stand when steering boat. 27, Standing cleats upon which officer stands when going on to a whale in order to get a longer view. 28, Cuddy-board. 29,29,29,29,29, Cuddy-boards; cedar boards filling up the stern of boat from the cuddy-board aft to stern-post. 30, Logger head strip, or lion's tongue. 31, Logger-head; an upright post with enlarged head, around the

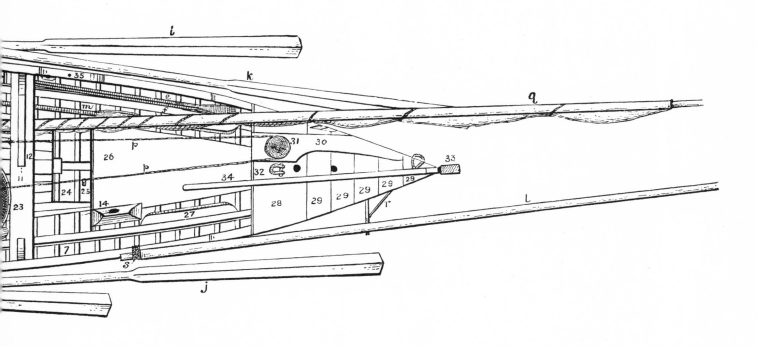

neck of which runs the tow-line when fast to a whale and by which the line is managed. 32, Boat-iron, or shackle, same as 6. 33, Rudder. 34, Tiller. 35,35,35, High and low rowlocks (wooden), with holes for the reception of shanks of rowlocks. 36,36, Bow-cleats; nailed to gunwales, and used in bowing on a whale, and also as safeguard in case the tow-line should jump from bow-chocks and preventing it from sweeping the boat aft.

A, First iron, shank resting in bow-chocks and handle in boat-crotch. B, Second iron, placed in same position as first iron; the handle of first iron, which is the first instrument used, is placed in the top crotch; the handle of second iron is p,laced in the lower crotch; the extreme end of tow-line is bent in the eye of the first iron strap; these two irons are known as the live irons or live harpoons. C,C, Spare irons on port side of boat above thwarts

(the two other spare irons, one on either side of boat under thwarts cannot be shown in the plan). D,D,D, Three lances (thrust by hand) on starboard side of boat, used in killing the whale. E, Boat spade on starboard side aft. G, Harpooner oar. H, Bow-oar. I, Mid-ship oar. J, Tub-oar. K, Stroke-oar. L, Steering-oar, manipulated by officer of boat when going on to a whale. M,M,M,M, M, Paddles. N, Small tub with tow-line coiled down, containing 75 fathoms of line. O, Large tub with tow-line coiled down, containing 225 fathoms of line. P,P,P, Tow-line extending aft from large tub around loggerhead and forward across the thwarts to box of boat (4), where it is coiled and known as box-warp (PP); thence extending to and bent in eye-splice of first iron strap. Q,Q, Mast and sail. R, Steering-oar brace. S, Lashing or strap for handle of steering-oar when not in use or fast to a whale.

Drawing *from* **THE FISHERIES & FISHERY INDUSTRIES OF THE UNITED STATES** *by George Brown Goode.*

Chapter VI

SAILING RIGS

Sail plans and rigs on whaleboats varied greatly as different whale fisheries developed rigs to suit different conditions. Styles changed over a period of time while captains and mates experimented and formed their preferences. Shore whaling, adapting to local weather conditions, or sometimes reflecting the influences of other types of local boats, added to the variety. In some cases sails were auxiliaries to the oars; in others, much of the operation was under sail. Some of the rigs were small and of limited effectiveness; others were well designed and efficient.*

By the 1850s the hinged mast step and centerboard were in use in American whaleboats. James Beetle is credited with both innovations, having first experimented with the hinged step in 1837 and with the centerboard in 1841. The former permitted a larger rig that could still be lowered, and made going on the whale under sail more practical. The centerboard made for a more weatherly boat. Both developments encouraged more sail area and greater use of sails. All rigs, however, remained simple and practical, and put heavy reliance on man power and live ballast. Wherever used, rigs were kept low and light, because all whaleboat masts were made to be lowered.

Early rigs were sometimes quite large. A sketch of the ship *France* in a log dated 1846 shows a whaleboat with a low spritsail, a topsail above it, and a balanced club jib that extends forward of the stem. It was a complicated rig for a whaleboat and, with the whole rig set, a large one. The spritsail itself is small, the peak low, and the head horizontal;

* The most casual rig was described in the New Bedford *Standard-Times*, November 22, 1924: there was no mast step in the boat; the mast was held upright, braced against a thwart, by a crew member. On nearing a whale, mast and sails and all were thrown overboard to be picked up later.

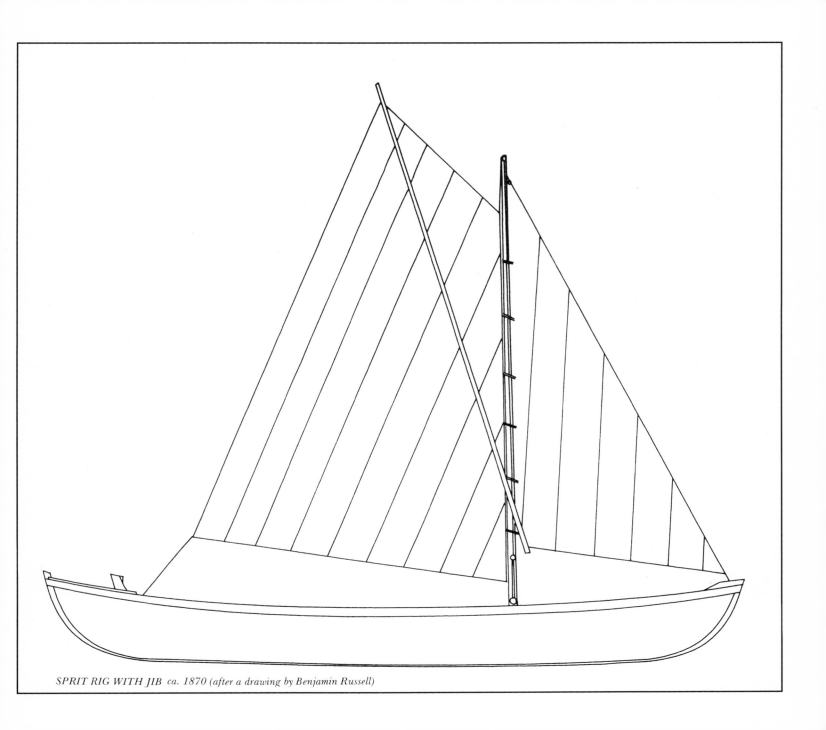

SPRIT RIG WITH JIB ca. 1870 (after a drawing by Benjamin Russell)

in the sketches this was used without the other sails when going on whales. Probably the short mast could be unstepped without a hinged step.

A larger, high-peaked spritsail with jib became a standard rig thirty years later. Prints of whaleboats in the Arctic in 1871 show about half with spritsails, the rest having a dipping lug. There were no booms, and a sheet tended from the quarter went to a single block at the clew. Six mast hoops were used. The jibs were larger and had a lower foot (about one-third the sail area of the main) than those used in later American boats. Jib sheets went to cleats abaft the mast. All the boats in this series of lithographs, whether sprit- or lug-rigged, used steering oars while under sail. None show rudders.

A half-scale Delano whaleboat at the New Bedford Whaling Museum is sprit-rigged. Full-sized, the mast would measure nineteen feet, six inches and the sprit nineteen feet. There is no jib, and the rig has no halyard. In lowering the mast, the sheet was allowed to run, the sprit was laid up against the mast, the sail was furled around both and secured with the sheet and shrouds. The mast was then unstepped.

The Edwards boat at East Hampton has a small spritsail. Its mast is eleven feet and its sprit fifteen feet, eleven inches. The foot is short and the sail is laced to the mast. There are no reef points, shrouds, centerboard, or rudder. The mast steps through a hole in the second thwart. In lowering, the sail was furled against the mast, secured with two half-hitches of the sheet, and lifted out of the step. This simple, reduced rig was apparently the

best for local conditions. The boat was launched off the beach with the wind generally onshore. The sail was used in reaching parallel to the shore and for running toward the beach; the crew pulled to windward.

The whaleboats of Bequia today have a high-peaked, boomed spritsail and jib, both of which appear to have been influenced by other local boat types. They have centerboards, and can beat to windward against the trades—in fact, until the advent of power they only took whales seen to windward of the island as it was an impossible task to tow a dead whale back if it was to leeward. These boats are ballasted with rocks, which are removed on beaching and piled beside the boat for the next run. If the boat is capsized, the rocks are rolled out to keep them from sinking the boat. In the strong prevailing trades, such ballasting has proved practical. The boats are launched from well-sheltered beaches where the rocks can be put in the boats just after they are waterborne and taken out as they ground. Ballast could not be used in boats launched through surf or lowered from whaleships.

The boom of one boat at Bequia measured twenty-two feet three inches and the sprit twenty-three feet six inches: both were of bamboo. The mast measured eighteen feet nine inches. The jib was a near-perfect equilateral triangle, with the clew overlapping the mast about five feet. The mainsail was laced to the boom and the mast. The tack of the main was cut off, making a sail with five sides. To strike the mast, the jib was first taken in, the main sheet started and the sail allowed to fly out to leeward. The sprit was unshipped, the boom layed up against the mast, and the halyards and sheets were wrapped around the sail, boom, and mast. The mast was then lowered. The whole oper-

* Henry Hall notes the use of gaff topsails in 1880. He also says masts were twenty-four feet high and that the boats carried thirty-five to fifty-five square yards of canvas. *Rudder* in March, 1900, has an article in which it is stated that forty-seven square yards of duck were required to make a suit of sails.

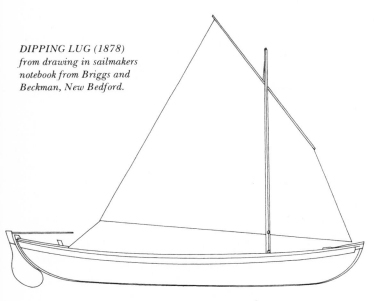

DIPPING LUG (1878)
from drawing in sailmakers
notebook from Briggs and
Beckman, New Bedford.

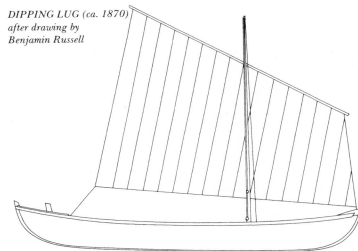

DIPPING LUG (ca. 1870)
after drawing by
Benjamin Russell

ation, according to an observer, was very fast and seamanlike.

Lug rigs aboard whaleboats were used at the same time as sprit sails and continued in use to the end of American whaling. The dipping lug was earlier, and was a type preferred by some for Arctic, bowhead whaling. The standing lug, which was simpler to rig and use, was still found on the *Manta* and *Daisy* in the last days of the whaleships.*

Captain Bodfish in *Chasing the Bowhead* wrote that the dipping lug was the best for Arctic whaling. Improper handling of the jib in other rigs, he wrote, was responsible for losing many whales. The dipping lug has no jib, as the tack of the sail is fas-

tened to the stem of the boat. The portion of the sail forward of the mast acts as a backed jib in coming about, causing it to swing through the wind very quickly. Tacking required alert handling, because as soon as the boat swung through the wind, the tack had to be cast off and brought around the shrouds and behind the mast, while the gaff was dipped to the other side, and the tack then again secured to the stem. Probably two men would be needed to handle the sail smartly. Whaleboats had the advantage of a large crew.

The earlier lug rigs on whaleboats, such as the dipping lugs of 1871, had a short mast and a long gaff. The angle of the gaff is rather flat, which gives the rig a low appearance, and the mast is near the middle of the gaff.

A whaleboat from the schooner *Manta* at the Kendall Whaling Museum has a standing lug with boom. The mast is twenty-two feet ten inches, the gaff sixteen feet nine inches; the mainsail rather

---

* I once rigged a boat with a standing lug rig. It was extremely simple and very fast to get up and down, with only one halyard that passed through a sheave at the masthead and then down to the gaff. Releasing the halyard brought down the gaff and sail. There were no hoops, parrels, or gaff jaws to bind or jam.

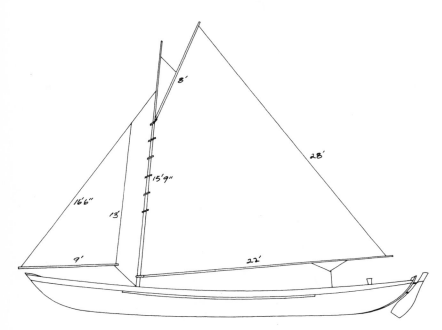

large and high-peaked. The gaff was raised by a single halyard attached to it about one-third the distance from the forward end. There is a parrel at the gaff's lower end, and the foot of the sail is laced to the boom. The boat had a small jib with a high-cut foot. Shrouds went to the masthead.

The gaff rig appeared later than the sprit and lug rig in whaleboats, and is the rig still used in the Azorean boats. Early rigs were low; later the gaff was peaked very high.* Jibs were often used, but in later boats they were small compared to the mainsail. In the sail plan of one American boat the jib has only 70 square feet, and the main 280 square feet. The foot of the jibs was cut high in most rigs. The mainsail of American gaff-rigged boats was

* The high-peaked gaff sails were called leg-of-mutton sails, though they had the four sides and gaff of the standard gaff rig.

Whaleboats of the U. S. Navy were often rigged with a sliding gunter. There was not much difference between this and the high-peaked gaff sails.

boomed and either loose-footed or laced. Mast hoops were rather widely spaced and in some cases were left off at the bottom of the reef cringles. The sail was laced to the gaff. One, two, or three sets of reef points were sewed in the main. The jib, if carried, was sometimes rigged with a toggle at the head for quick release from an eye at the end of the halyard. In going on the whale, the jib was generally taken in first, then the main halyard was released, the gaff and sail lowered, the shrouds released, and the mast lowered.

The gaff-rigged Azorean boats give the appearance of being over-canvassed. Often they were not equipped with centerboards. A balanced club jib was set flying—according to a model, some boats carried three sizes of jibs. The rest of the rig is the same as the gaff rig of American whaleboats.

Whaleboat spars were simple, practical, and often crude. Masts were generally spruce. Gaffs were spruce or sometimes bamboo. Masts were

OPPOSITE PAGE LEFT: Azorean Boat. The jib, with club, is set flying. Sailplan taken from a model at Mystic Seaport. The model was equipped with jibs of three sizes; the one shown is the middle-sized.

OPPOSITE PAGE, RIGHT: A comparison of early and late gaff rigs. Solid line—low rig with large jib. Boat length: 29' ca. 1870 (from sailmaker's notebook, Kendall Whaling Museum). Dotted line—high-peaked main with small jib. Boat length: 29' 10 1/2" represents a sail plan in use after 1900 (From plan by William Hand and R. O. Davis. Drawn in 1935).

UPPER LEFT: Standing lug sail. W. H. Tripp Collection, Mystic Seaport.

UPPER RIGHT: Whaleboat with lug rig from JOHN R. MANTA. Note steering oar is boated and helmsman is using rudder. Courtesy of Kendall Whaling Museum.

RIGHT: A photograph taken from the CHARLES W. MORGAN shows standing lug mainsails with jibs. Courtesy of Mr. and Mrs. Jack McNatt.

Boat from JOHN R. MANTA *with reefed mainsail. Note one more set of reef points. The sail is a high-peaked gaff or gunter rig. Courtesy of Kendall Whaling Museum.*

Whaleboats on sleds being transported over ice for floe whaling. Sails, men, and dogs provide the motive power. Boats are from the topsail schooner **ERA** *whaling in Hudson Bay, ca. 1900. Photograph by Captain George Comer, Comer Collection, Mystic Seaport.*

sharply tapered below the hinged partners or tabernacle so that they would not jam as they were unstepped. The heel was round. Some masts had a straight taper from the partners to the head, others maintained a more or less constant diameter for one-third or one-half the height of the mast before tapering to the head. The masts of American gaff and lug-rigged boats were from eighteen to twenty-four feet in length; the diameter at the heel was two and one-quarter to two and one-half inches. The diameter at the partners was four to four and three-quarters inches and at the head two and one-quarter to two and one-half inches. Azorean boats have taller, heavier masts; one boat that was small by Azorean standards had a mast twenty-four feet six inches in height with a diameter at the thickest point of five and three-quarter inches.

Fittings on the masts were very simple. The masts often had a single sheave for the main halyard, generally two and one-half inches in diameter and about five inches below the head. The head was square to make shoulders for the shrouds and a strop for a thimble or block for the halyard. A pin athwartships above the shrouds prevented them from slipping off when the mast was lowered. Some boats had a galvanized band with eyes at the head, or wooden shoulders or stops fastened to each side of the mast for the shrouds to lie on. There were generally no other fittings at the head. At the foot, if the rig did not have a boom, an eye was fastened to the mast for the tack of the main-sail.

Booms were spruce or bamboo and in some American rigs were twenty-three feet long. Azorean booms went to twenty-six feet or more. The booms were thin and limber, bending considerably in a fresh breeze. They measured two and one-quarter inches to two and three-quarter inches at the jaws, two and five-eighths to three inches in the thickest section, and two to two and a quarter inches at the outboard end. Bamboo booms had a natural taper. Boom jaws were either conventional

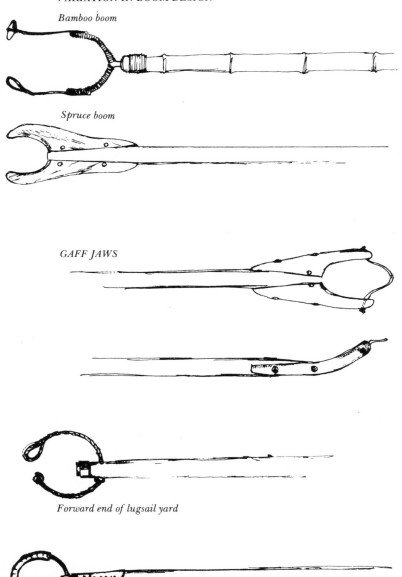

VARIATION IN BOOM DESIGN

Bamboo boom

Spruce boom

GAFF JAWS

Forward end of lugsail yard

Parrel on high-peaked gaff

wooden ones or were made of a forged iron fork with a pin driven in the end of the boom. The iron fork was served and had a toggle and eye to act as parrel. This arrangement allowed the boom to be quickly freed from the mast to avoid binding when lowering the mast. In later boats, an eye in the end of the main sheet was spliced around a thimble on a bridle on the boom. The bridle was only about three feet long and was held to the boom by seizing at about three-quarters of the distance out on the boom, centered over the sheet cleats.

Gaffs were of spruce or bamboo and their lengths varied with the sail plan. In boats with high-peaked gaffs, some were fifteen feet long. Jaws were of wood. On the gaffs of some lug-rigged boats a parrel made of a forged iron hoop circled the mast; an eye with a pin in the end of the gaff held it. The forged hoop was served or had leather sewn around it for chafing gear.

The rigging of whaleboats was simple and strong. Fewer lines meant less opportunity for fouling when lowering and raising the masts. The smaller rigs had no shrouds. Larger rigs had a single set that could be quickly set up and released. The shrouds were of hemp and manila, five-eighths of an inch or nine-sixteenths of an inch in diameter. Usually both shrouds were continuous, with an eye spliced in the middle that slipped over the head of the mast. Lanyards for setting up the shrouds were of five-sixteenths of an inch line and about eight feet long. These were spliced in above the eye at the lower end of the shroud and ran down through a thimble in a grommet at the gunwale. The lanyard was made fast to its standing part with a slipped hitch, allowing the shrouds to be released quickly. Some Azorean boats now have two sets of shrouds going to cast iron chain plates.

The main sheet and halyard was of half-inch

manila, the jib of three-eighths of an inch. Both sheets were usually single lines without mechanical advantage.

There was great variation in the quality, cut, weight, and design of the sails on whaleboats. Some were made ashore by professional sailmakers, while others were made aboard ship. In all cases, the sails had panels running parallel to the leech in both main and jib. Panel widths varied. On mainsails, boltropes on the head, foot, and luff were universal and they were sometimes used on the leech. Some spritsails used lacings and others used hoops, even though the sail was not usually lowered. The gaff-rigged boats had hoops; on one Azorean boat I examind, they were made of bone. If not loose-footed, the sails were secured to gaffs and booms by lacing or a seizing at each grommet.

Spars, sail, and rigging on whaleboats had hard usage. The gear remained in the boats at all times during a voyage; wet sails were dried only when used; raising and lowering the masts chafed gear. Some photographs indicate that there was little overhauling until something broke. Exceptions were the boats used in shore whaling—here the sails and rigging were generally maintained in excellent condition. In sailing the gaff-rigged boats at Mystic Seaport, it was our conclusion that the system of staying the mast, which allowed it to be raised and lowered quickly, did not provide the strongest support. Though the shrouds were taken up, masts showed a strong bend in a breeze. The mains were loose-footed, which put all the tension on the ends of the thin booms, producing a hard bend between the bridle and the clew.*

* In the course of sailing a whaleboat one year at Mystic Seaport, two masts and two booms were broken. One mast, which was of fir, broke at a large knot; the other broke while attempting to careen the boat on a beach.

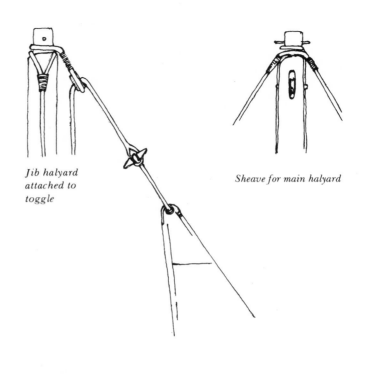

Jib halyard attached to toggle

Sheave for main halyard

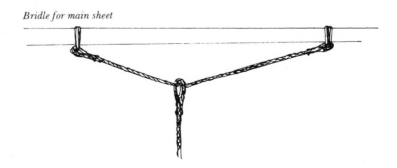

Bridle for main sheet

Chapter VII

WHALEBOAT PRODUCTION

At one time or another whaleboats were built in the United States along the coast from Long Island to Maine and, late in the story, in San Francisco Bay. The greatest building activity was near the whaling centers, but because the boats were light and could be easily transported, they were sometimes built some distance inland and brought to the ports on special boat wagons. While it seems an exaggeration to call the building of 100 or so stock boats a year in one of the small shops "mass production," it does represent an early example of efficiency in applying basic assembly line methods on a small scale. The result was that small shops employing only a few men, with a small capital investment, low overhead, and the most casual record keeping,* produced a considerable number of boats quickly at very low cost. Howard Chapelle writes:

> Mass production in boatshops seems to have begun about New York in the 1830's and 40's in the construction of the Whitehall boat and similar small craft. The idea slowly took hold and quantity production of dories, yawls, whaleboats and seine boats began at various towns along the coasts; by 1880 the practice was very widespread all over the United Sates.[1]

In the decade of the 1850s the number of American whaleships in service rarely dropped below 600. These were 3-, 4-, and 5-boat ships. With spares, they carried altogether from 3,000 to 3,500 boats. At the same time additional whaleboats were employed in shore whaling. By the 1880s, the number of whaleships had dropped to little more than 100 ships and barks and about 60 brigs and schooners. Together they carried about 1,000

---

* James and Charles Beetle kept records on scraps of cedar boat boards.

76

boats. Assuming that one-fifth of the boats were replaced each year, the demand in the 1850s would have been for 600 to 700 boats a year and in the 1880s for 200 or less.*

In the *Census Report* for 1880 Henry Hall wrote that whaleboat building thirty years before had provided a good living, producing a "prosperous class of men," but that in later years the few surviving builders had to struggle to make a modest income. Formerly, he wrote, William Smith of New Bedford and others had built 100 to 120 boats a year.[2] James Beetle, according to his own account, built nearly 1,000 boats between 1834 and 1854, or about fifty a year.** Little capital was needed, Hall noted, to become a builder. A shed near the water and $100 worth of tools was all that was required; the place of building did not even have to be on the water.

The market for boats declined steadily after 1860, though not as quickly in the New Bedford area as in other whaling centers. The Civil War hurt the builders and orders fell after the large-scale ship losses in the Arctic in 1871 and 1876. With the decline in demand for first oil and then whalebone, the whaleships passed and with them the need for large numbers of whaleboats. Between 1900 and 1913 the number of whaling vessels dropped from twenty-four to thirteen. They still whaled in the Atlantic and the Arctic, often operating in the former on a marginal basis with little spent on new boats or other equipment.[3] Beetle and Pierce and Kilburn in New Bedford had a

* Henry Hall writes in 1880 that 900 boats were in service and not over 150 were needed each year as replacements.

** James Beetle carved a serial number in Roman numerals on the lion's tongue and on top of the loggerhead when whaleboat production was in full swing. After the Civil War, he started each year with "I".

Recently completed boat being lowered from loft at the Beetle boat shop, Clarks Point, New Bedford. Courtesy of Harold Beetle.

few last orders for boats for Alaskan Eskimos,* or for research vessels or some special purpose, but after 1910 the market had almost disappeared. As the demand declined, the builders entered other trades, retired, or diversified.

The builders did little advertising, expanding and contracting their operation as demand fluctuated. A few ran advertisements in the *New Bedford Directory*. John Cranston's in 1865 reads: "Whaleboats constantly on hand, or built to order, as good as the best, as cheap as the cheapest." In the 1869-70 *Directory* William F. Butler and Theodore Tripp also advertised whaleboats in stock or built to order.

James Beetle met incoming ships or dropped by the offices of the whaleship owners and agents to look for business. He described getting a verbal order for forty boats, a one year's supply for the Howland whaleships. The builders also were ready

to take orders for other types of boats: George Rogers of New London built surf boats, seal boats, quarter boats, yachts, and fishing boats. Beetle also diversified, building lifeboats for ships, lifesaving boats, Noman's Land and other fishing boats, and pleasure craft.

Most of the shops were small and employed few men, though the J. C. Beetle shop in California was a sizable building.* It looks prosperous under a coat of white paint and has sixteen or seventeen men lined up in front to be photographed. The shops of James and Charles Beetle in New Bedford were somewhat ramshackle, unpainted buildings on the outside, but inside in the lofts where the boats were built, they were models of efficiency. Llewellyn Howland, who worked there as a boy, wrote that the loft was specially arranged and reserved for whaleboat building. It was clean, orderly, and well lighted, with stock parts in special bins.

* In the 1920s it became a matter of prestige for an Eskimo to own a whaleboat. When fox skins brought cash, they bought boats.

* J. C. Beetle moved to Alameda, California, to build whaleboats for the New England whaleships when they shifted to San Francisco at the end of the nineteenth century.

LEFT: Some of the last whaleboats built, 1920. The rails on top of the wales mark these as boats built for the Arctic, possibly for Eskimos in Alaska. Note that the boat in the background will have an engine installed. Boats were built by Pierce and Kilburn, New Bedford. Courtesy of Kendall Whaling Museum.

BELOW: The J.C. Beetle shop in Alameda, California. J C. Beetle was a brother of Charles, who remained to build boats in New Bedford. W. H. Tripp Collection, Mystic Seaport.

Charles Beetle, whaleboat builder of New Bedford. Courtesy of Harold Beetle.

Old photographs of the interiors of the Pierce and Kilburn shop and other unidentified shops present a somewhat more cluttered and less organized appearance.

The number of men employed was small. James and Charles Beetle hired extras to make a total of five or six when larger orders came in. A photograph of the Leonard shop shows Ebenezer Leonard and his two sons, and one of the Pierce and Kilburn shop shows five men at work. From most descriptions and our experience at Mystic Seaport, it appears four men can work effectively on one boat. Undoubtedly many shops employed only two, as did we for most of the building at the Seaport.*

Building costs doubled between 1850 and 1890. In 1844 George Rogers sold lapstrake boats for $50 and "smooth" boats for $55. Some builders charged an extra $10 for the smooth or combination batten-seam and lapstrake boats. In 1855 the boats for the *Mermaid* cost $60 if lapstrake; $10 extra if centerboard. Beetle wrote that in the 1860s a boat sold for $75 and the materials in it were worth $30. In 1880, J. R. Brown wrote in the *Fish Commission Report* that a twenty-eight foot boat cost $90 and a thirty foot boat $100. Boats built at Prov-

* Outside of New Bedford, the names of only a few builders are known. New London had George W. Rogers, Reeves & Kelly, Gordon Bros. originally of Sag Harbor, Asa Comstock, and Nathan Steward. Eben Leonard and his sons were in Long Plains or Acushnet, Massachusetts. Uriah Morse was in Edgartown.

The *New Bedford Directory* of 1852 lists thirty-six boatbuilders, most of whom presumably built whaleboats. In the 1850s the demand for these boats was at its peak in New Bedford, 450 being the number required to outfit the whaleships from there in 1858, according to Starbuck in *History of the Whale Fishery.* In 1852 four of the builders are listed as having hired employees: Thomas N. Allen, W. H. Smith, George Hart, and R. C. Topham. In the *Directory* of 1869-1870,

incetown cost $110 to $120. Beetle said that boats in the 1880s sold for $85 to $100 and cost $65 to make. Hall gives selling prices as from $90 to $100 with $45 to $50 as the value of the materials. Spears notes that in 1908 a new boat cost "far above $100." In 1924 the price had risen to $250 and in 1933 Beetle's last whaleboat, built for a museum with sails and fully equipped, cost $440.

Wages and costs of materials appear to have ranged from 40 per cent to 60 per cent of the selling price. In 1879 George Rogers was charging customers $.30 an hour for labor and Beetle was paying his men $1.50 a day, which meant the price of labor was from 20 per cent to 25 percent of the selling price of the boat. His men worked a ten-hour day, six days a week—a sixty-hour week being standard at the time.

The following gives some idea of the cost of materials in the 1880s: galvanized boat nails and cut nails about $.10 a pound; putty, $.07 a pound; set of oars for a whaleboat, $8.50; mast and sail, $8.00; mast hinge, $4.00; rowlocks, $6.50; whaleboat jib and topsail, $3.00. Hall wrote that a large, particularly fine whaleboat, fully equipped, could cost $212.* Bills for outfitting the bark *Mermaid* in 1855 give the following prices: whaleboat masts, $.50 each; oars, $0.75 a foot; clench nails, $.27 a pound.

twenty-seven builders are listed, ten of whom were also listed in 1852. In the *Directory* of 1869-1870, five Allens, three Cranstons, two Warrens, and Wm. Smith & Wm. Smith, Jr. are among the names.

The best known of the New Bedford builders were James Beetle and his son Charles. James, born in 1812, learned boat-building from Wm. Cranston, and in the course of many years of building made many improvements to the boats. His son followed him in the trade, and today the Beetle Catboat bears his name.

* It is interesting to note this is slightly less than half of what Beetle charged for a rigged and equipped boat fifty years later.

Walter F. Chase, whaleboat builder of New Bedford. W. H. Tripp collection, Mystic Seaport.

81

ABOVE: *Whaleboats in Charles Beetle's yard. Courtesy of Harold Beetle.*

RIGHT: *Brand used by Charles Beetle. The name was burned into the wood on the lion's tongue and on the inside edge of the thigh board. Photograph by the author.*

Hall listed the following materials used in the construction of one boat:

150-200 board feet of oak
550-700 board feet of cedar
200 board feet of pine (The boats he describes are ceiled with pine)
18-20 pounds of nails

Hall's list is close to the amounts used at Mystic Seaport in whaleboat construction. He wrote that one-quarter to one-third of the lumber was lost in cutting. Leo Telesmanick was an apprentice under Charles Beetle and today is foreman of the shop where Beetle Catboats are built. He practices the economy learned in the whaleboat shop; the best cedar is used for planking, second best for ceiling, and scraps make up the decking. In whaleboat building, smaller scraps might be used in making the box and smaller pieces in the end of the ceiling. The use of patterns for many of these pieces meant great savings in lumber as well as time.

The speed of building in many of the small shops was impressive, though there are some contradictions in the statements about the exact time it took to build a whaleboat. Hall wrote that it took a single man twenty to twenty-five days. James Beetle said that prior to 1835 it required twenty day's labor because planks had to be prepared by hand; with machinery, "we can build a boat with 120 hours of labor." Charles Beetle, his son, wrote that his shop could turn out one boat a day and, in a rush, seven in six days. In a newspaper article, Charles Beetle is quoted as saying four men could build a whaleboat in twenty-eight hours. This figure is about the same as that cited in *Rudder* of March, 1900, which says four men could build one in three days. Llewellyn Howland describes building a boat non-stop. Charles Beetle, with four men and young Howland, whose responsibility was to keep up steam in the donkey engine and bring drinking water, worked on the boat one day, on through the night, and the following day and night. The boat was finished and delivered the morning of the third day after forty-eight hours of labor, with time off only for meals.

The men were assigned specialized tasks and worked as a well-drilled team. One got out planks and four did most of the actual construction. If several boats were being built, one man did all the caulking, puttying, and painting. With patterns, standardized parts, a division of labor, special forms and jigs, the building was very efficient. As Howland wrote, "The 'knocking up' of a whaleboat at Beetle's when I worked there was planned and executed with exactness and rapidity of an assembly job today."[4]

A boat carpenter from Mystic Seaport who had worked on whaleboats observed the production of wooden Beetle Catboats under the direction of Mr. Telesmanick. The same rules of economy and efficiency were applied as in the old shop; there was no lost motion, idle talk, or hesitation among the men, and the work proceeded very rapidly. It was this observer's conclusion that the claims for the speed in production of whaleboats had not been exaggerated.

1. Howard I. Chapelle, *American Small Sailing Craft* (New York: W. W. Norton and Co., 1951), p. 192.

2. Henry Hall, *Report of the Shipbuilding Industry in the United States*, in Fourth Census, Vol. 8 (Washington: Government Printing Office, 1884), p. 25.

3. William Henry Tripp, *There Goes Flukes* (New Bedford: Reynolds Printing, 1938), p. 173.

4. Llewellyn Howland, *West by Southwest of Cape Cod* (Harvard University Press, 1948), p. 84.

Chapter VIII

BUILDING METHODS

The methods and techniques used in whaleboat building were in some ways unique. Competition and a demand over the years for a relatively large number of stock boats encouraged efficient production in the small shops. Standardized parts, patterns, jigs, and forms were used wherever possible, as the design of the whaleboat lent itself to quick, cheap building. It also forced a certain sequence and technique in building.

Variations are found in the boats of a builder using the same molds. Some of these were deliberate and others resulted from the methods used. Two Beetle-built boats of approximately the same length have different sheers and different amounts of flare to the sides, although Beetle used the same molds and probably the same plank patterns. The experienced builder could vary the lines of boats from the same molds with the use of shims and by shifting the molds fore and aft. Such flexibility was desirable in meeting a buyer's requirements.

Other variations between boats were accidental. The steam-bent stem and stern posts, which were overbent on the bending form, straightened or held their shape in varying degrees. Molds, which were held in place with stays to the overhead and with a few longitudinal battens, did not have the rigidity of a jig that might be used in the construction of other boats. The wales, which had much to do with the shape, might not take and hold the same bend from boat to boat.

In our whaleboat construction at Mystic Seaport we had experience with most of these sources of variation. Hegarty writes that there was no great concern if planking stood a ways off the molds,[1] and an article in *Rudder* states: "These boats are usually built in a slambang manner; everything goes that can be covered with paint and putty. Still

ABOVE LEFT: Whaleboat under construction being planked up. Garboards have been fitted. Note iron horse for holding stem to shop floor, plank pattern on the floor and adjustable molds. Courtesy of Harold Beetle.

ABOVE RIGHT: Boat planked and ready for framing. Courtesy of Harold Beetle.

LEFT: Boat framed, with wales, bow chocks, and clumsy cleat installed. Risers and ceiling will follow. Note centerboard across the horses to the left. Courtesy of Harold Beetle.

Stem bent over form, with bending strap used on the outside of the curve, during construction at Mystic Seaport. Photograph by Mary Anne Stets, Mystic Seaport.

they hold together, and their qualities as sea boats are too well-known to be questioned."[2] In inspecting a number of boats, my impression was the boats were built roughly but sturdily. In some the fits, such as where frames notch over battens, were very close. There certainly was no effort to produce a yachtlike finish or build to yacht standards. The approach to building, like the design itself, was utilitarian.

Whaleboats were built upright on a keel plate or bearer secured to the shop floor. The bearer has a slight curve cut in the top edge to give a rocker to the sprung keel. The bearer is low to the floor, which makes working under it difficult in the early stages of building, but is a convenience later as the boatbuilder leans over the side to work inside.

Before the keel was placed on the bearer, it was tapered at both ends, a rabbet was cut on the bottom for the garboards and two cuts were made for the centerboard slot. The builder had wooden gauges that gave the depth and bevel of the rabbet at points along the keel. The fore and aft cuts for the centerboard slot were made by laying the plank on a table saw. The wood in the slot was not cut out at this point, but left as a plug, with a bridge in the middle to prevent the keel from spreading or pinching together during planking. The keel was then fastened to the bearer with carriage bolts driven into straps on the bearer. The bearer, with straps and bolts like the iron horses to hold the stem and stern, was part of the equipment of the shop and was used in the building of many boats.

Stem and stern posts were steamed and bent over the same form or bending horse. The pieces were generally sided one and one-half to one and three-quarter inches and molded three to three and one-quarter inches. The bend was strong, so the stock for bending had to be clear, straight-grained, green timber with annual rings at right angles to the plane of the bend. The rabbet was sometimes cut before bending. The builder could make gauges and patterns for cutting the rabbet, which was a very shallow S curve on a whaleboat's stem and stern post. The pieces were steamed for two hours and then bent over a form with an iron backing strap.*

Builders often made the bent stem and stern posts in advance and stocked them. A stay was nailed across to prevent them from straightening. In the boats built at Mystic Seaport the pieces were left on the form overnight and then a steel band was fastened inside like a bow string from the stem head to the heel to prevent straightening while building. This could be left on without inconvenience until the boats had been planked and framed.

A scarf joint ten to twelve inches long fastened with quarter-inch-thick rivets connected stem and stern post to the keel. The rabbets were faired into each other and a stopwater was placed in the rabbet at the seam. Stem and stern were held in position at the bottom with iron horses fastened to the shop floor, and at the top with stays to the shop rafters. Without such bracing, the limber stem and stern posts could be sprung out of alignment during planking.

Molds were then set on the keel. Five molds were the conventional number, though seven were sometimes used; the builders in Bequia use three. These were temporarily fastened to the keel with

---

* Henry Hall writes of a stem apron being used. Undoubtedly some builders made stems of two pieces as was sometimes done in surf boats and the U.S. Navy whaleboats. He also says that a keelson was laid on top of the heels of the frames. This may have been an earlier practice, but I did not see it in any of the original construction of the boats I examined.

Garboard being fitted. At Mystic Seaport garboards were steamed. Photograph by Mary Anne Stets, Mystic Seaport.

Scarf in garboard. These are 3'' long; a small butt block is placed behind the joint, which is held with clench nails. Photograph by Mary Anne Stets, Mystic Seaport.

bolts and stayed at the top to the shop rafters. Beetle used the same molds; the tops of which were pivoted and could be moved in and out to adjust the beam for whaleboats of different lengths.**

Planking followed. The cedar was sometimes a "scant" one-half inch, except for the sheer strake, which was a full one-half inch. Whaleboats generally had eight planks to the side. Builders used plank patterns, which made possible great savings in time and materials, and tended to standardize somewhat the lines of the boats. In the construction of the first boat at Mystic Seaport, battens were temporarily sprung over the molds and shifted up and down to the straightest, fair plank lines. The molds were then marked and measured to find plank widths. The bottom edge of each plank was spiled, and the top edge established by measuring up from the bottom. Thus planks were made and fitted as we proceeded. A builder with patterns cut all his planks at once, or had someone cutting planks as other men planked up the boat—a much faster process than the one we followed.

The garboards were fitted first.* Steaming the planks for fifteen minutes made the ends pliable where they had a twist. Clamps held the plank as it was fastened with one-inch galvanized boat nails spaced three inches along the keel and about two inches in the stem and stern posts. The butts in the planks were scarfed with a three-inch joint, with the

** The molds Charles Beetle used were destroyed in a fire in the 1930s. However, tracings were made of them, which I was able to examine. They show two positions: one apparently for boats twenty-seven to twenty-eight feet, the other for boats twenty-nine to thirty feet.

* Henry Hall describes a sequence of planking that would seem impossible: the sheer strake was first, planks beneath followed, molds were then removed, battens fitted and fastened, and the boat then framed. He apparently misunderstood the builder's explanation.

feather edge aft on the outside. The usual way was to lay the plank on the bench and cut the scarf with a slick. A small butt block with grain running vertically was placed behind the scarf and the joint was fastened with galvanized clench nails.

A dory lap was made at the ends between the garboard and second plank, which laps it. Beginning about three feet from the stem, the outboard upper edge of the garboard was beveled. The inboard, lower edge of the second strake was given the same bevel. Put together, the lap disappeared at the rabbet. The amount of the lap of the planks was three-quarters to an inch. Galvanized clench nails were used as fastenings.

Clench nailing is fast and strong. A hole is made through the cedar with an awl and the nail started with the chisel point directed so the point will turn at an angle to the grain of the wood. The nail is driven until the point projects about one-sixteenth of an inch; the backing iron is then held against it. The iron is allowed to bounce with the blows and the point turns back into the wood across the grain. The point can be directed by holding the face of the backing iron at a slight angle. The last blows set the head of the nail and draw the planks tightly together.

The batten-seam construction made a carvel-planked side between the laps at the garboard and the sheer. The battens behind the seams were cedar, cut from the same half-inch stock as the planking, and one and seven-eighths to two inches in width. Clench nails fastened planking to battens, which were scarfed to run the full length of the seam. At the turn of the bilge at the boat's midsection, the battens were given slight bevels above and below the seam.

Three strakes at the turn of the bilge, which is hard in whaleboats, had to be cupped by warping

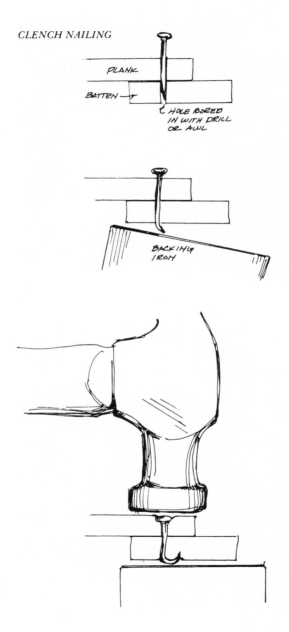

CLENCH NAILING

PLANK

BATTEN

HOLE BORED IN WITH DRILL OR AWL

BACKING IRON

Warping planks at the turn of the bilge. These were steamed. The clamps and forms were left on overnight. Photograph by Mary Anne Stets, Mystic Seaport.

Tools of Charles Beetle. The drawknife with the "V" in the blade was used for cutting the rabbet in the stem and stern. Photograph by the author.

to make a fair curve of the sides. In most boat construction, a backing-out plane hollowed the inside of the plank, and the outside was planed at the edges. In contrast, the thin, wide planks used in whaleboat construction were steamed and warped in a form and then hung on the boat. At Mystic Seaport it was found that the plank could be cut to shape, steamed, clamped to the molds, and then warped in place with curved forms clamped at intervals along the plank. The planks were immediately fastened with clench nails. We left the forms on for the night while the cedar set. In cutting the planks and warping them, the builders were mindful of their tendency to warp in a direction that would straighten annual rings. The rule was to hang up the planks so that sapwood, if there were any, would be on the inside.*

The knottiest piece of cedar, Mr. Telesmanick tells me, was saved for the sheer strake, as a split will stop at a knot. The sheer strake is the widest in the boat and is the one that takes the most punishment. There is structural weakness between the tops of the frames and the wales, and here is where splits occur.

After planking was complete and the sheer made fair, the bow chocks, which could be made in advance, were fitted, followed by the oak wales. Some builders steamed and bent these over a form. At Mystic Seaport they were steamed and bent around the molds inside the sheer strake and clamped while being fastened with nails driven at three-inch intervals through the sheer strake. We found some of the wales could be bent in cold. Later rivets were

* Charles Beetle had a hammer with a large, round face. With it, it was said, he could "mold" the cedar planks to make fair, smooth sides. The boat in the Mariners Museum at Newport News, Virginia, was built by him for the museum and was never battered and scarred by service. The smooth seams are evidence of his skill.

added which passed through the sheer strake, rubbing strips, and seat knees.

The builder then framed the boat. The oak frames were sided three-quarters of an inch and molded one and three-quarter inches at the heel and one and one-quarter inches at the top. The pieces for bending were cut from patterns. Frames were steamed for an hour and bent over a trap having a curvature somewhat greater than the extreme curve in the midsection of the boat. They could easily be straightened, if necessary, to fit in the boat. One curve was sufficient for framing the entire boat. The curve diminished toward the bow and stern; the last frames in the stern had no bend. In the shop the frames taken off the trap were immediately fitted in the boat, or they were stayed and stocked.*

The top of the frame was cut with a chisel point which was thrust up between the wale and the planking. The frame was then pushed down against the inside of the planking and scribed at the laps and battens. It was then taken out and notched on the bench by hand or on a band saw. The foot was cut to lap the keel and the top of the frame at the heel was sawn flat for a fastening into the keel and for the middle piece of the ceiling to lie on. Notches were not cut to the full depth of the batten, but left shallow; therefore, the planking between battens stood slightly off the frame.**There

Frames bent over a trap. Photograph by Mary Anne Stets, Mystic Seaport.

* The trap made for frames at Mystic Seaport held fifteen frames. On the average we broke three frames in bending fifteen.

** The technique of getting close fits over laps and battens was described by Mr. Telesmanick, but we found it difficult to apply at the Seaport. Our method was to spring a thin batten against the inside of the planking on top of the battens and laps and mark it, then hold the batten along the edge of the frame to transfer the marks to the frame for cutting.

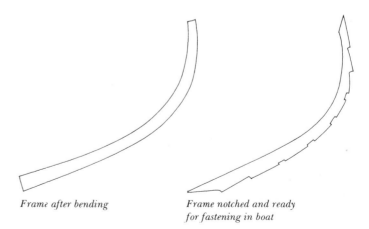

Frame after bending   *Frame notched and ready for fastening in boat*

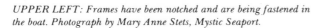

UPPER LEFT: *Frames have been notched and are being fastened in the boat. Photograph by Mary Anne Stets, Mystic Seaport.*

UPPER RIGHT: *Frames in place. Note notches over laps and battens. Photograph by Mary Anne Stets, Mystic Seaport.*

ABOVE: *Steam-bent seat knees being riveted. Note filler pieces behind. Photograph by Mary Anne Stets, Mystic Seaport.*

RIGHT: *Hinged mast tabernacle and partners. Photograph by Mary Anne Stets, Mystic Seaport.*

Whaleboat nearing completion at Mystic Seaport. Rubbing strips and guards will be fastened next. Photograph by Mary Anne Stets, Mystic Seaport.

was no bevel on the frames, and those at the ends of the boat were slightly canted. The frames were fastened with one nail into the keel, one nail in each lap, and two in each batten. The molds were taken out as the boat was framed.

Risers were then sprung in the boat and fastened at the frames. Ceiling planks, made of leftovers from planking, were cut from patterns and nailed in below the risers. Head and stern sheets followed. Thwarts were cut and laid on the risers and on the outside rubbing strips, and guards were fastened with boat nails.

Seat or thwart knees were then fitted. These were steam bent, made to a standard size and bent to the same curve. As the bend was hard, about 90° with a radius of six inches, the knees were sawn with a kerf before bending. The kerf followed the grain from the bottom, but as the knee was molded less at the bottom than at the top, the cut began on one side and ended in the center. The knees were fastened through the top and throat with one-quarter inch galvanized rivets. On the thwarts they were clench-nailed.

The construction of the cuddy board aft and the warp box forward was simple and quick. The lion's tongue, loggerhead—which was sometimes turned—and steering oar brackets were made in advance and stocked. Mast partners and tabernacle pieces were made from patterns.

The centerboard slot, previously sawn, was cut out and the case fitted. Canvas folded with white lead between was laid between the keel and the case. The toes at the ends of the sides of the case held a fastening into the keel, enough to hold the case in place until four-and-a-half inch galvanized nails could be driven up through the bottom of the keel into the sides. The case was then bored for a five-eighths-of-an-inch bolt for the centerboard pivot. The boards themselves could be made up in advance.

The garboard, the stem and stern rabbet, and the batten seams were caulked, the latter with a strand of cotton wicking rolled into the seams. Loose knots in the wood were reamed out and plugged with cedar. The seams were run with paint and puttied, nail heads were puttied, and the boats given a coat of primer. Some were delivered without further painting, while other builders gave their boats a finish coat.

1. Reginald B. Hegarty, *Birth of a Whaleship* (New Bedford: Free Public Library, 1964), p. 149.

2. *Rudder*, vol. 11, no. 3, March, 1900, p. 124.

Chapter IX

PAINTING, REPAIRS, AND MAINTENANCE OF WHALEBOATS

Whaleboats were painted for preservation, identification, camouflage, and appearance. By the end of the nineteenth century the outside of the hull was generally painted white below the sheer strake; the sheer strake and wales were black or some color.* It was common practice to paint the insides a variety of colors. Some builders left the painting of the finish coat to the whaleship, whose officers might have their own preferences or color code for identification. Port boats were sometimes painted with sheer strake of one color and starboard boats of another.

Charles Beetle generally painted new boats white with umber tops and yellow ceiling: an example is the new boat he built for the Mariners Museum in Newport News. He also painted the "tops" of used boats black. The Beetle whaleboat at the Nantucket Whaling Museum has a black sheer strake and wales; the guards and rubbing strips are blue, and the warp box and cuddy board are salmon with black trim along the edges.

The Edwards boat used in shore whaling on Long Island is all-white, perhaps reflecting an influence from the surf boats of the Lifesaving Service. The inside of the Edwards boat is also painted white. The Dominy boat used along the same stretch of beach has a white hull and green sheer strake; the inside is green to the bottom of the risers, while the ceiling below is unpainted.

The boat from the *Daisy* at Cold Spring Harbor Whaling Museum has a white hull, and umber

* Early in the nineteenth century boats were more colorful. Many had red bows, the red ending in a diagonal slash with the rest of the hull white. In some, the colors were reversed. Shades of blue and green were often used for the hull. Paintings show boats with white sheer strake and blue below, white below the waterline with green above, and many other combinations.

sheer strake, wales, warp box, and cuddy board. The inside is grey from below the wales to the bottom of the riser; thwarts and centerboard case are also grey while the ceiling is umber. Photographs of the *Daisy*'s other boats by Robert Cushman Murphy show an entirely different scheme with the second strake white and the planking above and below dark. The *Manta*'s boat at the Kendall Whaling Museum has a white hull, black sheer strake and wales, umber cuddy boards and thigh board; umber below the wales to the bottom of the risers, buff warp box and blue ceiling. Photographs of other boats show rubbing strips and guards in black or some dark color, and the rest of the hull—including the sheer strake—white. The effect is two narrow, dark stripes along the sides.

Scammon describes the unusual colors of the boats and sails in the California grey whale fishery in the 1870s. Sails were sometimes colored or had crosses, balls, stars, crescents, numbers, or letters on the mainsails. Boats were white, black, lead colored, or painted with stripes of three colors. The bows might be red, blue, or green. Some had eyes on the bows.[1]

James Templeman Brown, writing of the boats in the 1880s, notes that they were generally white below but depending on the whaling grounds, they might be other colors. Whaleships sailing in the Gulf Stream painted their boats a salmon pink, a leather tint, lead color, or light blue.[2] Clifford Ashley says much the same thing about the outside of the boats, though he recalls one ship whose boats had a red sheer strake, and says black boats were used in sealing.[3]

Ashley also writes that interiors were often lumber-wagon blue, light umber, gunboat grey, or salmon pink. The cuddy board was usually painted the same color as the outside of the boat, while the warp box was a different color. The ceiling was light so that the equipment could be easily seen. Bow and stern sheets were left unpainted to provide better footing, and were sometimes covered with mats.

Azorean boats today are brightly painted: they are white below the sheer strake, and the color of the tops depends on the island to which the boat belongs. Pico boats are blue and Fayal boats red, with rubbing strips and guards often a different color. The edges of the thigh board, including the clumsy cleat, and the cuddy board are outlined with a contrasting strip. Interiors are sometimes varnished; however, some are painted the same color as the sheer strake down to the lower edge of the riser. Below, the ceiling is another color. Identification numbers are painted on the bows, and the boat's name, sometimes in gilt in a scroll, on the quarters. The mast is sometimes white; oars and paddles may be painted blue or another color. More attention was given to painting and color in the Azorean boats than was the practice of whaleships.

Boats belonging to Alaskan Eskimos today generally have their hulls painted white, with the sheer strake and guard in black, dark green, or some other color. There is one, however, at St. Lawrence Island that has an ochre hull.

Shipboard repairs to whaleboats were quick and rough. Damage and wear resulted from ice in Arctic whaling, from raising and lowering the boats, towing, and, of course, from the whales themselves.* Boats towed into the ice had planking cut and bows stove. Raising and lowering in rough

---

* A freakish accident that happened more than once was a boat being stove in by a dead whale. Whales that sank in shallow water after being killed were buoyed and raised after gasses formed. Often a tug brought them shooting to the surface under the boat.

weather smashed them against the ship's sides, splitting strakes, breaking wales, and racking the boats. Crews sometimes got the water out of a half-swamped boat by hoisting the bow until the water emptied out of the stern. Besides hoisting them with their full load of gear, boats were often raised with heavy loads of provisions. Being towed by whales into a head sea sometimes started the fastenings, and Charles Beetle wrote that a boat strained by fast towing could seldom be made usable for a second voyage.

Beetle said that boats stove in by whales were usually too damaged to make repairs practical. He always looked at the keel first: if it was broken, it was a question whether repairs were worthwhile. He did, however, replace stems, and mentioned repairing one boat stove in from keel to wale. He made a regular business of boat storage and repair. Once when 100 boats came to his shop in one week from incoming ships, he rented a neighboring lot and stored them there, bottom up. After repairs, some refastening and painting, they were sent out again as spare boats. A majority of the boats he built, he wrote, returned to him for repairs.

Brown noted that some ships returned with the same boats they had taken out, but that generally these had undergone so many repairs at sea and were so battered as to be unusable for a second voyage. Considerable swapping of boats and trading with other whaleships and natives went on. William Davis mentions a damaged boat that was repaired at sea by the captain. "Tinkering" and earlier repairs made it so heavy that it could not be used for whaling, so it was traded for provisions in Hawaii. He wrote that all boats were "delapidated" toward the end.

Ship carpenters aboard whaleships were skilled in whaleboat repair. Charles M. Scammon gives a

Boats in the Beetle yard at Clarks Point, New Bedford, for storage and repairs. Courtesy of Harold Beetle.

Spare whaleboat being launched through break in bulwark at cutting-stage. Note cranes and gripes of the boat in the davits. Photograph taken from the CHARLES W. MORGAN. Courtesy of Mr. and Mrs. Jack McNatt.

97

A used boat at Beetle's yard for repairs.
Courtesy of Harold Beetle.

list of materials taken on a whaleship for making repairs. It includes 900 feet of cedar planks, 24 frames, 12 seat knees, 2 stems, 1 keel, oak planks for wales, 20 pounds of clench nails, 10 pounds of ceiling nails, and 40 spruce poles for spare spars.* The materials were stored on the whaleship between the carlings between the forward and main hatch. Beetle mentions delivering spare, prebent frames and stems to whaleships, and the outfit of the *Mermaid* in 1855 included spare timbers at $.08 each, knees at $.33 each and gunwales at $2.50 a pair.

Repairs were made as quickly as possible in order to get the boat back in service. Robert Ferguson mentions a boat with its bow cut clean off by a whale's flukes. As the bow oarsman was hurt, damage to the boat must have extended well aft. The cooper and the carpenter, however, had it back in the davits after one day's work. One man drove nails from the outside while the other was on the inside holding the turning iron. Davis wrote that if the keel and gunwale were not broken, a boat could be put back in use in a few days by using prebent frames. When skilled carpenters became scarce, ships began carrying more spare boats.

The boats in some museums today show patches and rough repairs. Planking was patched with dutchmen and short lengths of plank backed with large butt blocks. For emergency repairs away from the ship, the boats were supplied with a roll of canvas and tacks. Eskimos today sometimes patch their boats with sealskin, and the Azoreans still carry canvas for covering holes. Necessity is the mother of invention: in one account of American whalers, the mate kept his whaleboat from filling as it was under tow by stuffing the jib into a hole stove

* Except for there not being enough frames, this amount of material was enough to make a new boat.

Evidence of longevity of whaleboats in the Arctic. This photograph was taken in 1973 at St. Lawrence Island, Alaska. The boat came from the steam whaleship BALAENA which was lost in the ice off the island May 1, 1901. The boat is now at the New Bedford Whaling Museum. Courtesy of the photographer, John Bockstoce. Copyrighted.

in the bow, the same trick as using a sail as a collision mat. Often boats were so shattered that the whaleship did not hoist the wreckage back aboard—just picked up the men and floating gear and abandoned the rest.*

The boatsteerer, under the direction of the mate, was responsible for the upkeep of the boats and gear. There was no fancy work on boats the whaleships carried; thrum mats and rigging might be neat and competently done, but they were not showy. The gig tackles which secured the bow when in the davits sometimes were fancy, according to Brown, but these were a part of the ship rather than of the boat.

* Sometimes the men in a stove, swamped boat climbed on the dead whale and waited there for rescue. It was standard practice if stove and swamped in a rough sea for the crew to lash the oars and sometimes the spars athwartships across the gunwales to keep the boat from rolling over. They could then sit inside on the thwarts until they were picked up.

Boats were carried ready for use on the cranes or overturned on the skids.** The skids were racks built over the deck between the main and mizzen

** Boats were named according to their position aboard the whaleship. The captain's or starboard boat was on the starboard quarter; the mate's or larboard boat was on the port quarter; the second mate's or waist boat was on the port side in the waist; the bow boat was the third mate's and was on the port bow.

The waist boat was often shorter than the other boats because of restricted space and closer davit spacing.

In some ships and barks a fifth boat was carried on the starboard bow. A schooner might have two or three boats as crane boats and one spare across the stern.

On the half scale model *Lagoda*, the boat equipment was marked:

    S.B.B. (Star'b. Bow Boat)
    S. B. (Starboard Boat)
    L. B. (Larboard Boat)
    W. B. (Waist Boat)
    P.B.B. (Port Bow Boat)

Used boats, carried as spares, on the skids aboard a whale ship. Oars and spars are stacked between. Note bearers with gripes and cranes for boats in davits. Courtesy of Kendall Whaling Museum.

mast of ships and barks. The overhead boats were often old and were sometimes used for making landings ashore if there was danger of damage to the boat. The spare boat across the tail feathers on the stern of schooners was sometimes overturned but more often was upright. Crane boats were ready for lowering unless there was heavy weather, and the boats were swung inboard or turned on their gunwales so the seas would not fill them. The keels of the boats at the davits were supported at two points by the cranes and were kept secure by gig tackles at the bow and two gripes that held them against the davits as the ship rolled. Line tubs were removed to reduce sagging while on the cranes. The rest of the equipment had to be ready in the boat.

The boats in davits were exposed to weather and sun. In the tropics, Brown writes, wooden spreaders were jammed anthwartships at the gripes between the wales to keep the boat's shape. Drain plugs were taken out to eliminate the weight of accumulated water. Ships in port put their boats over the side to soak up; and at sea, lowering for whales or drilling the crews probably prevented them from drying out under normal circumstances. In shore whaling, the boats were often kept in sheds or protected by boat covers.

1. Charles M. Scammon, *The Marine Mammals of the Northwestern Coast of North America and the American Whale Fishery* (Riverside: Manessier Publishing Co., 1969), Reprint ed., p. 271.

2. James Templeman Brown, *Whalemen, Vessels, Apparatus, Methods of the Fishery.* vol. 2, part 15 (Washington: Government Printing Office, 1883), p. 242.

3. Clifford W. Ashley, *The Yankee Whaler* (Garden City: Halcyon House, 1942), p. 63.

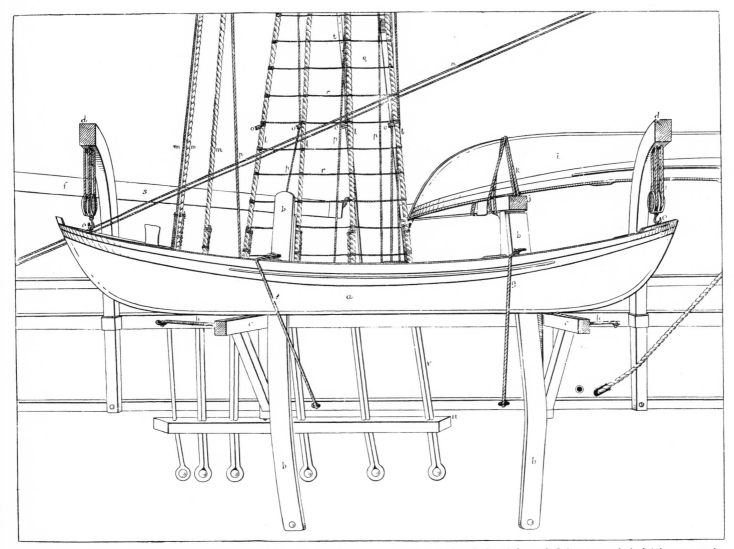

Whaleboat on the cranes. Cranes (c) support the keel of the boat. They are hinged to swing inboard when the boat is lowered. Gripes (g) are lashed tight to secure the boat. The bearers (b) keep the boat clear of channels and chainplates while the boat is lowered and raised. Davits (d) and davit falls (f) are for hoisting and lowering. Gigtackles, not shown, were rigged from the bow chocks to the bearers to prevent fore and aft movement of the boat.

Drawing from THE FISHERIES & FISHERY INDUSTRIES OF THE UNITED STATES *by George Brown Goode.*

Chapter X

THE
WHALEBOAT
AND
RELATED TYPES

There are similarities in construction and lines between whaleboats and a number of other boat types, although the degree and direction of influence is somewhat difficult to judge. Builders often built several related boats, and the men who used one type usually were familiar with similar boats. Whaleboats in American shore whaling, for example, often used the same beaches as surf boats, and men who went whaling were occasionally part-time sealers.

The types most similar to the whaleboats were sealing boats, seine boats, surf boats, and certain ship's boats of the British, French, and U. S. Navy. Whaleboat features were also copied by island boatbuilders in the Atlantic, Pacific, and Indian Oceans.

Surf boats of the nineteenth century on Cape Cod and Long Island were light and double-ended. They influenced some types of boats built for organized lifesaving, for these, like the whaleboats, often had a short deck forward and a cuddy board aft, with bow and stern sheets, five thwarts with single-banked oars, and a steering oar. Both lapstrake and batten-seam construction were used. Lines showed local variations, but in general they had greater beam, depth, and a rocker to the keel. In the lifesaving boats, the beam gave greater stiffness and carrying capacity, an important feature in a boat designed to rescue as many people as possible on each trip from a wreck. The depth provided greater freeboard in breaking seas and also increased carrying capacity. The sheer in most was stronger than in a whaleboat; the higher ends produced a righting effect in rough seas. The entrance was finer with bow and stern sections almost identical, and this fine entrance improved the surf boat as a pulling boat. Because it was launched off a beach through surf, and often had to be trans-

Surf boat of the U.S. Lifesaving Service.

ported a distance along the beach, the size and weight were limited.

A comparison of the whaleboat of the period to the plans of a Monomoy surf boat of 1893 shows the latter to be beamier, deeper, with greater sheer, greater fullness to the hull, and rounder bilges. The forward and after sections of the Monomoy are nearly the same. The rocker to the keel is not extreme, but is slightly greater. The boat is lapstrake-built and has a centerboard. The ceiling is not solid, as in the whaleboat, and there are four thwarts with double knees on each. Stem and stern posts are heavier than the steam-bent members of the whaleboat.

Comparing a whaleboat to the Humane Society boat used at Sankaty, Nantucket, which is now at the Mariners Museum in Newport News, Virginia, close similarities are found in details. The seat knees of kerfed, steam-bent oak with filler pieces

behind are the same, and the pattern of planking in ceiling, bow, and stern sheets is the same. Such details as peaking cleats, chamfer on tops of seat knees, cuddy board and oarlock socket blocks are common to both. The boat has chocking pieces aft and, in imitation of a whaleboat, the Sankaty boat has bow chocks which are, however, nonfunctional. Differences are in the greater flare to the sides, greater sheer, and proportionately greater beam. The lapstrake, half-inch planking is fastened with copper rivets. It is probable that the builder of this boat built whaleboats as well. It is known that Charles Beetle built boats for the U. S. Lifesaving Station at Chatham, and that in the 1870s George Rogers, builder of whaleboats and seal boats, also built surf boats.

Some seal boats had a close resemblance to whaleboats. Many whaleships also hunted seal in high southern latitudes. Writing in the 1880s, A.

103

Seine boats at former Higgins and Gifford shop, Gloucester, 1912. Henry D. Fisher Collection at Mystic Seaport.

Howard Clark in *The Fisheries and Fishery Industries of the U. S.*, says the boats carried by the sealing vessels "are about the same as the ordinary 28 foot whaleboat. They are made a little stouter and more burdensome than the whaleboat, but of the same general style, and are used in transporting men, skins and apparatus from the vessels to the shore." Later, smaller boats were used for the pursuit of seals in the water; this was known as pelagic sealing.

The pelagic sealing boats, except for some dugout Indian canoes from the Pacific Northwest, had the general lines of a small whaleboat. They were double-ended, nineteen feet long with a four and one-half foot beam, and a schooner might carry seven of them. Considered good pulling boats and sea boats, they carried two or three men: a hunter, a boatsteerer, and sometimes a "puller." Seals on the surface were approached quietly under sail or oars. At a range of 100 or 150 feet the hunter fired his shotgun; the dead seal was gaffed and pulled aboard and often skinned in the boat.

The East Coast seal boats were carvel-planked with one-half inch pine. Keel, stem, and stern posts were birch or maple; frames were ash, twelve inches on centers. The West Coast boats were lapstrake cedar and were considered to be better pulling and sailing boats but not as maneuverable. They had either a gaff mainsail or a spritsail with jib, and carried rudders but no centerboards. A "pushing board" was used as a paddle for quiet approaches.[1]

The seine boat evolved directly from the whaleboat. In 1856, an ordinary whaleboat was used on a menhaden purse seiner by Captain George Merchant, Jr., of Gloucester. It pulled, towed, and maneuvered easily; therefore, Merchant had a boat built specially the following year by Higgins and Gifford of Gloucester that resembled the whaleboat but was wider aft in order to take the weight of the seine. It proved very successful and was copied. The boats in 1857 were twenty-eight feet; in 1880 the average boat was thirty-four feet with a beam of seven feet five inches and a depth of thirty-three inches; later they grew to thirty-eight feet. The boats were lapstrake until 1872; thereafter they were made batten seam, which was said to make them more durable, increase their speed, and reduce the likelihood of nets catching. On the other hand, the lapstrake was stiffer.

The function of the seine boat was to carry the purse seine, which on some vessels was 225 fathoms in length. The boat was pulled with seven, eight, or nine single-banked oars thirteen or fourteen feet long. The net was shot or set while the boat was pulled in a circle around the fish. Besides the oarsmen, the boat held three men to shoot the net, and the captain, who steered with the steering oar. After pursing the net, it was pulled aboard the seine boat to constrict the enclosed fish, which were then bailed out with a large dip net onto the schooner.

Three features were important to a seine boat. First, it had to tow well at speeds of up to ten and twelve knots. Normally, seine boats were towed behind the schooner, but sometimes they were brought aboard in heavy weather. Second, unlike whaleboats, they had to be fine forward and full aft; this improved them as pulling boats, gave them carrying capacity aft, and reduced squatting under tow. Third, they had to be stiff and steady because of the movement while shooting and then pulling aboard the heavy seine of fish.[2]

The U. S. Navy has had boats called whaleboats on the allowances of vessels since the 1840s. Frigates of a class built between 1835 and 1845 carried, among other boats, a whaleboat and a barge. Despite the nomenclature, the latter was closer to the whaleboat of the period than the former. The whaleboat was twenty-eight feet in length, two feet five inches deep, and had a beam of seven feet two inches, which is about one foot wider than whaleboats of the period. The barge was twenty-eight feet in length, two feet four inches deep, with a six foot beam. The sections of the barge are close to that of a whaleboat, though it has a finer entrance. The boats have deadwood aft, which continued to be a feature of Navy whaleboats.

By the 1890s, the U. S. Navy had twenty, twenty-four, twenty-six, twenty-eight, twenty-nine, and thirty foot whaleboats, and twenty-eight and thirty foot "Gig whaleboats." The latter were slightly lighter and cheaper; the standard thirty-foot "whaleboat" cost $1,092 for the bare boat, as opposed to about $100 for a thirty-foot whaleboat for a whaleship. The beam, six feet ten inches, and the depth, two feet five inches, were roughly the same as those of the working whaleboats, but the Navy's boat was more burdensome with fuller sections, rounder bilges, and less overhang to the ends. The scantlings were for a far heavier boat; total weight was 1,767 pounds as opposed to about 1,000. Planking of the Navy's boat was three-quarter inch, frames are sided one inch, stem and stern sided two and one-quarter inches. The finish of the boat was elegant, having some mahogany trim and turned stanchions under thwarts and turned awning stanchions. The stern sheets had benches for officer passengers. The Navy's smaller whaleboats had single-banked oars; the oars of the thirty-foot boat were double-banked. The sail plan for all the boats was that of a ketch with a sliding gunter. The thirty-foot boat carried 278 square feet of sail. With no centerboards, the boats could not have been very weatherly.

A surf boat carried aboard the U.S.S. *Ranger* in 1893 was closer to the true whaleboat than were the Navy's whaleboats. Its length was twenty-nine feet three inches, beam six feet three and one-half inches, depth two feet two inches, sheer eighteen inches, and it weighed 1,430 pounds "with outfit." It had five thwarts, single-banked oars, and used a steering oar. The entrance was finer than a whaleboat's, even having a slight hollow. The sheer was very strong: the crew had the opinion there was not enough freeboard as the boat shipped water amidships in rough seas. The boat was carvel-planked and painted whaleboat-style with black sheer strake and white below.

Engines were installed in the Navy whaleboats early in the 1900s, although the boats aboard destroyers were still equipped with sails into the 1930s. Today the standard "motor whaleboat" is of wood or plastic. It is twenty-six feet three-quarters of an inch in length; the beam of the wooden boat is seven feet two inches and that of the plastic, eight feet one and three-quarter inches. The present boats weigh more than 5,000 pounds with engine, or some five times the weight of those used in whaling. Until recently, the Navy had a few whaleboats of a different design which were used for training; these had a length of twenty-eight feet, a beam of seven feet eight inches, were ketch-rigged with lug sails and equipped with twelve, double-banked oars.*

* My father rigged a twenty-four foot Navy whaleboat as a sloop around 1930. It had no centerboard, so he tried to make it more weatherly and add ballast by fastening an iron rail on the bottom of the keel. This helped, but I gather the boat never did go to weather very well. Later he raced the whaleboats off destroyers.

Until recently, the whaleboats used by the British Navy had preserved some features of the old whaleboats, but now they, too, have gone to plastics. The British boats were twenty-seven feet long, with a beam of six feet, a depth of two feet six and one-half inches; they had little sheer and high freeboard, and the ends had less overhang and were fuller than the working whaleboats. Planking was three-eighths of an inch elm or mahogany. Their weight, with full equipment and two men aboard, was 2,600 pounds. They were pulled with five single-banked oars: the stroke oar was sixteen feet and the rest seventeen feet. These oars were said to work very well in rough seas, better than the shorter oars used in other ships' boats of the British Navy. They had centerboards and were yawl-rigged with a foresail, standing lug main, a leg-of-mutton mizzen, and a trysail. Some of the boats had been built for the Navy in Malta, and these had a high reputation and were much sought after by the captains of the ships.*

A boat which evolved from the whaleboat is the modern motorized whale and towing boat of the Azores. Its lines are somewhat closer to older

My brother-in-law, while captain of a naval vessel in the 1960s, rigged a motor whaleboat as a ketch with sliding gunters. The spars were improvised from dunnage. The boat was not weatherly; in fact once while sailing in the Bay of Naples they could not make it back to the ship. The engine could not be started, so they crossed the Bay more or less at the mercy of the elements and landed on a stone mole, where one stayed to guard the boat while my brother-in-law went off for aid on a borrowed bicycle. He said they had a more successful sail later in the harbor at St. Thomas. These, perhaps, were the last attempts to sail a whaleboat in the U.S. Navy.

* Information on the British Navy whaleboats was supplied by Harold Kimber and Commander J. E. G. McKee of the Greenwich Museum. The latter used to sail the boats during World War II in races at Scapa Flow. He writes that they stood up very well in the blowing weather found there.

CORTES LONGITUDINAIS

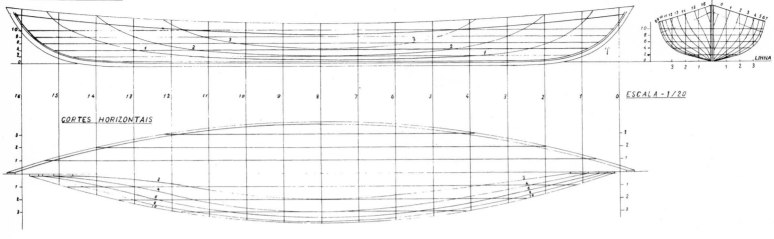

ESCALA - 1/20

CORTES HORIZONTAIS

LIHNA

ABOVE: Lines plan of Azorean whaleboat. Length 37'. Beam 6' 3''. The boat is proportionately narrower and the ends are finer with greater overhang than American whaleboats.

The boat is equipped with a centerboard. There are six thwarts; thus allowing six men pulling oars rather than the five which was standard for American boats.

The whaleboat has batten-seam construction except for the sheer strake, which laps the strake beneath. Keel and wales are made of a species of pine. Stem, stern, thwart knees, frames are a type of acacia.

RIGHT: 30' U.S. Navy whaleboat, 1895.

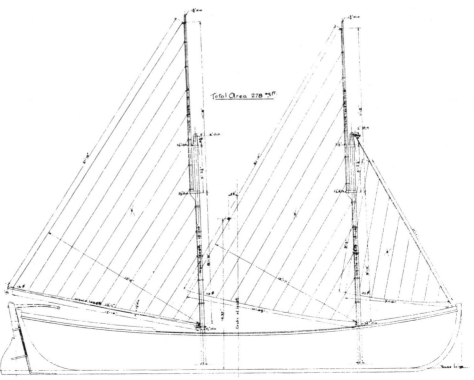

Total Area 278 sq. ft.

Modern diesel-powered Azorean whaleboat. Courtesy of the photographer, Peter F. Tripp.

American whaleboats than to the contemporary, non-motorized Azorean boats. The ends are less fine and the overhang less extreme. The construction is molded plywood, a material also used to build some of the contemporary non-motorized whaleboats. The engine is a Diesel that is said to move it at fourteen knots. The boat also carries oars. Other conventional whaleboat features are bow chocks, clumsy cleat, warp box forward, and lion's tongue and loggerhead aft. An oarlock for a steering oar is mounted to starboard.

A boat with an expensive engine would not be exposed to the usual risks of a whaleboat. Presumably the main role of the boat is to tow other boats out and dead whales back. Since it is also equipped to kill whales, under unusual circumstances the engine could be cut off and the boat go on whales under oars, or it might assist in killing a whale another boat was fast to. Such use of a motorized whaleboat is not new, the experimental use of boats with engines is described by Brown in the 1880s.[3]

According to local sources, the boats of Tristan da Cunha are derived from whaleboats. Whaleships often stopped at the island, and the islanders themselves have been building a boat patterned after whaleboat lines since about 1886. Their measurements are: twenty-eight to thirty feet, depth twenty-four to thirty inches, and beam of six to seven feet. Weight is estimated at between 1,200 and 1,500 pounds, which seems heavy for a canvas-covered boat unless gear is included. Canvas is used because wood is scarce and because lightness is an advantage in surf. The boats last eight to eleven years and are now recanvased every two seasons—it is said that better canvas than today's was formerly obtained from visiting ships of the Royal Navy. The boats are pulled with six oars or sailed. In 1973, there were eight on the island.

The whaleboats of Bequia used for shore whaling reflect the influence of American whaleboats. Whaleships from New England often stopped in the Grenadines and recruited crewmen in the early 1900s. In 1911, Frederic A. Fenger, a naval architect cruising the Carribean in his sailing canoe, described the boats as the "same large double-ended sea-canoe of the Yankee but it has lost the graceful ends and the easy lines of the New Bedford craft." The boats are "almost uncouth in their roughness."[4]

Two boats still whale in Bequia. Scantlings, lines, rig, and hull construction are closer to the local fishing craft than to the American whaleboat, but fittings and the arrangement inside are much the same. The profiles of stem and stern are much different from the American whaleboat because of the deadwood and a four inch deep keel. Sections at bow and stern are hollow at the waterline. Sheer is slight and the beam proportionately greater, making a heavier-looking boat than the American whaleboat.* In construction, scantlings of the Bequian boat are heavy. Frames are bent on the flat and widely spaced. They reach to the top of the sheer, and wales are fastened to the inside face. Thwart knees and stem and stern posts are natural crook. The bow chocks are massive. The boats are carvel-planked with three-quarter inch planking; there are no laps. The boats are ballasted with about 400 pounds of rock ballast. They have cen-

terboards, and with the relatively large spritsail, mainsail, and jib, perform well and are fast in the strong prevailing winds around the island.

Elsewhere in the Atlantic, it is reported that there are whaleboat-like craft on the coast of Brazil, but whether there is a connection between these and the boats used by Azoreans who attempted to set up shore whaling in Brazil, or the boats used earlier by whaleships, I do not know. On various islands in the Pacific and Indian Oceans, certain whaleboat features have been adapted by builders. The Pitcairn Islanders use large, double-ended longboats with features that appear to be copied from whaleboats. These are launched from ramps into the exposed waters of Bounty Bay and carry passengers and freight between the island ships lying to offshore when men can be found to man them. And in the Indian Ocean at Keeling-Cocos, boats are built that derive from whaleboats, as do some of the boats of the Seychelles.

* I have seen a half model of a whaleboat obtained from a builder, C. B. Magras of St. Lucia. It is a lift model with the top layer missing at the sheer. The scale is three-quarters inch to the foot. Lines of the model are similar to those of an American boat, and it does not appear to have much resemblance to the existing boats in Bequia. The latter, I am told, are closer to the boats used for fishing. I am indebted to Mr. John McVitty, of Stonington, Connecticut, for information on the Bequian boats.

1. A. Alfred Mattsson, "Fur Seal Hunting in the South Atlantic," *The American Neptune* (April, 1942), p. 154, *idem.* "Sealing Boats," *ibid* (October, 1943), p. 327.

2. G. Brown Goode and J. W. Collins, "The Mackerel Fishery," *The Fisheries and Fishery Industries of the United States* (Washington: Government Printing Office, 1887), pp. 250-52.

3. James Templeman Brown, *The Fisheries and Fishery Industries of the United States* (Washington: Government Printing Office, 1887), p. 246.

4. Frederic A. Fenger, *Alone in the Caribbean* (Belmont, Mass., Wellington Books, 1958), p 49.

Chapter XI
BUILDING A BEETLE WHALEBOAT REPLICA AT MYSTIC SEAPORT WITH WILLITS ANSEL IN 2002

Walter Ansel

My father, Willits Ansel, returned to Mystic Seaport in mid-August 2002 to teach four shipwrights how to build a traditional Beetle whaleboat. As his son and a Mystic Seaport shipwright myself, I was chosen to be the new boat's project leader. This new chapter in my father's book is intended to present an overview and trouble-shooting guide for those who someday would like to build a Beetle whaleboat replica. The information is taken from a daily log that I kept during the three-month construction period, and also from a video of the process shot by Markham Starr.

The best surviving example of a Beetle whaleboat is in the collections of the Mariners' Museum at Newport News, Virginia. It was built by Charlie Beetle in 1933 specifically for exhibition and has never been used. This design has become a favorite of Mystic Seaport's because of its stunning beauty and its reputation for handling. In 1973, Willits Ansel and Mystic Seaport's naval architect, Robert Allyn, traveled to Newport News and measured this boat, and Bob Allyn produced a lines drawing (#138), a construction plan (#139), and a sail plan (#153). These lines are so accurate and so superbly drawn that a boat can be built from them with a minimum of lofting. Copies of these drawings are available from the Ships Plans Collection at Mystic Seaport.

Like nineteenth-century whaleboats, the traditionally built whaleboats that Willits had constructed during the 1970s had relatively short lifespans because of their authentic but quickly rusting iron fastenings. Today, with whaleboat construction costs approaching $100,000 each, we opted for longer-lasting copper clench nails and bronze screws, the former being available from the Strawbery Banke Museum in Portsmouth, New Hampshire.

Historically, whaleboats were planked with northern white cedar, a marvelously tough, resilient wood that was known for its "leathery" qualities when wet. Unfortunately, clear wood of this species is practically unobtainable today. Instead, we used Atlantic white cedar in the flatter areas of the boat where the planks are widest, and accepted the knotty, but less-prone-to-split, northern white cedar at the bilge where the planks had to be cupped or warped with steam.

Because of his faith in, and experience with Bob Allyn's drawings, Willits chose to loft only the ends of the boat; that is, eight feet of the bow and stern in plan and profile. He then lofted the entire body plan and constructed a mold for each station. The molds were notched for the garboard lap and the plank battens. Since the lines are drawn to the outside of the planking, one half inch must be subtracted from them to account for the planking thickness. The stem and sternpost were gotten out of clear white oak eight feet long and one and one-half by three inches in section. These pieces were kerfed lengthwise along the middle or apex line so they'd bend easier. They were bent over a "trap" with some over-bend that allowed for springback (see drawing). Copper rivets one-quarter inch in diameter were used after bending to hold the kerf closed. The stem's rabbet was established using the five six-inch waterlines from the lofting along with station #1. Intermediate short stations drawn 90 degrees to the rabbet between waterlines four and three, and between three and two, gave additional rabbet shape information. The sternpost rabbet was established in the same way.

The keel was made from a white oak piece two inches by seven inches by twenty-one feet long. The sided keel, looked at in plan view—which resembles a cigar—was marked out using the half-breadth plan. Its rabbet shape was established from the lofting in the following way: At each station or mold on the body plan, the keel rabbet shape was drawn using a one-half-inch fid block that represented the planking.

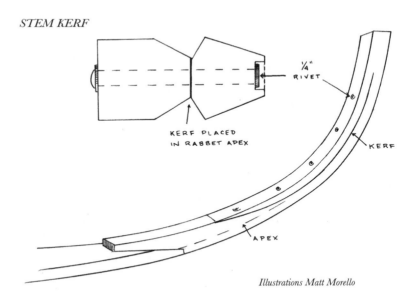

¼" RIVET

KERF PLACED IN RABBET APEX

KERF

APEX

Illustrations Matt Morello

This established the rabbet's depth and angle. Tracings were made of these keel sections, and their shapes were marked on the side and bottom of the keel timber as points and were connected with battens (see drawing). The keel rabbet was rough-cut square with a skill saw, and then finished with a slick, chisels, and finally a rabbet plane until the planking fid fit (see drawing).

The heels of the stem and sternposts were slathered with 3M 5200 adhesive sealant and riveted to the keel, creating a backbone unit that was then sprung down and temporarily screwed to the rockered strongback. It was then plumbed and squared, ready to receive the molds and planking. We used steel angle brackets (horses), forged by the Museum's blacksmith, to brace the stem and sternpost. At this point, the new whaleboat's profile had been locked in. Variations in the curves of steam-bent stems and sternposts give

111

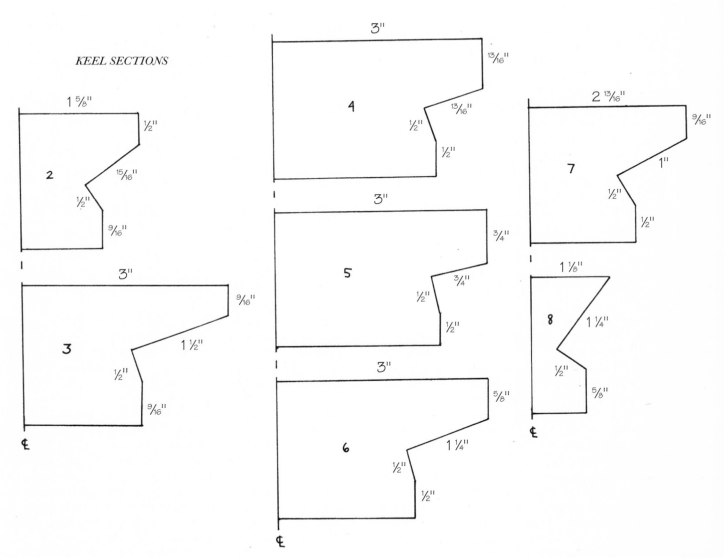

KEEL SECTIONS

Illustrations Matt Morello

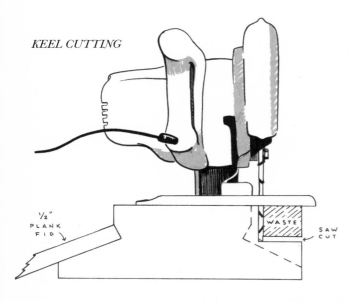

KEEL CUTTING

½" PLANK FID

WASTE

SAW CUT

Illustration Matt Morello

this type of building a bit of the "free form method" according to Willits.

While the lofting and mold and backbone construction were taking place, seventy-five six-foot-long, three-quarter-by-one-and-three-quarter-inch green (unseasoned) white oak frame blanks were sawn out. The frames are tapered in their molded dimension, being one-half inch thinner at the top than at the heel. We created this taper with a purpose-built table-saw jig. Unfortunately, most of our white oak was of the old-growth variety and too stiff to bend very well on the frame trap. But the trap was built with enough over-bend to make the released frame closely match the boat's midsection. Once again, John Gardner's advice held true: Fast-grown white oak with wide ring spacing is the best and strongest bending stock. We seemed to have better luck with blanks that had been stored in the river until steaming time. On our worst day we broke 70 percent of the frames we bent! Other builders have resorted to metal bending straps to compression-end their frames, a very reliable trick when you don't have much extra material on hand.

It should be noted that Barry Thomas and Bill Sauerbrey built a Beetle whaleboat for Mystic Seaport back in 1993. Bill described an economical Beetle method of making frames—which we did not use—whereby the frames were sawn from a wider piece of flat stock, the tapers overlapping with a heel swell at the butt (see photos).

We used the same measurements that Willits and Bob Allyn took off in 1973 to lay out our plank widths in 2002. These widths, marked on every mold, gave the sheer at the bow a nice kickup that didn't always show up on the existing older boats (see chart).

The keel and forefoot back rabbets required some tuning after set up. The gain in the ends of the garboard (a non-rabbetted dory lap) was thirty-six inches long and was cut after hanging the plank. Willits passed on some pearls of wisdom from Leo Telesmanick, who used to work in the Beetle Boat Shop. On quickly scarfing: "Cut the plank scarfs with a slick and give them a few licks with a plane." On clench-nailing the planks: "Just a couple of twists with an awl to make a hole for a nail," and "let your dolly bounce when you're clenching, it helps turn the nail." We found that the full-length clench nails were too big for the gains, so we had to resort to shorter, smaller ones to keep from splitting the cedar. We also found that two apprentice clenchers can do a better job if one of them drives the nail and the other turns it. The nailing became considerably neater as planking progressed and they gained experience.

In a nod to modernity and for ease of maintenance, the 2002 boat's plank scarfs were bedded with 3M 5200. The hood end and backbone plank fasteners

Beetle frame. Photograph by Bill Sauerbrey

BETTLE PLANK WIDTHS

	1	2	3	4	5	6	7	8	9
8 SHEER	34 3/8	39 3/4	45 3/4	49 1/8	49	46 1/2	41 7/8	37 1/2	27 3/4
7	29	33 3/4	39	41 3/4	41 5/8	39 3/8	35 3/8	32	23 1/4
6	26	29 3/4	33 3/4	36 1/2	36 1/4	34	30 3/4	28 1/4	20 3/4
5	22 5/8	25 5/8	28 3/4	30 5/8	30 3/4	29 1/4	26 5/8	25	18
4	18 1/2	20 7/8	22 3/4	24	24 1/2	23 1/2	22 1/8	21	14 1/4
3	14 3/8	16 1/4	17 1/2	18	18	17 1/2	17	16 1/2	10
2	9	11	11 1/2	11 1/2	11 1/2	11 3/8	11 1/4	11	4 3/8
1 GARBOARD	3	5 1/8	5 1/2	5 1/4	5 1/4	5 1/4	5 1/2	5 1/2	—

S T A T I O N S

P L A N K S

GIRTH MEASUREMENTS TO PLANK SEAMS

Illustration Matt Morello

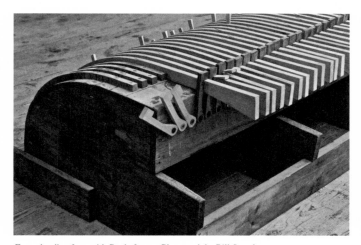

Frame bending form with Beetle frames. Photograph by Bill Sauerbrey

Wumping a plank. Photograph by Bill Sauerbrey

used in 2002 were #9 flathead silicon bronze wood screws instead of the traditional galvanized steel nails.

Beetle whaleboats, as mentioned earlier, have eight planks per side. We did not have to start cupping, or "wumping," planks until we reached the fourth plank up from the garboard, as planks four, five, and six form the turn of the bilge. Wumping is a term used by Beetle boatbuilders. In preparation for this, we planed a shy one-eighth inch off the upper, outer edge of the plank seam batten so that a stick laid on the mold would lay tight against it. This is similar to the way the top edge of a lapstrake plank is beveled. It should be noted that, traditionally, all of a whaleboat's battens butt tight against the backs of the stem and sternpost. To wump the plank, it was clamped to the molds with long bar clamps and then softened with boiling water poured onto piles of rags draped on the plank edge. At times, we wrapped the planks in plastic held in place with spring clamps to hold in the steam. After a half hour, the matching wumper blocks were clamped on and left to coax the plank into the desired cupped shape. Clenching to the batten was done soon thereafter to take advantage of the flexibility of the still-soft plank. It should be mentioned that the Beetle wumping method was different. The planks were steamed and cupped on the bench and later fitted to the boat after they were cold. Leo Telesmanick told Willits that in the Beetle Boat Shop the wide and curved-face clenching hammer might be used to "mash and mold the plank while clenching"! It's astounding how much abuse northern white cedar will take without splitting. We found the Atlantic white cedar to be less tough, more brittle, and easily split.

With planking completed, the white-oak inwales were sawn out and installed. Willits felt it was important to have the support of the molds while fastening and fitting the inwales. The one-and-five-eighths-by-one-and-seven-eighths-inch inwales were pre-bent to blocks temporarily fastened to the shop floor. The molds were then notched for the inwales, which were inserted inside the sheer strakes, then clamped and screwed into place. Willits cut out the bow chocks and riveted them to the stem and inwales. To fit the bow chocks, a notch has to be sawn in the forward part of the sheerstrake, and to no one's surprise—perhaps because it was discussed beforehand—a split appeared. This was not critical, however, because the plank is well supported by the rails and the warp box (see photo).

With the inwales in place and fastened, all of the molds were removed for installing the frames—with the exception of station #1. That one was locked in, so it had to be disassembled later.

Whaleboat frames, numbering thirty-two pairs in the Beetle whaleboat, are a challenge to install quickly. It was Willits's firm opinion (backed by much experience) that the inwales should always be installed first, to act as a backstop in which to jam the tops of the frames so that the notches for the battens and laps could be established during fitting. Fitting a curved, notched piece to a curve is akin to stringing a bow, and involves both bending and sideslipping. If you don't have the top jammed under the inwale, the frame will be very hard to position properly.

The thwart positions determine the frame spacing, which is not consistent. With that thought in mind, Willits drew the thwart locations on top of the recently installed inwales, then divided up the space in between. He used a long one-eighth-inch-by-three-quarter-inch oak batten to draw the position of each frame on the planking (and seam battens) from the inwale down to the keel. It should be noted that on plan #139 five frames are shown between each thwart. Frames on either side of a thwart lie about one-half inch away from the thwart's edge. Forward of the forward-most (harpooner's) thwart, there are five frames

Bow chock cut out. Photograph by Bill Sauerbrey

that are more widely spaced and canted as well, having their tops pitched forward. This is mirrored aft, except there are seven cant frames, with their tops pitched aft.

We framed the 2002 boat in four days with three experienced shipwrights. One man was inside the boat marking and fitting while the other two were outside selecting the frames, sawing the notches with a fourteen-inch band saw (positioned close by), and screw-fastening after the final fitting. Fastenings were #9 one-and-three-quarter-inch flathead silicon bronze wood screws.

The following method for framing was developed with Willits's advice: We started with a thin storystrip (a one-eighth-inch-by-three-quarter-inch batten) that was sprung into the boat at the frame location and tacked in place with light wire nails. On its edge we marked the batten and lap positions. A pre-bent frame that best conformed to the hull at that location was then selected. Two positions of the frame were established: the tightest curve in the hull, and where the frame top would land. The unseasoned, more-recently bent frames straightened out more easily, and this was

done in a bench vise. A three-eighths-inch line was scribed on the side of the frame with a combination square in the place where the battens would land. The storystrip was next wrapped around the outside of the frame, aligned to the number-two batten mark, and the batten and lap positions were transferred to the frame. Then the four batten notches were cut, as well as the frame heel, which was roughly chopped off at the opposite side of the keel. The frame top curve (a chisel shape) was drawn from a pattern and sawn. At this point the frame was ready for its first fitting (see drawing).

Willits told us to start the frame in at an angle, with its top in the correct position and its upper notch aligned with the topmost batten. Then we were to tap sideways, picking up the other battens as the frame moved toward its position. He said that you cannot pound the frame directly in against the hull because the battens' corners will be chipped off. The angled approach worked very well for us, and got the frame into position for the first scribing. With pencil dividers we scribed the edge of the frame to fit to the three lapped planks as well as the angled fit against the keel. We found that a frame would fit better if this operation was done twice in small increments: a three-eighths-inch scribe first, then a one-quarter-inch scribe. The top of the frame often had to be clamped against the sheerstrake because of the over-bend. Other whaleboats studied at Mystic Seaport over the years had too much cut away from their frame heels where they fitted to the keel. This resulted in a weak and unsupported garboard plank that often leaked, or a keel that dished in. Our frame heels were secured with a single #9 screw driven through the frame and into the top of the keel. Often, at the ends of the boat, we would resort to twisting the cant frames with a crescent wrench so they'd lie tight against the planking. We added oak wedges (glued with 3M 5200) under the frames, where needed, for more garboard support. (The Beetle Boat Shop's swelled-frame-foot method does not require wedges). The inside man resorted to knee or foot pressure to hold the frame down tight against the seam battens while the screws were being driven from the outside. We opted for good working fits, not chalked-marked perfect fits. As a whaleboat's frames do not contact the planks between the battens, this is not too hard to achieve. We installed twenty frames on our most productive day.

While putting in the seat risers, Willits observed that it's the sum of many long, light parts working together that gives a whaleboat its strength. Leo Telesmanick said that the Beetles referred to this as "basket construction." The three-quarter-inch-by-three-and-one-half-inch eastern spruce seat risers were scarfed, glued, and installed as one piece. The cedar ceiling planking was installed next, following plan #139 from the Mariners' Museum.

The centerboard trunk was installed at this point, and for watertightness and longevity, it was thru-bolted with five-sixteenths-inch threaded bronze rod. The mast step was also bolted through the keel with five-sixteenths-inch bronze carriage bolts.

The very wide and short ceiling plank that covers the frames directly above the stern sheets was an interesting piece to fit and install. I nailed a spiling board just below the last upper ceiling plank. Using this as a reference, I picked up the widths, the butt locations (scarf), and then the bevels between the deck beams and frames. This information was transferred to the plank stock and a plank was cut out. This piece has considerable twist, so I had to screw-fasten one end, then soak it with boiling water and rags for about twenty minutes before I could push the other end into place with my foot and quickly fasten it.

We made the thwarts from eastern white pine. After

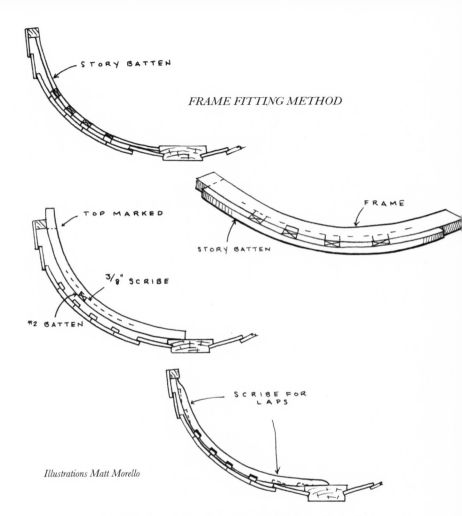

FRAME FITTING METHOD

Illustrations Matt Morello

they were installed, their knees were fitted and fastened. The fourteen thwart knees are vital to the gunwale strength on a whaleboat, as the frames are not fastened to the inwales. In the middle of the boat, Willits used the pre-bent knees having the tightest bend. In order to fit a knee, he first set it on top of the thwart, then clamped it to the inwale so that it stuck up above the sheer. He then made a cardboard pattern for the pine filler block that occupies the space behind the knee. When the filler was fitted tightly, the knee was then riveted through the thwart, inwale, sheerstrake, and guardrail. The six-inch-long rivet, a diagonal one through the throat of the knee, was essential to tying the whole gunwale together structurally. We used one-quarter-inch-diameter copper rod for this in the 2002 boat.

It should be noted that in the Beetle construction plan #139 there are many small wooden fittings such as chocks, pads, cleats, sockets, braces, and oarlock pads that have to be made and installed. The loggerhead was made from a seven-inch-by-seven-inch-by-thirty-six-inch blank of white oak that was then turned on a wood lathe. We had the good fortune of having a skilled shipwright who devoted himself to this sort of bench work, so we could concentrate on locating and installing the fittings as he produced them. This was a big timesaver.

With the completion of all the whaling fittings, the boat was caulked and painted with Kirby paint in the traditional way.

We worried about the possible failure of the old-style iron rods used for hoisting the whaleboat on the whaleship's davits. Since the boat was to be hauled up on davits again and again by Mystic Seaport's Special Demonstration Squad for as many as twenty years, we were concerned that the iron rod would react with the tannin in the oak stem and corrode, causing the stem to rot. Therefore, we decided to make the rods of five-eighths-inch silicon bronze with cold-bent eyes that were welded closed with the tungsten-inert-gas (TIG) process. The rods were installed the traditional way: drilled for, then riveted over a washer (clench ring) that was outside the boat's forefoot.

Whaleboat construction requires a fairly high level of skill from its builders. It should be said that traditional methods are proven and work well. This should not discourage the less-experienced or those who cannot obtain oak and cedar. In upstate New York, a very fine modern version of the Beetle whaleboat was built of lapped plywood planks glued with epoxy. This boat has brought great pleasure to a group of sailing and rowing enthusiasts.

The 2002 "Ansel Boat" has seen continuous use since its construction and is now more than ten years old. It has been rowed and sailed several times a week, yet it has held its shape and is still watertight. There is impressive wear on the steering oar brace and where oarsmen have placed their feet. The many oak fittings inside the boat have come loose from drying out and should be refastened. Other than that, I think a Yankee whaleman would gladly take her on a voyage, even though, back then, at ten years old she would be considered antique.

Afterword
THE YANKEE WHALEBOAT IN THE TWENTY-FIRST CENTURY

Evelyn Ansel

Introduction

The legacy of the Yankee whaleboat has proved to be tenacious. The subject is at turns arcane and brutal, the boats themselves complex to build and a challenge to handle. One might expect the topic to have faded from public interest as the whaling industry itself declined over a century ago. And yet, the elegant minimalism of its design, and the working narrative of the whaleboat, continue to enthrall amateur and professional historians, boatbuilders, rowers, and sailors alike. Today, the historically commercial and highly evolved Yankee whaleboat is preserved primarily in museums. Known extant historical examples of Yankee whaleboats (see appendix) are appropriately presented as artifacts for display and study only. While interest in plans, articles, and books relating to whaleboats has remained steady since the publication of this monograph in 1978, the production of the boats themselves had become increasingly rare. The active survival of the type at Mystic Seaport was due entirely to the presence of the Museum's flagship and last remaining wooden whaleship in the world, the *Charles W. Morgan,* and the particular attention and interest of a few key individuals within the Museum.

Charles W. Morgan Restoration and the Thirty-Eighth Voyage

Since the inception of this book nearly forty years ago, ten traditional whaleboats have been built and used extensively at Mystic Seaport to complement the interpretation and study of the *Morgan.* These boats were constructed by shipwrights working in both the Henry B. duPont Shipyard and the John Gardner Small Boat Shop at the Museum. Several were

The Alexandria Seaport Foundation boat under construction. There was much lively debate among builders about the relative merits of building right-side up (the traditional Beetle method) versus upside down. In the end, most of the builders chose the Beetle method, though several noted they would do the opposite were they to build a second. Photograph by Evelyn Ansel.

displayed on the *Morgan*'s characteristic davits, as they would have been in service. Others were used seasonally by the Museum's Special Demonstration Squad to demonstrate and interpret the use of whaleboats in the whale hunt. On a couple of notable occasions, these boats were used for international competitions between Mystic Seaport and Australian crews.

However, as the new millennium neared, the Museum found that few of the boats were serviceable enough for regular use. The boats built in the 1970s and '80s were constructed in much the same way that the New Bedford boats would have been built at the peak of whaling in the mid 1800s, with few changes in materials or construction techniques. This meant that though the Mystic Seaport boats were not subjected to anywhere near the stresses imposed upon whaleboats carried on ships, after two to three decades

of use their galvanized fastenings were long past a working whaleboat's normal five-year lifespan. The few boats left in the Museum "fleet" were in very poor condition, and the boatbuilders and shipwrights who built them had since retired or moved on. While descendants of the whaleboat could still be found, built in modern strip planking and fiberglass in the New Bedford racing community, the legacy of the traditionally constructed New England whaleboat was growing increasingly tenuous.

Aware that the type was on the edge of extinction, Mystic Seaport asked author Willits Ansel to come out of retirement in 2002 to build "one last whaleboat," so the Museum might thoroughly record the building process. The level of careful documentation throughout construction stands as testament to the fact that those involved at the time were unsure of the future of these boats. It was also an effort to capture something of the relationship Will had had with Leo Telesmanick, whom he had worked and had interviewed in the 1970s, and who was regarded as the last link to the days of commercial whaleboat construction in the Beetle Boat Shop. There was much speculation at the time that this was the end of the line.

But the turn of the twenty-first century proved to be a pivotal time for the continued existence of both whaleship and whaleboat. It had been clear since the late 1990s that the *Morgan* needed a significant restoration. She was still floating on much of her original 1841 bottom, and she had not been hauled for restoration since the late 1980s. Following the construction of a new lift dock at the Museum's Henry B. duPont Shipyard (a huge project in it's own right), the *Morgan* was hauled in the fall of 2008 for what would become a five-year restoration, with an additional year allowed for rerigging the ship. After much internal discussion and extensive consultation with the international maritime heritage community at large, it was an-

Apprentices close in on the sheer at Lowell's Boat Shop in Amesbury, Massachusetts. Lowell's is one of the oldest continuously running shops in the country, and its relationship to the dory parallels that of the Beetles to the whaleboat. The Lowell family refined both the design and the process for the scaled production of dories, supplying great numbers for the New England fishing fleets. When fishing technology changed and demand for traditional dories all but disappeared, the shop survived by adapting its designs for recreational use. Now operated by Lowell's Maritime Foundation, it is part apprenticeship program, part museum, and part commercial shop. Photograph by Evelyn Ansel.

nounced that the goal of this restoration would be to return the *Morgan* to sea for her thirty-eighth—and likely final—voyage during the summer of 2014.

While this decision may have surprised some in the maritime community, this goal was a hugely significant factor in the overall success of the restoration. Deciding to sail the *Morgan* again not only provided a concrete rallying point for support locally, nationally, and internationally, but it also ensured that the restoration was conducted with a very high level of attention to the overall structural integrity of the ship. Because she would sail again, this restoration could not be in any way cosmetic or superficial. The Shipyard would be required to address a few peculiarities of previous

restorations as well as fundamental aspects of her original construction that might have been adequate if she were simply returning to exhibition at Chubb's Wharf, but would need to be addressed if she were going to sea. Some of these structural elements had not been exposed since her keel was laid in 1841, and much was learned in the process of restoration.

A planned voyage helped create a firm deadline for the completion of the project. While logistics were discussed and timber was located and obtained, one idea in particular was emphasized over and over again throughout the planning process: if the *Morgan*'s return to sea were to be meaningful within the scope of the Museum's mission—and worth the minimal (but

Detail of the tabernacle of the single Leonard-style boat built for the fleet. It was built by students at the Apprenticeshop boatbuilding school in Rockland, Maine. The reinforcing elements between thwarts are particular to the Leonard boat and support the heavier rig that this design traditionally carried. Photograph by Evelyn Ansel.

Alternative tabernacle arrangement in the Gannon & Benjamin-built Beetle-syle boat. The bronze tabernacle hinges, oarlock socket fittings, and gudgeons were all sand-cast at the Mystic River Foundry in Mystic, Connecticut. Photograph by Evelyn Ansel.

present) risk involved in taking her to sea again—it would be vital that she be properly outfitted for the voyage. While ensuring that she went to sea appropriately equipped is in part an issue of historical accuracy and good stewardship, it is also a question of best practice and even safety. She would not be a theatrical prop for an exhibition; she would be the exhibition. This meant that she would need, in addition to a complete rig and a new suit of sails, a full complement of whaleboats. After all, a whaleship without her whaleboats is just a ship.

Birth of the National Whaleboat Project

At the start of the *Morgan* restoration in 2008, it was unclear how and to what extent whaleboats could be included in the 2014 voyage. Though the staff felt that whaleboats would be a key interpretive component during the voyage, it was clear that the Museum Shipyard could spare neither the manpower nor the capital from the *Morgan* restoration to gather materials and build a full fleet of boats. In 2008, there were only two whaleboats left in the water at the Museum. These were being used actively for interpretation and therefore were unavailable for summer voyaging. How could the Museum ensure that the *Morgan* would go to sea with even a fraction of the seven whaleboats she would have carried? Who might be willing or able to help?

This question was posed to the annual meeting of the Council of American Maritime Museums, held at Mystic Seaport in May of 2010. Was there any interest among the maritime community at large in building whaleboats for the *Morgan*? Over the following three years, nine institutions would volunteer to build a total of ten whaleboats. This unprecedented collaboration drew a diverse group of people together with the commercial, the historical, and the educational sectors of maritime heritage all well represented. Soon after the initial proposal to the community in 2010, the National Whaleboat Project grew beyond expectation. In fact, the project gained such momentum in the following two years that after the tenth commitment-to-build, Mystic Seaport had to turn down new inquiries. Ten boats is a small number in comparison to the thousands that were regularly shipping on whaling voyages at the height of whaling. However, ten becomes a number worth noting when one considers that in the span of three years, the National Whaleboat Project would manage to assemble as many Yankee whaleboats as had likely been seen since the bark *Wanderer* left New Bedford in 1924.

The Shops

Historically, whaleboats were built in the regions surrounding ports that harbored whaling fleets. New Bedford was the epicenter of production in New England, but whaleboat shops also flourished from New London, Connecticut, to San Francisco on the West Coast to meet the needs of the Arctic whalers. While none of the thirty-eighth-voyage fleet hailed from California, their range in the Northeast was greater than it would have been historically. Two of the boats came from New Bedford and Martha's Vineyard, Massachusetts, regions with deep ties to whaling and to the *Morgan* in particular. The rest of the fleet hailed from as far south as Virginia, as far north as Midcoast Maine, and west to the Great Lakes. All were located near—or in one case, surrounded by—rivers, lakes, or sea. Almost half of the whaleboats were built in the hearts of cities, which may seem counterintuitive but is actually nicely aligned with historical precedent.

While the shops renowned for mass production of whaleboats in the nineteenth century were purely commercial ventures, the builders involved in the thirty-eighth-voyage project reflect the variety in mission and purpose one finds in institutions dedicated to preserving wooden boat building and maritime heritage in the twenty-first century. Seven of the nine participating shops were education-focused nonprofit organizations. Two of the shops were "career college" institutions whose students and apprentices leave their two-year programs ready to work in commercial yards. Another two were nonprofits primarily concerned with providing alternative skills and opportunities through boatbuilding to at-risk youth, while two more were maritime museums working with volunteers and local students. The two commercial shops had significant historical interest in the project based on their own histories, and each collaborated with museums. One shop represented a working combination of three types: part living history museum, part educational nonprofit, and part commercial shop. Despite the range in missions represented by these shops, in each case the local community support for the whaleboat project was almost overwhelming.

With the encouragement and direct support of Peter Kellogg, whose record of support for restoration and use of traditional boats is well known and respected, Independence Seaport Museum in Philadelphia and Rocking the Boat in New York City stepped forward and volunteered to build the first two whaleboats. This set an example that was embraced by the others, and was the important catalyst for this amazing story and result. Over the ensuing two years, each institution involved came up with creative methods to draw their communities into the project through various events, classes, open houses, and curriculum development, and all were ultimately successful.

It was easy to see why some of these local communities felt immediately connected to the project; for

Two boats were built at Independence Seaport Museum's Workshop on the Water in Philadelphia. The first boat completed for the National Whaleboat Project is pictured at left; on the right, volunteers fit thwart knees for the second boat. One of the two boats remains at Independence Seaport to be used for programming there, while the other has joined the permanent fleet at Mystic Seaport. Photograph by Evelyn Ansel.

example, one of the contributing shops was actually the Beetle Boat Shop, originally the producer of the Beetle-pattern whaleboat, working in collaboration with the New Bedford Whaling Museum. Martha's Vineyard, once home to countless whaling captains, six of whom commanded the *Morgan*, was another building site where the local historical connections were widely commented on. For some of the other shops involved in the National Whaleboat Project, the shared relevance was perhaps less obvious at first glance, but ultimately some surprising and interesting connections were made. For example, when asked why a boatbuilding school on the Great Lakes was building a *whale*boat—"There aren't any whales in the Great Lakes, right?"—*Charles W. Morgan* historian Matthew Stackpole noted that at one time there were more lighthouses on the Great Lakes than on the East and West Coasts combined. And what fueled lighthouse lamps? Until 1860 it was sperm whale oil, supplied by the whaling fleet.

Such connections, historical, geographical, and personal, were made over and over again by the boat-

BOATBUILDING PROGRAMS THAT
PARTICIPATED IN THE NATIONAL
WHALEBOAT PROJECT (in chronological order)

1. Independence Seaport Museum, Philadelphia,
   Pennsylvania (two boats)
2. Rocking the Boat, Bronx, New York
3. Lowell's Boat Shop, Amesbury, Massachusetts
4. Great Lakes Boat Building School, Cedarville,
   Michigan
5. The Apprenticeshop, Rockland, Maine
6. Gannon & Benjamin Marine Railway,
   Vineyard Haven, Massachusetts
7. Beetle Boat Shop/the New Bedford Whaling
   Museum, Wareham/New Bedford,
   Massachusetts
8. Alexandria Seaport Foundation, Alexandria,
   Virginia
9. Lake Champlain Maritime Museum,
   Vergennes, Vermont

The New Bedford Whaling Museum collaborated with the Beetle Boat Shop to produce a whaleboat for the fleet. Though currently located in Wareham, Massachusetts, and now known for its catboats, it is the same Beetle firm of whaleboat fame, and the only shop that once built the type which is still in operation today. The Whaling Museum loaned the now-accessioned original Beetle branding iron to the shop to officially mark the first whaleboat to leave the shop's doors since 1933. Photographs by Bill Sauerbrey.

builders, students, and volunteers in each of these shops with the visitors that came to see what they were working on throughout the project. Every shop, much like the duPont Shipyard at Mystic Seaport, was open and welcoming to visitors and community members. It is striking to imagine the numbers of people who witnessed this project in its various stages around the country. The builders, volunteers, administrators, students, and apprentices who had a hand in the ten boats number in the hundreds, not to mention the thousands of visitors who bore witness as the boats took shape. This level of engagement is particularly impressive when one considers that, until about four years ago, only a handful of people in the world had had direct experience with Yankee whaleboat construction. Education and outreach were key components of the success of the project at each location, and the fund-raising successes in each case stood as testament to a much larger collective community triumph.

The large crowds drawn to the launching of every whaleboat at its home port were a visible testament to the extent of community support in each case. All of the shops had the opportunity to launch and use their boats in their local waters before delivering them to Mystic. In the nineteenth century, finished whaleboats (primed, but unrigged) would likely have been unceremoniously delivered the short distance from the shop to the wharves stacked in wagons. Our "only children" were rather more pampered, with launchings that involved much fanfare, good cheer, well-deserved celebration, and plenty of local press coverage. Each whaleboat was a one-off, coming to Mystic from a much greater distance than they would have historically, and this presented some nontraditional and creative possibilities for delivery. The majority of the boats arrived in the summer of 2013 overland on trailers, but a few arrived by water. One was towed to Mystic behind a Vineyard Haven-designed-and-built schooner that belonged to the proprietor of the shop that produced both boats. The only shop to build a Leonard-pattern boat, located in Rockland, Maine, opted to deliver the boat under its own power. In an eight-day journey, five apprentices and one instructor from the shop rowed and sailed the roughly 350 nautical miles from Rockland to Mystic, with occasional assistance from the schooner that served as their chase boat. There was much anticipation and excitement as she finally pulled up the Mystic River on a Friday afternoon after a passage of more than a week. By this time, both boat and crew were nicely broken in. The wear and tear was as admired throughout the whaleboat-celebrating events that weekend as the unpainted, near-perfect, and as-yet unmarred workmanship visible in others on display. It will be both rewarding and informative to watch the entire whaleboat fleet gain the patina that comes from the combination of attentive care and regular hard use.

Mystic Seaport's Leadership Role

While the local communities were undeniably the driving force for the completion of each whaleboat, Mystic Seaport played a key role in ensuring that the lead boatbuilders at each shop had the technical and material support they needed throughout the building process. The builders gathered at Mystic Seaport for a series of meetings so they could consult with one another as well as with the Museum's shipwrights who had been involved with whaleboat construction in the past. These "gams"—the whalemen's term for the informational and recreational gatherings held when whaleships met at sea—allowed them to compare notes with one another while they were at different points in construction, and they also had the added benefit of letting them see the progress on the *Morgan* herself. The gams were particularly informative because the individual projects started at different times, and the boats progressed at their own pace. The commercial shops completed their boats in about three months each, while some of the educational programs took nearly two years from lofting to launch. This was more often the case in the programs that worked with younger apprentices. The relaxed pace allowed the students to learn as they progressed and be involved with the project every

The Apprenticeshop's Leonard boat arrives at Mystic Seaport after an eight-day, 350-nautical-mile delivery by sea. Photograph by Evelyn Ansel.

step of the way, and the results were impressive.

Aside from facilitating communications between builders during the construction process, Mystic Seaport also provided the Whaleboat Project shops with hardware kits, and with stock where necessary. Walter Ansel, Will's son, and by this time a senior shipwright at the Museum's duPont Shipyard, served as the primary contact and facilitator for the project on behalf of the Museum and helped coordinate the acquisition of materials for many of the shops. This allowed for some consistency and control among the boats even as they were being built hundreds of miles apart, and it also took into consideration the principal donor's desire that the boats be competitive across the fleet. The Museum's Shipyard furnished the stock that was more difficult for smaller shops to obtain. All of the hardware for the fleet was produced by Mystic Seaport. Patterns for oarlock fittings, rudder gudgeons and pintles, and mast-step tabernacles were produced at the duPont Shipyard and sand-cast at a local foundry. The fifty iron oarlocks for the boats were forged by two of the Museum's extremely

A freshly painted whaleboat awaits launch at the Gannon & Benjamin Marine Railway in Vineyard Haven, Massachusetts. Gannon & Benjamin was one of two solely commercial shops to participate in the project, the other being the Beetle Shop. Each boat in the National Whaleboat Project fleet has a different-colored sheer and a builder's plate or identifying mark carved or branded in the interior. Most of the builders chose colors associated with their individual shops. Photograph by Evelyn Ansel.

talented shipsmiths. This project alone took most of a winter, and was executed with great care and with beautiful results. The whaleboat sails were all produced by Nathaniel S. Wilson's traditional sail loft in East Boothbay, Maine, which would also sew sails for the *Morgan* herself, and the Museum's head rigger sent rigging kits and an explanatory DVD to each shop.

Challenges of Building a Twenty-First-Century Fleet

At the height of the whaling industry in the mid 1800s, dozens of shops built whaleboats, but today we have complete sets of lines for relatively few original boats. Furthermore, these lines were all taken by modern boatbuilders and drawn up by modern naval architects. By contrast, nineteenth-century whaleboat builders refined their designs by carving half models and wedging and shimming the molds around which they built their boats. Consequently, relatively standard dimensions were interpreted and built slightly differently by each shop. Three documented and identified types have been built at Mystic Seaport since the 1970s. Today they are identified as the Leonard pattern, the Beetle pattern, and the Arctic-style boat. Nine of the National Whaleboat Project boats were built to the lines taken off the Beetle-built boat at the Mariners' Museum in Newport News, Virginia, and one of the ten was built to William H. Hand's plans for a boat built at the Leonard shop.

It is estimated that James Beetle's shop turned out more than 1,000 whaleboats between 1834 and 1854, while his sons Charles and John built hundreds more into the 1900s. This remarkable output can be attributed to the scaled production methods he developed, where a boat was built like an exquisite corpse: pieces and patterns were worked up before hand, the same

Mystic Seaport shipsmith Michael Saari produced more than fifty oarlocks for the fleet. In order to make production as efficient and consistent as possible, he built a custom swedge (left) to shape the shanks, which were then riveted onto the horns (above). Each oarlock was then served with marline and tarred to prevent wear on the oars. Photographs by Evelyn Ansel.

molds were used over and over to shape the boats in record time, and a division of labor made each employee a specialist in some aspect of the construction. In this nearly production-line process, no single apprentice in the shop would have been skilled in all the steps to build a whaleboat from the ground up. The process of building ten boats for the current fleet diverges significantly from the manner in which the Beetle Boat Shop produced such a great number of boats. Each of the modern boats was a one-off, the only exception being Workshop on the Water at Independence Seaport, which built two. As is ever the case when approaching a design for the first time, one theme that arose again and again during the builders' gams at Mystic Seaport was the necessity for interpretation throughout the building process. From reading lines plans and construction plans to

aspects of equipment and use, each step is a sort of translation. A common theme in the meetings was also which peculiarities of whaleboat construction (and there are a few) might have been approached differently after the first boat was complete. As with any population of boatbuilders, if you pose a question to a group of nine you will receive ten different answers; breathing life into a fleet reconstituted largely from plans, with a few extant examples for comparison, will furnish the same results. Though the human chain of whaleboat builders remains unbroken, it is tenuous, and we are limited today to the specific knowledge and experience of a very small number of builders. Because our whaleboat-building population today is not comprised of a group of eighteenth- or nineteenth-century boatbuilders, some aspects of their methodology and problem-solving approach are

Rocking the Boat's whaleboat awaits rigging on the beach at a whaleboat race in New Bedford while Mystic Seaport crew members step the mast of the Gannon & Benjamin boat. In an effort to keep the National Whaleboat Project boats competitive across the fleet, the sails were all produced by Nathaniel Wilson's sail loft in East Boothbay, Maine. Photograph by Evelyn Ansel.

fundamentally different. It is important to acknowledge that in the practice of producing replicas we, today, are also contributors to what will one day be the historical record. Each of the whaleboats at this point is unique, and to some extent embodies the individual character of the shop where it was built. Each boat handles a little differently, has it's own builder's plate and marks, it's own quirks of construction. Though it may seem counterintuitive, this sort of variation and personality from a museum perspective is a valuable thing. The boats on any single whaleship would likely have been built by the same shop, but each mate was responsible for rigging his own

boat, there were differences in paint scheme for ready identification from the ship. Beyond differences within a single fleet, variation from whaleship to whaleship and between shops would have been noticeable. It is appropriate that the last wooden whaling ship in the world represents this diversity in her fleet.

The necessity for interpretation and reinterpretation was not only limited to reading plans and documenting work. It also required a fresh perspective when choosing materials and stock. Again, there was a desire to ensure that the boats would be competitive with one another across the fleet, so there was a fair amount of discussion among shops and at Mystic Seaport about the choice of materials. As the majority of the boats were going to end up in Mystic Seaport's care (two of the fleet would remain with their sponsoring institutions), some choices were also made to better facilitate future care with some consistency across the fleet. Historical accuracy was a priority, but certain conscious material changes were made to ensure that the Museum could be the best possible steward for what amounted to a monumental investment of time and resources. For example, to lengthen the overall lifespan of the boats, copper fasteners and bronze fittings were substituted for the galvanized hardware typical of late-nineteenth-century whaleboats. This was a departure from the methods employed with boats built at Mystic in the 1970s and '80s, virtually all of which are now gone. Some smaller cosmetic decisions were also made as deliberate departures from what we know to be historically true; for example, it was decided that the interiors of the boats would be oiled instead of painted. Historically, the ceiling, risers and floorboards would have been painted light colors so that tools and equipment would be easily visible in the bottom of the boat. However, it was decided that scraping and painting the interiors of eight whaleboats every season would create an unnecessary drain on

The Beetle-built Yankee whaleboat (left) squares off against an Azorean-style whaleboat in the 2013 Dabney Cup competition at New Bedford, Massachusetts. Photograph by Evelyn Ansel.

Shipyard staff and resources, whereas an oiled interior would not detract from their performance as museum reproductions and demonstration pieces.

Finding building stock was a challenge for many of the shops, and also required compromises in some cases. Mystic Seaport was able to furnish oak for bending stock stems and thwart knees, and some cedar for planking. Offcuts from three-inch-by-forty-foot white-oak planks milled for the restoration of the ship herself made excellent keels for the whaleboats. Many shops tried to use northern white cedar from Maine for planking, which was often cited as preferable by the New Bedford builders for its "tough and leathery" quality when wet, as opposed to the comparatively

brittle southern white cedar varieties. There was much lively conversation about the quality of stock furnished for the project, perhaps in part reflecting the market that contemporary builders of wooden boats must work in. "Workboat standards" is no longer a common benchmark among commercial builders. In the 1880s, New Bedford whaleboat-builders found oak timber from eastern Connecticut "better suited for their work as it is free from knots for a length of 30 feet or more."[1] Though this description sits in stark contrast with the material generally available today, the tone of the lament is all too familiar to the contemporary builder—in fact, one boatshop acknowledged receipt of a shipment of cedar with a

The Great Lakes Boat Building School collaborated with local maritime heritage organizations to outfit their boat with spars and oars. The Maritime Heritage Alliance in Traverse City, Michigan, built the spars, and the Michigan Maritime Museum chapter of the Traditional Small Craft Association in South Haven, Michigan, was responsible for the set of oars. The boat, complete with oars and spars, is pictured here at the 2013 WoodenBoat Show at Mystic Seaport. Photograph by Evelyn Ansel.

humorous note thanking the duPont Shipyard for "the loose bundle of knots, surrounded by a little cedar."

The notable exception was the boat from the Great Lakes, for which all of the lumber was obtained locally. This was an intentional decision on their part, partly reflecting changing ideas about supporting sustainable local forestry practices and cutting down on their carbon footprint by limiting unnecessary shipping when virtually all the materials they needed were available locally.

Spar stock was also particularly difficult to source, but the decision was made early on in the project to keep the rigs as consistent and historically accurate across the fleet as possible. With this in mind, it was decided that the spars would not be laminated. Many of the shops used Douglas fir for their masts and spars; eastern spruce would have been preferable, but was unobtainable. The Leonard boat did end up with laminated spars because the plans indicated that the rig was larger and heavier than those specified for the Beetle boats. This decision was made partly because it was difficult to find large-enough stock, but also because the prospect of regularly stepping and un-stepping a "telephone pole" in open water seemed like asking for trouble.

Planners also made a conscious decision to build each set of six oars of spruce instead of the much heavier, though more traditional, ash. This was a pragmatic choice, considering that programming would often involve children. Most of the sets of oars were purchased from Shaw & Tenney, the Maine shop famous for its oars. A few of the shops opted to build their own sets in-house or in collaboration with other local maritime heritage groups. In other shops, particularly those working with younger apprentices, the lead builders reported that having smaller groups break off to build oars and the rudder was a useful strategy in keeping everyone in a large group occupied and engaged. As time goes on and our definition of "traditional construction" continues to evolve, it is inevitable that further compromises will be made in regard to materials. However, this evolution represents a new chapter in the history of the whaleboat in it's own right.

Conclusion

Even before it was fully assembled in the spring of 2014, the fleet was used extensively for programming, both at Mystic Seaport and beyond. Many of the boats were present for the relaunch of the *Morgan* in the summer of 2013, and they participated in a cere-

monial row-by to salute her as she waited on the lift dock that morning. As the seven whaleboats—crewed by apprentices, students, shipwrights, boatbuilders, volunteers, and at least one museum director—jockeyed and sprinted in circles while waiting for the signal to fall into formation, some participants speculated that this many Yankee whaleboats probably hadn't rowed together in this manner in about a century (or, possibly ever, considering the lighthearted and celebratory nature of the day). During the summer and fall of 2013, several of the newly launched boats remained in their home waters to be used for programming within the communities where they were built. All of the boats will be carried aboard the *Morgan* for some leg of the journey during her voyage in the summer of 2014 and will be used in dockside programming at each port of call. After they have served on the thirty-eighth voyage, the whaleboats themselves will continue to present the Museum with a wealth of opportunities. The boats that will call Mystic Seaport their home port may serve as traveling exhibits when they aren't on the water working, and each museum, shop, and school that contributed a boat to the project will be welcome to reclaim their own boat on loan for programming and use at its original home port. In addition to traveling and out-of-water interpretive possibilities, the chance to test and experiment across the fleet at Mystic will also allow the Museum to enrich programs spanning from research to education. At the time of this writing, the

Regional high school students work with Lake Champlain Maritime Museum staff and community volunteers to build the twenty-nine-foot Beetle whaleboat for Mystic Seaport. Photograph by Buzz Kuhns, Lake Champlain Maritime Museum.

thirty-eighth-voyage fleet has had the opportunity to measure itself by oar and sail against its Azorean and fiberglass cousins in New Bedford, with much fanfare and excitement. Though the *Charles W. Morgan* will return to her berth after the thirty-eighth voyage, the whaleboats will serve as emissaries for her story for years to come.

Though the story of the National Whaleboat Project

is one rooted in a specific time and place, the outstanding success of the collaboration has given cause to hope that this cooperative model for maritime heritage preservation might be implemented elsewhere. The combination of context provided by historical and academic texts like this monograph, and hands-on experience gained through projects such as the assembly and use of the thirty-eighth-voyage fleet, ensures that this type of regional cultural heritage continues to persevere in a very active and real sense. The way in which we interact with these boats is fundamentally different today than it was at the height of the American whaling industry; how we document and record them, how we build them, the material choices we make, and how we use them after launch day have all evolved over time. Even our means of communicating between builders and shops has changed radically in the last ten years. Not only are we using plans and tables of offsets that would not have held much relevance for the Beetles or the Leonards in the 1800s, but the project was also documented and shared through countless blogs, emails, films, photographs, and cellphone calls. However, this is also an indication that the whaleboat— and more broadly, the connection to the heritage that it represents—is still very much alive today. Without either the context of the academic and historical research or the experience of building, using, and maintaining these boats with our own hands, our experience of these boats would be far less rich. Together, historical and academic context combined with the physical engagement with these forms ensures that we not only remember, acknowledge, study, and learn from history, but we also begin to see our own history evolve ahead of us.

1. James Templeman Brown, "The Whale Fishery," in George Brown Goode, ed., *The Fisheries and Fishery Industries of the United States*, Sect. V, vol. II (Washington: Government Printing Office, 1887), 241.

Appendix A

SAIL PLANS
AND RIGS

Replica of sprit-rigged Beetle whaleboat being sailed on Mystic River. Photograph by Ken Mahler, Mystic Seaport.

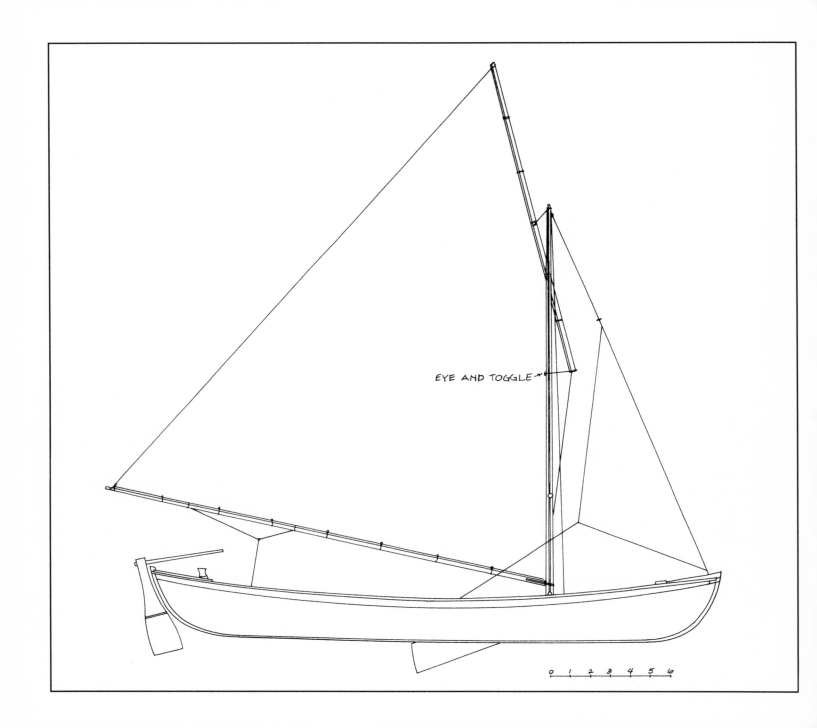

EYE AND TOGGLE

0 1 2 3 4 5 6

LUG SAIL WITH JIB (ca. 1910)

Boat from *John R. Manta* at Kendall Whaling Museum. The sail was not with the boat. Drawing of rig and sails is based on spar measurements and photograph.

MAST
The mast has shoulders at the head where the diameter is reduced for the shrouds and a strap with a galvanized block for the jib halyard. Below the shoulders a 2¼″ sheave is let in the mast for the main halyard.
   Length 22′5″
   Diameter at step 1¼″
      At partners 4″
      6′ above partners 4⅛″
      At head at shoulders 3″
      Above shoulders 1¾″

BOOM
Wooden jaws.
   Length 22′10″
   Diameter at jaws 2⅜″
      6′ from jaws 3″
      At end 2″

GAFF
Bamboo
   Length 16′9″
   Diameter at lower end 2″
      At peak 1½″
At lower end is a short lanyard with an eye and toggle which was used as a parrel around the mast.

MAINSAIL
   Foot 22′3″
   Luff 10′9″
   Head 16′3″
   Leech 29′
   Tack to peak 27′
   Area 318 square feet

JIB
   Luff 13′9″
   Foot 7′
   Leech 10′3″
   Area 34 square feet

TOTAL SAIL AREA
   352 square feet

SHROUDS
   9/16″ line, set up with lanyards

HALYARDS
Main halyard ⅝″ line, secured to gaff near the center. Jib halyard passed through block at masthead.

MAIN SHEET
Single line with eye and thimble at the end that rides on boom bridle.

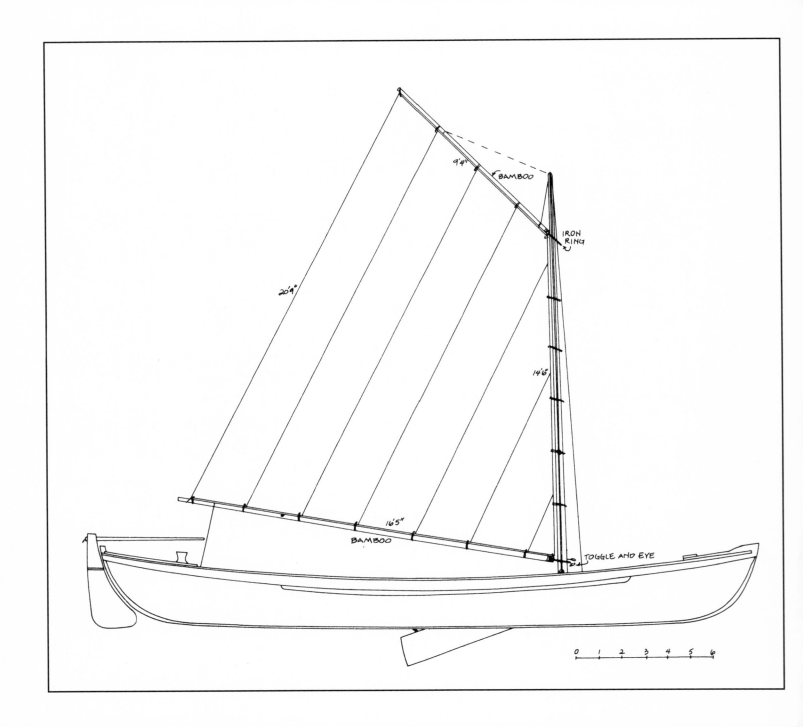

9'4"

BAMBOO

IRON
RING

20'9"

14'6"

16'5"

BAMBOO

TOGGLE AND EYE

0 1 2 3 4 5 6

GAFF MAINSAIL (ca. 1910)

Beetle Whaleboat, Nantucket Whaling Museum

MAST
The mast is spruce. Shoulders for the shrouds are formed by reducing the diameter at the head to 1⅝'' for the last 4 inches. A peg above the shoulder prevents the shrouds from slipping off when mast is lowered. A sheave for the halyard is below the shoulders. At the foot of the mast a hole is bored through; this may have been used for securing a downhaul.
> Length 19'11''
> Diameter at step 2¼''
>> At hinge 4''
>> 6' above hinge 3¾''
>> 12' above hinge 3''
>> At head at shoulders 2½''

BOOM
Bamboo. Forged jaws with pin driven into plug in the end of the boom. Jaws are wrapped with canvas and served. Toggle and eye splice act as a parrel.
> Length 16'9''
> Diameter at jaws 3''
> Natural taper
>> At end 2''

GAFF
Bamboo. Iron hoop acts as parrel. A pin on the hoop is driven into the end of the gaff. The hoop is served.
> Length 9'5''
> Diameter at jaws 3''
>> At peak 2''

SAIL
> Bolt rope of 5/16'' line on all edges. Panels 28'' wide. No reef points.
> Foot 16'5''
> Hoist 14'6''
> Head 9'4''
> Leech 20'9''
> Tack to peak 22'
> Area 210 square feet

SHROUDS
Made of a single piece of 9/16'' line with a piece spliced in the middle to make an eye to slip over the mast head. The splice on each side of the eye is served to prevent its enlarging. Lanyards of 5/16'' line to eyes in the wales take up the shrouds.

HALYARD
As the boat is rigged now, there is no peak halyard. A single halyard passes through a sheave at the masthead and is spliced around the gaff near the throat. There must originally have been a peak halyard, now lost, or a bridle for peaking the sail. In the drawing a peak halyard is shown with a dotted line.

SHEET
Single line attached to the boom about one foot from the end.

MAST HOOPS AND SEIZINGS TO SPARS
Five mast hoops irregularly spaced. Sail is seized to boom and gaff through grommets in the seams.

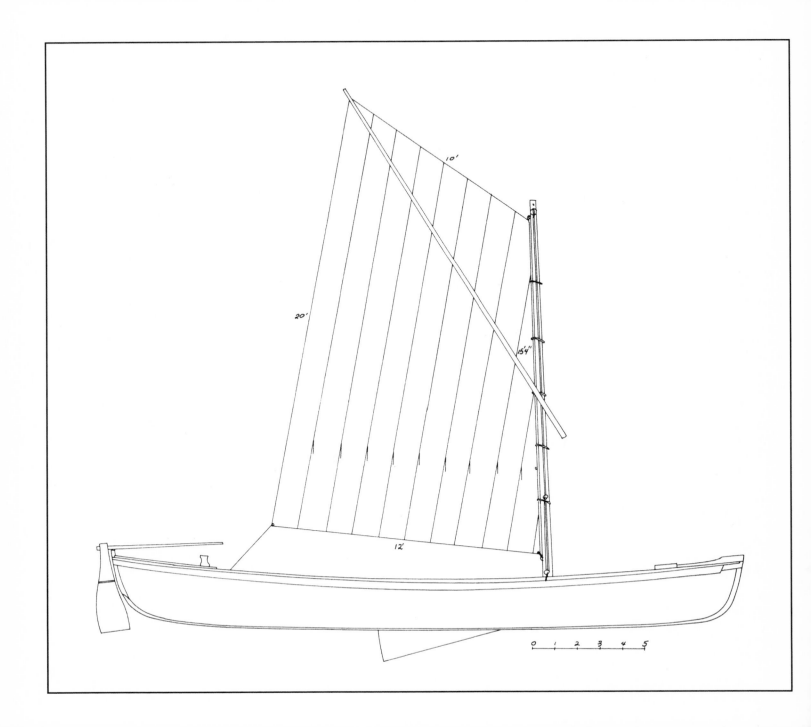

10'

20'

15'4"

12'

0 1 2 3 4 5

SPRITSAIL (ca. 1845)

The drawing is from a half-scale model whaleboat on the *Lagoda* at the New Bedford Whaling Museum. The model represents a whaleboat of the 1840s. Measurements below are full size.

MAST
　　Length 19'6''
　　Diameter at partners 3½''
　　　At head 3''
The mast has a staple at the head for securing the head of the sail, and stops and peg for holding the shrouds at the head. At the foot is a block of wood with a hole for securing the tack.

SPRIT
　　Length 19'
　　Diameter at lower end 2¼''
　　　At middle 2⅝''
　　　At peak 1¾''

SAIL
The sail is made of panels 14'' wide. It has one set of reef points four feet from the foot. The mast has five mast hoops.
The sail did not lower; there is no halyard. The sail was furled against the mast before unshipping the mast. In reefing, the sail was apparently simply reefed up to the row of reef points rather than being lowered and reefed.
　　Peak to tack 22'
　　Foot 12'
　　Hoist 15'4''
　　Head 10'
　　Leech 20'
　　Area 187 square feet

SHEET
Single line from the clew.

SHROUDS
Eyes at top slipped over the head of the mast and rested on stops on the sides of the mast. Shrouds were taken up by lanyards to straps in the wales.

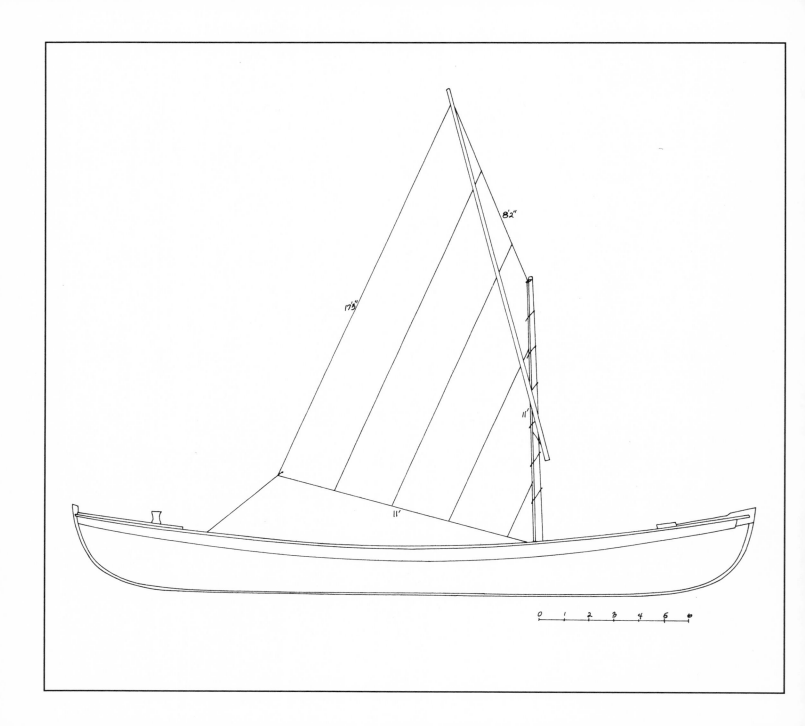

17'3"

8'2"

11'

11'

0 1 2 3 4 5 6

SMALL SPRITSAIL USED IN
SHORE WHALING (ca. 1900)

Edwards Boat, Amagansett, Long Island

MAST
Length 13'3''
Diameter at partners 3½''
At head 2''

SPRIT
Length 15'11''
Diameter in center 1½''
At each end 1''

SAIL
The sail did not lower, and was laced to the mast through grommets. Panels are 29'' wide. The sail does not have reef points. When unshipping the mast, the sail was furled against the mast, which was then unstepped.
Foot 11'
Hoist 11'
Leech 17'3''
Head 8'2''
Tack to peak 19'
Sail Area 110 square feet

SHEET
Single line from the clew

SHROUDS
None

HALYARD
A halyard passed through a sheave at the top of the mast.

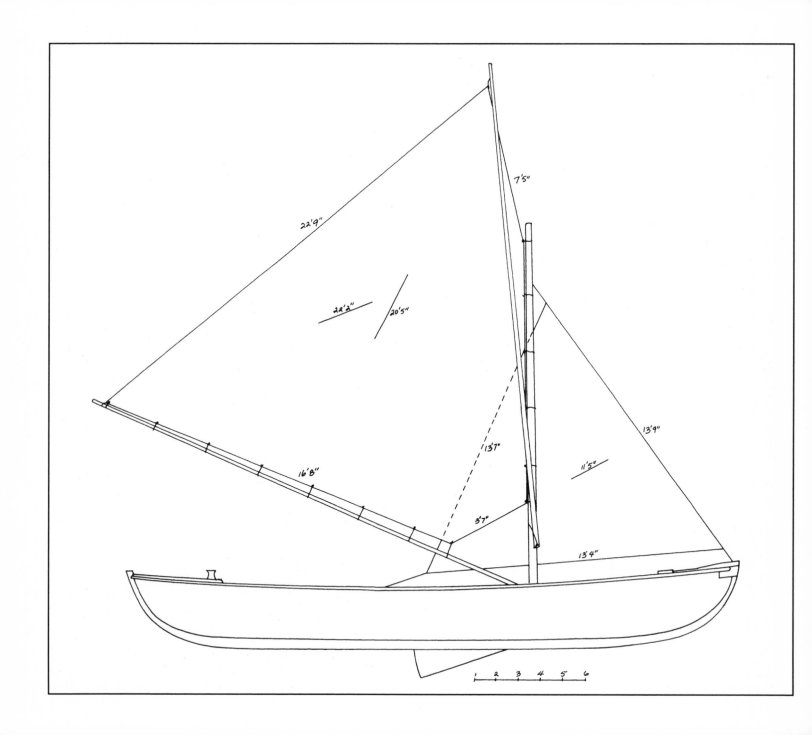

22'9"

7'5"

22'2"   20'5"

13'9"

13'7"

16'8"

11'5"

3'7"

13'4"

1 2 3 4 5 6

SPRITSAIL RIG FROM BEQUIA 1965

MAST
Length 18'9''

SPRIT
Length 23'½''
Material: Bamboo

BOOM
Length 22'3''
Material: Bamboo

MAINSAIL
Hoist 12'3''
Head 7'5''
Foot 16'8''
Leech 22'9''
Tack is cut off, making a fifth edge 3'7'' long
Area: 202 square feet

JIB
Luff 13'9''
Foot 13'4''
Leech 13'7''
Area: 78 square feet

TOTAL SAIL AREA
280 square feet

Appendix B

EXAMPLES OF TEN WHALEBOATS

Plans of the whaleboats in Appendix B are obtainable from Mystic Seaport. For prices and information write:
Curatorial Department
Mystic Seaport Museum, Inc.
Mystic
Connecticut 06355

Whaleboat at Madeira. Photograph by Peter Tripp.

SAG HARBOR WHALEBOAT

Location: Sag Harbor Whaling Museum, Sag Harbor, Long Island

The boat is said to have come from the whaleship *Concordia,* which last whaled in 1870, but there is no definite proof. If true, it is the oldest-known boat. It has had extensive rebuilding.

It differs from late model whaleboats in various respects, having thole pins and natural crook seat knees, which were characteristic of earlier whaleboats. The sheer is extreme, most being forward of the center of the boat, possibly the result of restoration work. The bow has more than the usual amount of flare at the rail, which makes the sides straighter in plan view. Midship sections are more rounded, lacking the usual hard bilge.

Length 27'4''
Beam 5'8''
Depth 2'
Sheer 17''

Lines taken off and rough lines plan by Willits Ansel; finished lines plans by Robert Allyn.

EDWARDS BOAT

Location: East Hampton Whaling Museum, East Hampton, Long Island

This boat was used in shore whaling at Amagansett, Long Island, until the early 1900s, and closely resembles another boat at the museum called the Dominy boat, used off the same stretch of beach. Family tradition has it that the Edwards boat was built in New London, though its similarity with the Dominy boat raises some doubt.

Both have construction features that are not found in New Bedford boats. There are seven planks to the side rather than the usual eight; the carvel planking is without battens; garboards are not lapped by the plank above. Frame spacing is even throughout and is approximately 12'', with frames notched into the wales. Workmanship is good.

The Edwards boat is a handsome, small whaleboat. A profile of the stem and stern shows a resemblance to the Beetle whaleboats, with an easy sweep up from the keel and a sharper bend high up the stem. The sheer is strong and runs in an even curve from bow to stern. The entrance is fine for a whaleboat and bow and stern sections are similar. The even sheer line, similar profiles of bow and stern, and similarity of bow and stern sections give a symmetry to the ends of this boat that is not found in others.

The boat carried a small spritsail, but had neither centerboard nor rudder.

Length 27'5''
Beam 5'10''
Depth 2'1''
Sheer 15½''

Lines taken off and rough lines plan by Willits Ansel; finished lines plan by Robert Allyn.

Whaleboat at Sag Harbor Whaling Museum, Long Island, shows evidence of considerable rebuilding. Photograph by author.

The Edwards boat used in shore whaling at Amagansett, Long Island. Photograph by author.

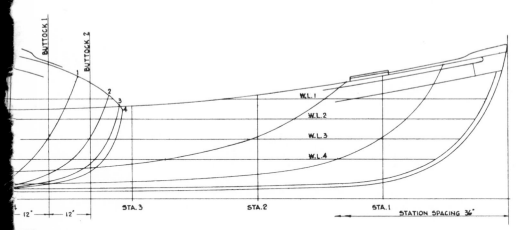

BUTTOCK 1
BUTTOCK 2

W.L.1
W.L.2
W.L.3
W.L.4

STA.3   STA.2   STA.1
STATION SPACING 36"

12"   12"

OAT
LING MUSEUM
T. 7IN. DEPTH 2FT. 0¾IN.

NOTE :- THESE LINES DRAWN FROM OFFSETS LIFTED FROM
ACTUAL WHALEBOATS BY WILLITS D. ANSEL. LINES
ARE TO OUTSIDE OF PLANKING.

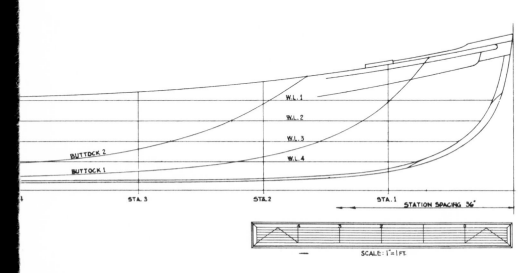

W.L.1
W.L.2
W.L.3
W.L.4

BUTTOCK 2
BUTTOCK 1

STA.3   STA.2   STA.1
STATION SPACING 36"

SCALE: 1"=1 FT.

THE MARINE HISTORICAL ASSOCIATION INC.
MYSTIC SEAPORT
MYSTIC CONNECTICUT
WHALEBOAT LINES
DRAWN BY R.C.ALLYN   DATE- JAN. 14. 1974

SERIAL NO. 148

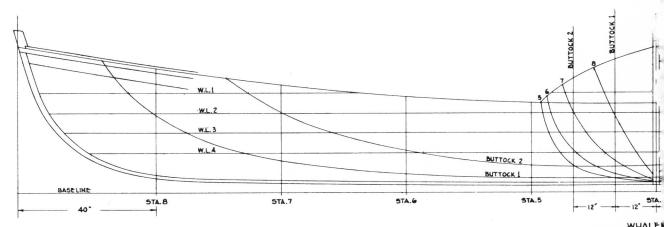

W.L.1
W.L.2
W.L.3
W.L.4
BASE LINE
40"
STA.8   STA.7   STA.6   STA.5   12"   12"   STA.
BUTTOCK 2   BUTTOCK 1   BUTTOCK 2   BUTTOCK 1
5   6   7   8

WHALE
SAG HARBOR WHA
LENGTH 27 FT. 4 IN BEAM 5

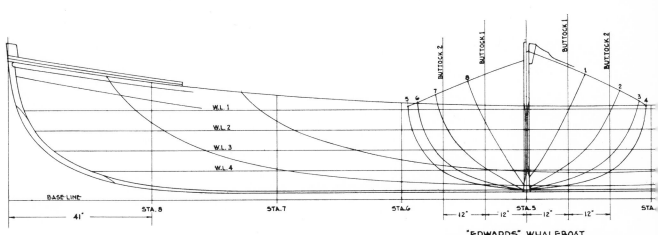

W.L.1
W.L.2
W.L.3
W.L.4
BASE LINE
41"
STA.8   STA.7   STA.6   12"   12"   STA.5   12"   12"   STA.
BUTTOCK 2   BUTTOCK 1   BUTTOCK 1   BUTTOCK 2
5   6   7   8   1   2   3   4

"EDWARDS" WHALEBOAT
USED IN SHORE WHALING AT AMAGANSETT, L.I.
LENGTH 27 FT. 5 IN. BEAM 5 FT. 9 IN DEPTH 2 FT. 1⅛ IN.

ARCTIC WHALEBOAT

Location: New Bedford Whaling Museum, New Bedford, Massachusetts

The builder and history of this boat are unknown, but it has the length and construction features of the Arctic whaleboat: a rail on the wale raises the sheer 1⅞'', and a heavy shelf under the thwarts gives greater strength than that provided by the seat risers alone. The shelf pieces are sawn to shape, sided 1⅛'' and molded 4'', and are riveted through the frames and planking at intervals of about one foot. Otherwise, construction and scantlings are standard.

The boat is out of shape. Stem and stern are about 2'' out of alignment; both sides were measured and at some points corresponding half breadths were off 2½''. The lines were faired between the half breadths of the port and starboard sides.

The boat is provided with a large gaff rig.

    Length 29'11½''
    Beam 6'5½''
    Depth 2'5''
    Sheer 12''

Lines taken off and rough lines plan by Willits Ansel; finished lines plan by Robert Allyn.

BEETLE WHALEBOAT

Location: Nantucket Whaling Museum, Nantucket, Massachusetts

The boat has the "Beetle" brand on the lion's tongue and the inside edge of the clumsy cleat, with characteristic bow chocks and stem and stern profiles. It has inner and outer wales with filler pieces between, giving a heavy appearance to the rail. Scantlings and construction are standard. The boat has seen considerable service and has shipboard patches and repairs.

It has moderate fullness in the bows and a long run. Midship sections have flat floors and a rather hard bilge. The sheer strakes, 7¾'' wide, are plumb at the midship sections. The profile at bow and stern has a gradual sweep up from the keel and a harder curve near the head.

The boat was provided with a rather small gaff rig and no jib.

    Length 28'11¾''
    Beam 6'7''
    Depth 2'2½''
    Sheer 14''

Lines taken off and rough lines plan by Willits Ansel; finished lines plan by Robert Allyn.

Beetle whaleboat at Nantucket Whaling Museum. The curvature of the
stem and bow chock construction is characteristic of the Beetle
boats. Photograph by author.

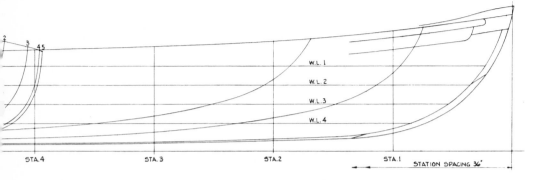

W.L. 1
W.L. 2
W.L. 3
W.L. 4

STA.4   STA.3   STA.2   STA.1   STATION SPACING 36"

NOTE :- THESE LINES DRAWN FROM OFFSETS LIFTED FROM
ACTUAL WHALEBOATS BY WILLITS D. ANSEL. LINES
ARE TO OUTSIDE OF PLANKING.

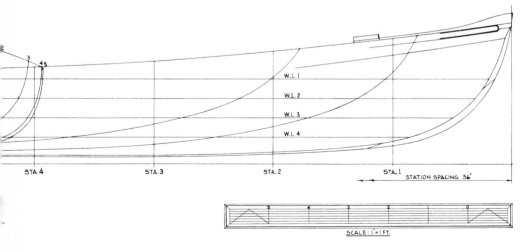

W.L. 1
W.L. 2
W.L. 3
W.L. 4

STA.4   STA.3   STA.2   STA.1   STATION SPACING 36"

SCALE : 1" = 1 FT.

THE MARINE HISTORICAL ASSOCIATION INC.
MYSTIC SEAPORT
MYSTIC CONNECTICUT
WHALEBOAT LINES

DRAWN BY R.C.ALLYN   DATE - JAN. 3, 1974

SERIAL NO. 147

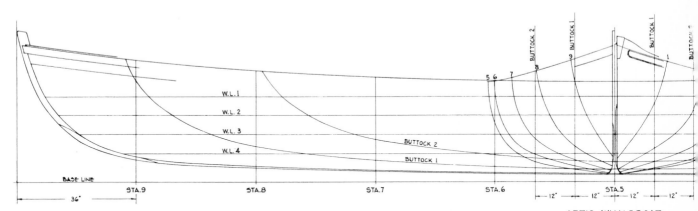

W.L.1
W.L.2
W.L.3
W.L.4
BUTTOCK 2
BUTTOCK 1
BASE LINE
36"
STA.9   STA.8   STA.7   STA.6   STA.5
12"   12"   12"   12"
BUTTOCK 2   BUTTOCK 1   BUTTOCK 1   BUTTOCK 2
5 6   7   8   9   1

ARTIC WHALEBOAT
NEW BEDFORD WHALING MUSEUM
LENGTH 30 FT. — BEAM 6 FT. 4½ IN. — DEPTH 2 FT. 5½ IN.

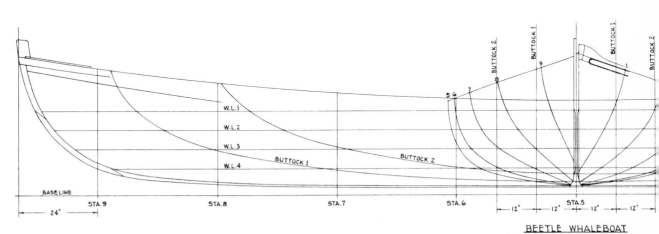

W.L.1
W.L.2
W.L.3
W.L.4
BUTTOCK 1
BUTTOCK 2
BASELINE
24"
STA.9   STA.8   STA.7   STA.6   STA.5
12"   12"   12"   12"
BUTTOCK 2   BUTTOCK 1   BUTTOCK 1   BUTTOCK 2
10   5 6   7   9   1

BEETLE WHALEBOAT
NANTUCKET WHALING MUSEUM
LENGTH 29 FT. — BEAM 6 FT. 5 IN. — DEPTH 2 FT. 3

BOAT FROM *CHARLES W. MORGAN*

Location: On exhibit, Mystic Seaport, Mystic, Connecticut

The builder and early history of this boat are unknown. It arrived at Mystic Seaport on the *Morgan* in 1941, and was restored there some years later. The ship carpenter who did the restoration said it was badly out of shape and the sides had to be pulled in.

The sheer of the boat is strong for later whaleboats. The entrance has the standard fullness; the run is long. Midships sections are standard with moderate flare at the rail—it is possible the flare and sheer developed during restoration. It has inner and outer wales, as do the other five boats which came aboard the *Morgan*. The scantlings and construction are conventional.

 Length 28'8¾''
 Beam 6'4¾''
 Depth 2'2''
 Sheer 15½''

Lines taken off and rough lines plan by Willits Ansel; finished lines plan by Robert Allyn.

BOAT FROM *JOHN R. MANTA*

Location: Kendall Whaling Museum, Sharon, Massachusetts

The builder is not known; Mr. Brewington, Director of the Museum, says there is an unconfirmed rumor that it was built by a Portuguese builder in New Bedford. The boat has seen hard use and some restoration work has been done on the thwarts to preserve its shape. The stern is twisted 1¼'' to starboard. The stem and stern posts are very different in profile, the stern being more plumb. Midsections have moderate dead rise; sides are plumb at the rail. The entrance is rather fine and the run full for a whaleboat. Sheer is slight. The construction and scantlings are standard for American boats.

 Length 29'1¾''
 Beam 6'2½''
 Depth 2'4½''
 Sheer 12''

Lines taken off and rough lines plan by Willits Ansel; finished lines plan by Robert Allyn.

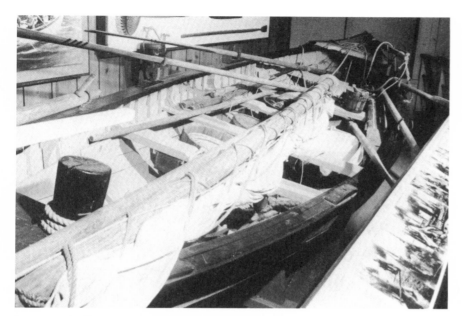

Boat from the CHARLES W. MORGAN *on exhibit at Mystic
Seaport, 1975. Photograph by Maynard Bray.*

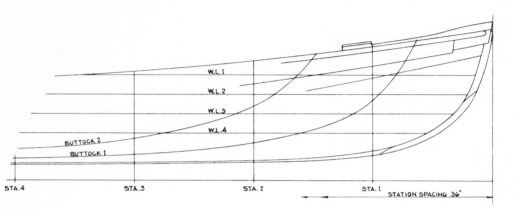

W.L.1
W.L.2
W.L.3
W.L.4

BUTTOCK 2
BUTTOCK 1

STA.4   STA.3   STA.2   STA.1

STATION SPACING 36"

NOTE :- THESE LINES DRAWN FROM OFFSETS LIFTED FROM
ACTUAL WHALEBOATS BY WILLITS D. ANSEL. LINES
ARE TO OUTSIDE OF PLANKING.

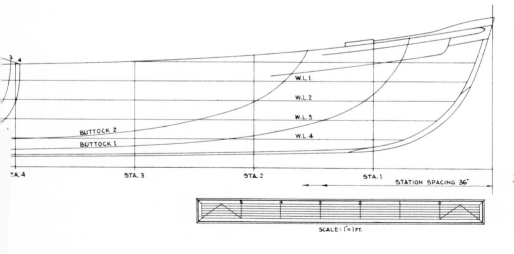

3 4

W.L.1
W.L.2
W.L.3
BUTTOCK 2
BUTTOCK 1
W.L.4

TA.4   STA.3   STA.2   STA.1

STATION SPACING 36"

SCALE: 1"=1 FT.

THE MARINE HISTORICAL ASSOCIATION INC.
MYSTIC SEAPORT
MYSTIC CONNECTICUT
WHALEBOAT LINES

DRAWN BY R.C.ALLYN   DATE - JAN. 30 1974

SERIAL NO. 149

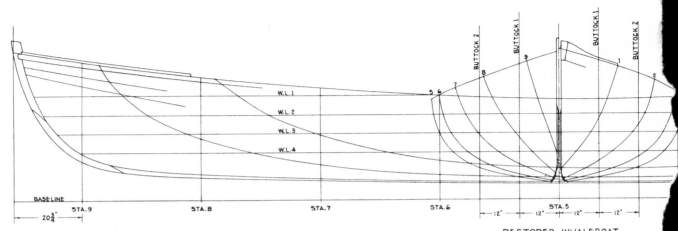

W.L.1
W.L.2
W.L.3
W.L.4

BASELINE

STA.9   STA.8   STA.7   STA.6   STA.5

20¾"

BUTTOCK 2   BUTTOCK 1   BUTTOCK 1   BUTTOCK 2

5 6 7   8   9   1   2

12" 12" 12" 12"

RESTORED WHALEBOAT
AT MYSTIC SEAPORT
LENGTH 28 FT. 8¾ IN. BEAM 6 FT. 4½ IN. DEPTH 2 FT. 3 IN.

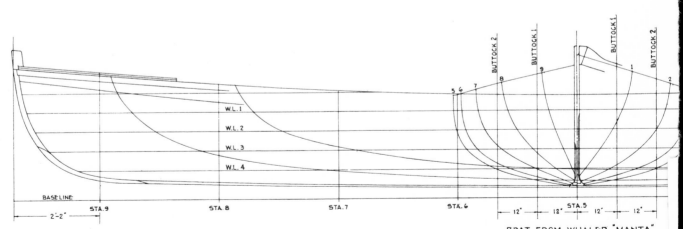

W.L.1
W.L.2
W.L.3
W.L.4

BASELINE

STA.9   STA.8   STA.7   STA.6   STA.5

2'-2"

BUTTOCK 2   BUTTOCK 1   BUTTOCK 1   BUTTOCK 2

5 6 7   8   9   1   2

12" 12" 12" 12"

BOAT FROM WHALER "MANTA"
AT KENDALL WHALING MUSEUM
LENGTH 29 FT. 2 IN. BEAM 6 FT. 2½ IN. DEPTH 2 FT. 4½ IN.

AZOREAN WHALEBOAT

Location: New Bedford, Massachusetts

This boat, which belongs to the New Bedford Whaling Museum, was examined while it was undergoing restoration at the Beetle Boat Division of the Concordia Company, South Dartmouth, Massachusetts. It was built in the Azores and was brought to the United States around 1967.

The boat is shorter than the average Azorean boat and originally had five rather than the usual six thwarts. It has been described as representing a transitional stage between the American boats and later Azorean boats. Earlier, the Azoreans got whaleboats from American whaleships or directly from builders in the United States. They then began building whaleboats themselves and modified the design to suit their own needs. The present Azorean boats are longer, have less sheer, greater flare to the sides, slacker bilges, are narrower proportionately, and have greater overhang at the ends.

The workmanship and finishing is good. An example of the care in building is a bead cut in the seat riser. The riser is copper-riveted rather than fastened with galvanized clench nails. As is common with Azorean boats, it has a short shelf for strengthening along the sides between the first, second and third thwarts. The sheer strake laps the strake beneath; the rest of the planking is carvel. Frames are evenly spaced. The keel is narrower on the underside than in American boats generally. This boat has a centerboard, which is rather uncommon on Azorean whaleboats.

    Length 30'8½"
    Beam 5'11"
    Depth 2'2"
    Sheer 11"

Lines taken off and rough lines plan by Willits Ansel; finished lines plan by Robert Allyn.

POLARIS WHALEBOAT

Location: Stony Brook Community Fund, Stony Brook, Long Island, New York

This is the oldest whaleboat type that can be documented with certainty. There is a possibility that the boat was built by George Rogers of New London, a whaleboat builder who specialized in boats for Arctic exploration. It was taken to the Arctic in 1871 by Arctic explorer Charles F. Hall aboard the steamer *Polaris,* and abandoned at Newman Bay, Greenland, in July 1872. Commander Peary brought it back to the United States in 1906.

Workmanship and materials are of a high order. The boat is fastened throughout with copper rivets; the breasthook is bronze; iron knees brace the thwarts; sheer strake, wales, ceiling, and thwarts are beaded. Stem and stern posts are natural crooks. Frames are light, ⅝" x ¾", and widely spaced at 10". Frame heads notched into the inwales and intermediate floors between the regular frames add strength. A keelson is notched over the frames and floors. The top two strakes are lapped, the rest are smooth; there are no battens. An iron shoe runs the length of the relatively flat keel.

The boat is small by whaleboat standards; the lines are delicate, with finer ends and slacker bilges than the boats carried aboard whaleships. Though built with bow chocks and loggerhead for whaling, the boat seems to have been designed primarily for pulling under oars and lightness for carrying over ice.

    Length 24'3"
    Beam 5'5"
    Depth 2'4"

Lines taken off by Willits Ansel. Plans drawn by Robert Allyn.

POLARIS *whaleboat as found by Peary's expedition in 1905. Robert E. Peary Papers,*
Record Group 401/1, National Archives, Washington, D.C.

POLARIS *whaleboat at Stony Brook, Long Island, in 1981. Photograph by Author.*

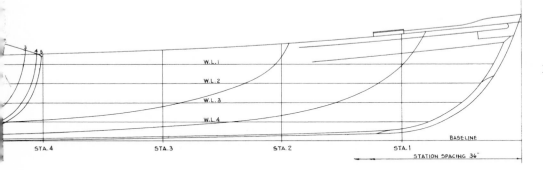

W.L.1
W.L.2
W.L.3
W.L.4

BASELINE

STA.4   STA.3   STA.2   STA.1

STATION SPACING 36"

THE MARINE HISTORICAL ASSOCIATION INC.
MYSTIC SEAPORT
MYSTIC CONNECTICUT
WHALEBOAT LINES

DRAWN BY R.C.ALLYN   DATE - JULY 9, 1974

SERIAL NO. 154

SCALE: 1"=1 FT.

NOTE:— THESE LINES DRAWN FROM OFFSETS LIFTED FROM
ACTUAL BOAT BY WILLITS D. ANSEL. LINES
ARE TO OUTSIDE OF PLANKING.

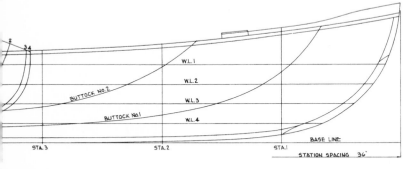

W.L.1
W.L.2
BUTTOCK No.2
W.L.3
BUTTOCK No.1
W.L.4

BASE LINE

STA.3   STA.2   STA.1

STATION SPACING 36"

XPEDITION—1871

THE MARINE HISTORICAL ASSOCIATION INC.
MYSTIC SEAPORT
MYSTIC CONNECTICUT
WHALEBOAT LINES

DRAWN BY R.C.ALLYN   JUNE 1982

SERIAL NO. 183

SCALE: 1"=1 FT.

NOTE:— THESE LINES DRAWN FROM OFFSETS LIFTED FROM
ACTUAL BOAT BY WILLITS D. ANSEL. LINES
ARE TO OUTSIDE OF PLANKING.

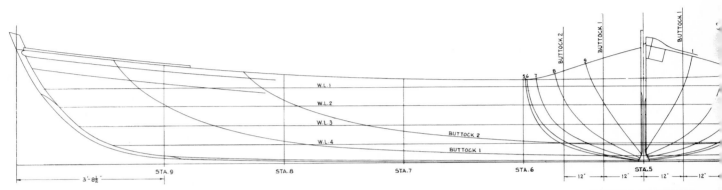

W.L.1
W.L.2
W.L.3
BUTTOCK 2
W.L.4
BUTTOCK 1

STA.9   STA.8   STA.7   STA.6   STA.5

BUTTOCK 2
BUTTOCK 1
BUTTOCK 1

3'-8½"   12"   12"   12"   12"

AZOREAN WHALEBOAT
LENGTH 30'-8½" – BEAM 5'-11¼" – DEPTH 2'-2½

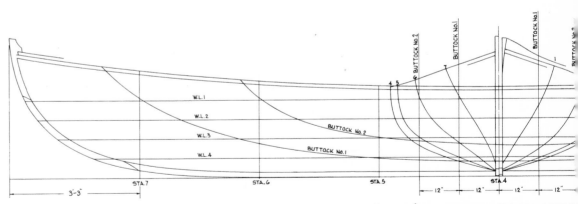

W.L.1
W.L.2
BUTTOCK No.2
W.L.3
BUTTOCK No.1
W.L.4

STA.7   STA.6   STA.5   STA.4

BUTTOCK No.2
BUTTOCK No.1
BUTTOCK No.1

3'-3"   12"   12"   12"   12"

"POLARIS" WHALEBOAT FROM THE HALL ARTIC E
LENGTH 24'-3" – BEAM 5'-5" – DEPTH 2'-4"
AT STONY BROOK L.I.

BEETLE WHALEBOAT

Location: Mariners Museum, Newport News, Virginia

This boat was built in 1933 for the museum by Charles Beetle, and represents a boat for the sperm fishery. Its lines are finer than those of most of the later whaleboats. Beetle may have had in mind the earlier boats built primarily for pulling. He admired these particularly. It has never been used and has always been kept inside. There is some slight unfairness at the shores, but the shape is truest and the condition is the best of any original boats. The workmanship is of a high order; since it was known the boat was to become a museum piece, very likely special care was taken in its building. Any refinements, however, were a matter of degree rather than kind, for all the features found in it are also found in Beetle's working whaleboats.

It has the fullness in the bow sections developed by James Beetle to give buoyancy as the whale sounded. Midship sections have the characteristic flat floors and hard turn of the bilge. There is somewhat more flare to the sides in the midsections than in most other boats, including Beetle-built ones, that were examined. The run is long. The profiles of bow and stern are characteristic of Beetle, with an easy sweep up from the keel and a harder curve near the head.

Construction and scantlings are conventional.

The boat is equipped with a large gaff main and a small jib.

Length 28'5¾"
Beam 6'5"
Depth 2'2"
Sheer 15"

Lines taken off and construction details recorded by Willits Ansel and Robert Allyn. Plans drawn by Robert Allyn.

Whaleboat at Mariners Museum, Newport News, Virginia, which was built by Charles Beetle for the Museum. Photograph by author.

OFFSETS-FEET-INCHES-EIGHTHS TO OUTSIDE OF PLANKING

ION	SHEER	KEEL RABBET	WL.1	WL.2	WL.3	WL.4	DIAG.A	DIAG.B	DIAG.C	DIAG.D	SHEER	KEEL BOTTOM	BUT K.1	BUT K.2
			HALF BREADTHS								HEIGHTS			
1	1-5-1	0-0-6	0-11-4+	0-8-2	0-4-6	0-0-6+	0-7-7+	0-10-6	1-1-0	1-2-3+	3-0-2+	0-4-5+	2-1-2+	—
2	2-4-0+	0-1-1+	2-0-4	1-8-0+	1-2-0+	0-6-1+	1-1-3+	1-6-2	1-11-1+	2-2-1	2-7-7	0-1-6+	0-10-2	1-11-3
3	2-10-1	0-1-6	2-8-7	2-5-7	2-0-6+	1-2-2	1-4-6	1-11-2+	2-6-4+	2-9-7+	2-5-2+	0-0-6	0-5-1+	0-11-4
4	3-1-0	0-2-2	3-0-4+	2-11-0	2-7-4	1-10-0+	1-6-5	2-2-0+	2-11-1+	3-2-1	2-3-5	0-0-2-	0-3-0	0-6-7
5	3-1-6	0-2-2	3-1-4	3-0-0	2-8-5	1-11-5	1-7-1	2-2-5	2-11-7	3-3-0	2-2-6+	0-0-0	0-2-4	0-6-2
6	3-0-2	0-1-7+	2-11-5	2-9-3	2-4-4+	1-6-0	1-5-7	2-0-6	2-9-0+	3-0-6	2-3-1+	0-0-4	0-3-7-	0-9-0-
7	2-7-4	0-1-4+	2-5-3	2-1-4+	1-7-1	0-9-4+	1-3-1	1-8-6	2-3-0+	2-6-3+	2-4-7	0-1-2	0-7-4-	1-4-2
8	1-9-7	0-0-6	1-5-7+	1-2-7	0-8-6	0-3-3	0-10-7	1-2-5	1-6-2	1-8-3-	2-8-6	0-2-1	1-3-6	
9	0-7-7	0-0-6	0-4-1	0-2-0+	—	—	0-2-2+	0-4-3+	0-6-0+	0-6-5+	3-3-0	1-0-1	—	—

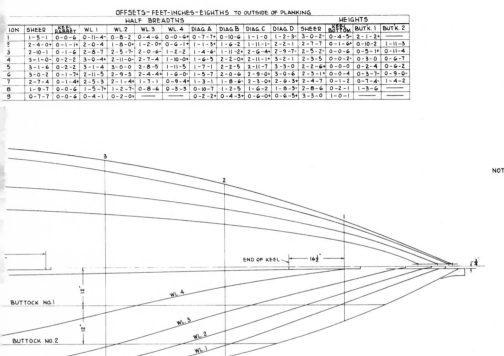

NOTE –

THESE LINES LIFTED MAY 1973 FROM BOAT EXHIBITED AT THE
MARINERS' MUSEUM, NEWPORT NEWS VA. THE BOAT WAS BUILT
IN 1933 AND IS THE LAST ONE MADE BY CHARLES D. BEETLE.
IT WAS NEVER USED AND IS IN MINT CONDITION.

END OF KEEL — 16½"

BUTTOCK NO.1

BUTTOCK NO.2

WL. 4
WL. 3
WL. 2
WL. 1
SHEER

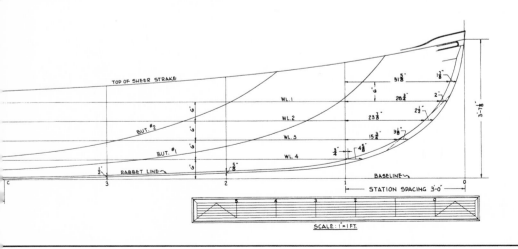

TOP OF SHEER STRAKE

BUT. #2
BUT. #1
RABBET LINE

WL.1
WL.2
WL.3
WL.4

BASELINE

STATION SPACING 3'-0"

SCALE: 1"=1 FT.

THE MARINE HISTORICAL ASSOCIATION INC.
MYSTIC SEAPORT
MYSTIC CONNECTICUT
BEETLE WHALEBOAT
LINES & OFFSETS

DRAWN BY R.C.ALLYN   DATE – JUNE 15,1973
SCALE: 1"=1 FT.

SERIAL NO. 138

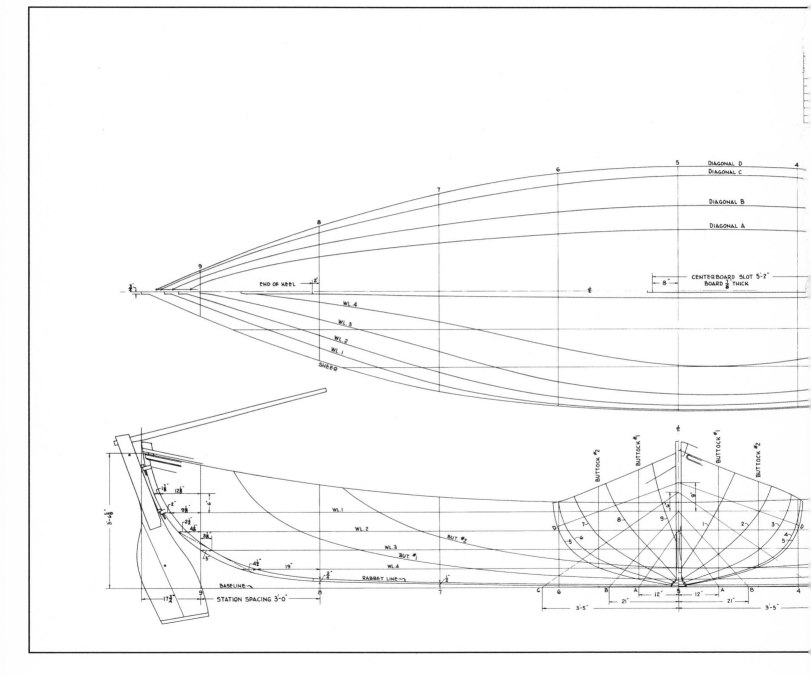

DIAGONAL D
DIAGONAL C
DIAGONAL B
DIAGONAL A

CENTERBOARD SLOT 5'-2"
BOARD ⅛ THICK

END OF KEEL

WL.4
WL.3
WL.2
WL.1
SHEER

BUTTOCK #2   BUTTOCK #1   BUTTOCK #1   BUTTOCK #2

WL.1
WL.2   BUT. #2
WL.3   BUT. #1
WL.4
BASELINE   RABBET LINE

STATION SPACING 3'-0"

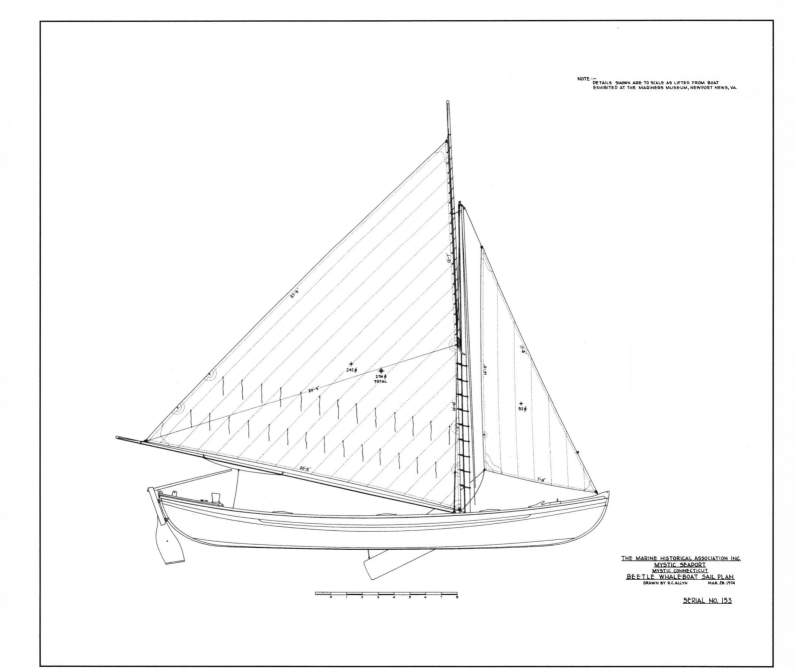

NOTE:—
DETAILS SHOWN ARE TO SCALE AS LIFTED FROM BOAT
EXHIBITED AT THE MARINERS MUSEUM, NEWPORT NEWS, VA.

THE MARINE HISTORICAL ASSOCIATION INC.
MYSTIC SEAPORT
MYSTIC CONNECTICUT
BEETLE WHALEBOAT SAIL PLAN
DRAWN BY R.C.ALLYN   MAR. 28. 1974

SERIAL NO. 153

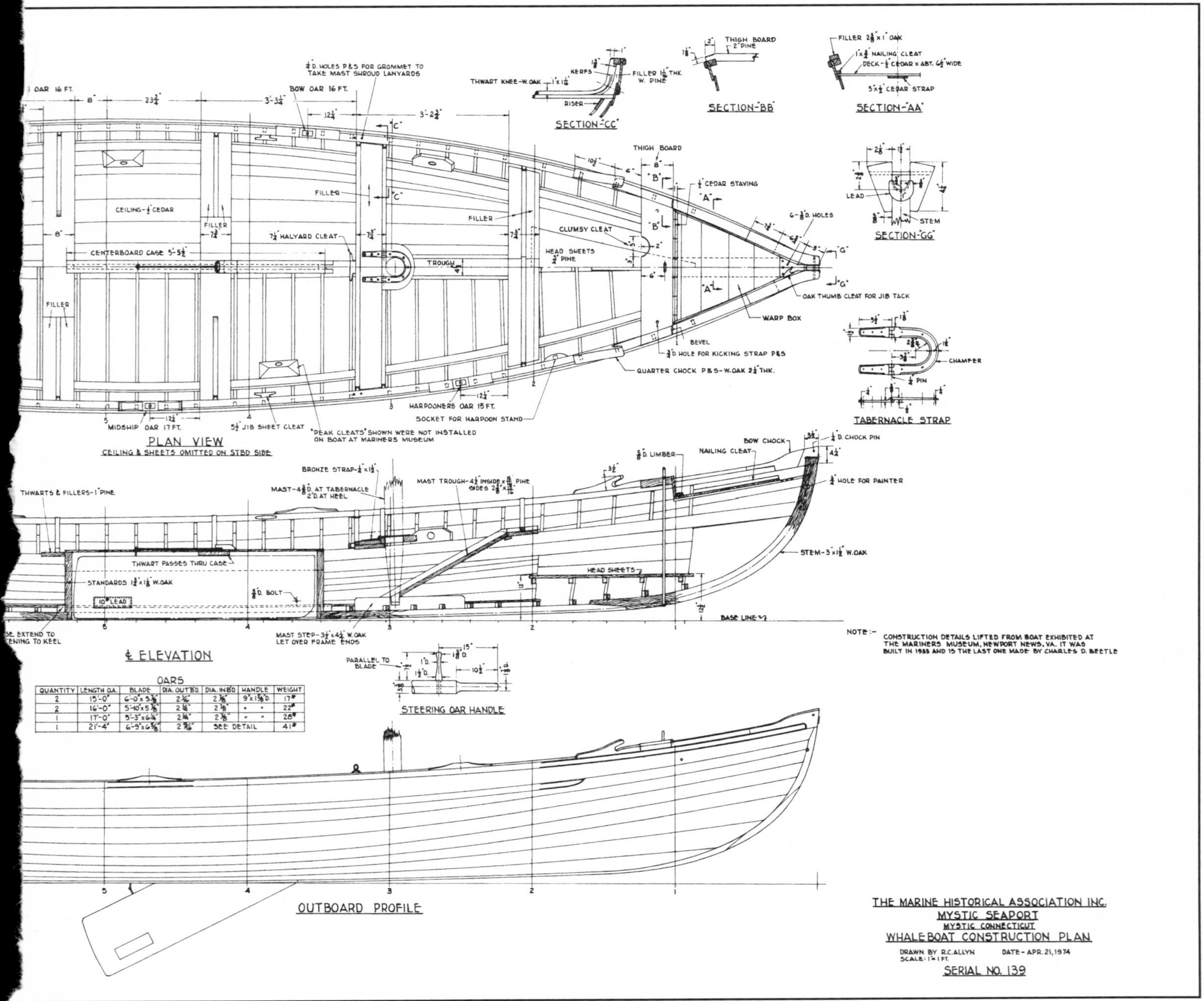

SECTION-"CC"
THWART KNEE-W.OAK 1"x1½"
KERFS
FILLER 1½" THK. W. PINE
RISER
SECTION-"BB"
THIGH BOARD 2" PINE
SECTION-"AA"
FILLER 2⅝" x 1" OAK
1"x¾" NAILING CLEAT
DECK-½" CEDAR x ABT. 6½" WIDE
5"x½" CEDAR STRAP
SECTION-"GG"
LEAD
STEM
TABERNACLE STRAP
CHAMFER
PIN
¾"D. HOLES P&S FOR GROMMET TO TAKE MAST SHROUD LANYARDS
BOW OAR 16 FT.
OAR 16 FT.
CEILING-½" CEDAR
FILLER
CENTERBOARD CASE 5'-5½"
7¼" HALYARD CLEAT
TROUGH
HEAD SHEETS ½" PINE
CLUMSY CLEAT
THIGH BOARD
½" CEDAR STAVING
6-⅜"D. HOLES
OAK THUMB CLEAT FOR JIB TACK
WARP BOX
BEVEL
⅜"D. HOLE FOR KICKING STRAP P&S
QUARTER CHOCK P&S-W.OAK 2¼" THK.
HARPOONERS OAR 15 FT.
SOCKET FOR HARPOON STAND
MIDSHIP OAR 17 FT.
5½" JIB SHEET CLEAT
"PEAK CLEATS" SHOWN WERE NOT INSTALLED ON BOAT AT MARINERS MUSEUM
PLAN VIEW
CEILING & SHEETS OMITTED ON STBD SIDE
BOW CHOCK
¼"D. CHOCK PIN
⅝"D. LIMBER
NAILING CLEAT
¾" HOLE FOR PAINTER
BRONZE STRAP-¼"x1½"
MAST-4⅜"D. AT TABERNACLE 2"D. AT HEEL
MAST TROUGH-4½" INSIDE x ⅞" PINE SIDES
THWARTS & FILLERS-1" PINE
THWART PASSES THRU CASE
STANDARDS 1¼"x1½" W.OAK
10# LEAD
⅜"D. BOLT
HEAD SHEETS
STEM-3"x1½" W.OAK
BASE LINE
MAST STEP-3½"x4½" W.OAK LET OVER FRAME ENDS
& ELEVATION
PARALLEL TO BLADE
STEERING OAR HANDLE
OUTBOARD PROFILE

NOTE:- CONSTRUCTION DETAILS LIFTED FROM BOAT EXHIBITED AT THE MARINERS MUSEUM, NEWPORT NEWS, VA. IT WAS BUILT IN 1933 AND IS THE LAST ONE MADE BY CHARLES D. BEETLE

OARS

QUANTITY	LENGTH O.A.	BLADE	DIA. OUT'BD.	DIA. IN'BD.	HANDLE	WEIGHT
2	15'-0"	6'-0" x 5⅞"	2 1/16"	2⅛"	9" x 1⅝" D.	17#
2	16'-0"	5'-10" x 5⅞"	2¼"	2⅛"	" "	22#
1	17'-0"	5'-3" x 6¼"	2¼"	2⅛"	" "	28#
1	21'-4"	6'-9" x 6⅝"	2 9/16"	SEE DETAIL		41#

THE MARINE HISTORICAL ASSOCIATION INC.
MYSTIC SEAPORT
MYSTIC CONNECTICUT

WHALEBOAT CONSTRUCTION PLAN

DRAWN BY R.C.ALLYN — DATE - APR. 21, 1974
SCALE: 1" = 1 FT.

SERIAL NO. 139

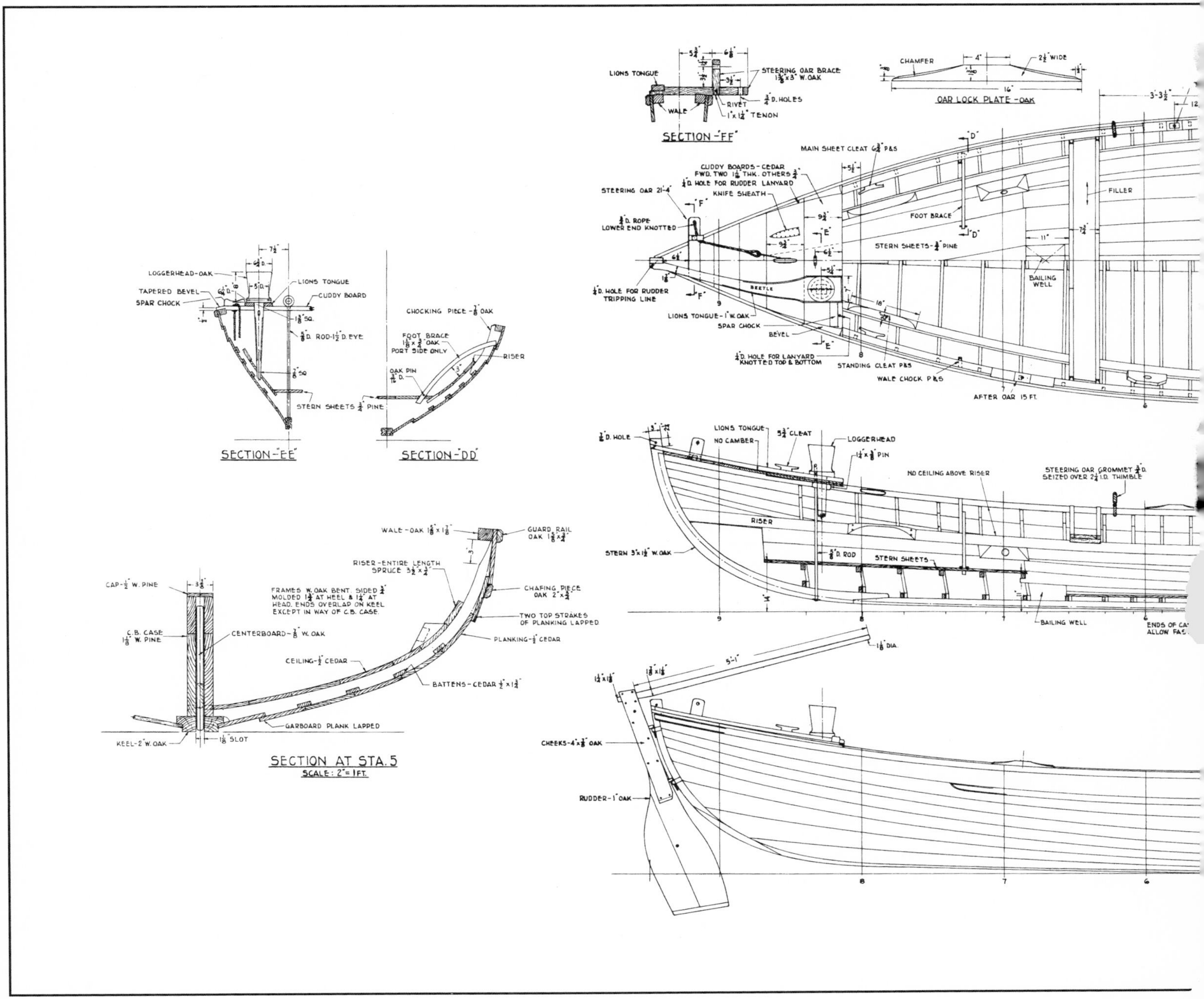

SECTION "FF"
LIONS TONGUE
STEERING OAR BRACE 1⅝"x3" W. OAK
¾" D. HOLES
RIVET
WALE
1"x1¼" TENON
CHAMFER
2½" WIDE
OAR LOCK PLATE - OAK
MAIN SHEET CLEAT 6¾" P&S
CUDDY BOARDS - CEDAR FWD. TWO 1¼" THK. OTHERS ¾"
¾" D. HOLE FOR RUDDER LANYARD
KNIFE SHEATH
STEERING OAR 21'-4"
⅜" D. ROPE LOWER END KNOTTED
FOOT BRACE
STERN SHEETS - ¾" PINE
FILLER
BAILING WELL
½" D. HOLE FOR RUDDER TRIPPING LINE
BEETLE
LIONS TONGUE - 1" W. OAK
SPAR CHOCK
BEVEL
¾" D. HOLE FOR LANYARD KNOTTED TOP & BOTTOM
STANDING CLEAT P&S
WALE CHOCK P&S
AFTER OAR 15 FT.
LOGGERHEAD - OAK
TAPERED BEVEL
SPAR CHOCK
LIONS TONGUE
CUDDY BOARD
⅝" D. ROD - 1½" D. EYE
STERN SHEETS ¾" PINE
SECTION "EE"
CHOCKING PIECE - ⅞" OAK
FOOT BRACE 1⅛" x ¾" OAK PORT SIDE ONLY
RISER
OAK PIN
SECTION "DD"
⅞" D. HOLE
LIONS TONGUE
NO CAMBER
5¾" CLEAT
LOGGERHEAD
1¼"x⅜" PIN
NO CEILING ABOVE RISER
STEERING OAR GROMMET ¾" D. SEIZED OVER 2¼" I.D. THIMBLE
RISER
STERN 3"x1½" W. OAK
⅝" D. ROD
STERN SHEETS
BAILING WELL
ENDS OF CA
ALLOW FAS
WALE - OAK 1⅝" x 1⅞"
GUARD RAIL OAK 1⅝" x ¾"
RISER - ENTIRE LENGTH SPRUCE 3½" x ¾"
CAP - ½" W. PINE
FRAMES W. OAK BENT. SIDED ¾" MOLDED 1¾" AT HEEL & 1¼" AT HEAD. ENDS OVERLAP ON KEEL EXCEPT IN WAY OF C.B. CASE.
CHAFING PIECE OAK 2"x¾"
TWO TOP STRAKES OF PLANKING LAPPED
C.B. CASE 1⅛" W. PINE
CENTERBOARD - ⅞" W. OAK
PLANKING - ½" CEDAR
CEILING - ½" CEDAR
BATTENS - CEDAR ½" x 1¼"
GARBOARD PLANK LAPPED
KEEL - 2" W. OAK
1⅛" SLOT
SECTION AT STA. 5
SCALE: 2" = 1 FT.
1⅛" DIA.
CHEEKS - 4"x⅜" OAK
RUDDER - 1" OAK

WHALEBOAT PLANS BY R. O. DAVIS AND WILLIAM H. HAND.

The lines in these plans may be those of a boat built by Eben Leonard—there is now no known Leonard-built whaleboat in existence. The accompanying plans, showing lines, construction and sail plan, were drawn by R. O. Davis and checked by William H. Hand in 1935. Three replicas were built and tested at Mystic Seaport in 1972 and 1973.

The plans show moderate sheer, the sweep of which appears symmetrical fore and aft, though the lowest point is slightly aft of midships. Stem and stern posts have considerable rake and make an even curve from keel to head. Bow sections are full, giving a codhead appearance when viewed from the quarter. Midship sections are plumb at the rail, the bilge is characteristically hard with little deadrise. The run is long.

Construction and scantlings are conventional.

The sail plan calls for a large gaff mainsail and small jib.

The plan appears to be in error with respect to the nomenclature and lengths of pulling oars.

The boats tested performed well under oars and sail. They were ballasted with 1,000 pounds of lead, approximately the equivalent weight of equipment aboard a whaleboat, and the rudder of the second boat was made deeper. Without the ballast, the boats were tender, made considerable leeway, and failed to come through the wind in tacking. Ballast brought them down to their lines and made them more stable and weatherly.

Length 29'10½''
Beam 6'7''
Depth 2'4½''
Sheer 15''

OFFSET TABLE
DESIGN #615
WM. H. HAND. JR. _____ M.A.
NEW BEDFORD
May 1935

	STATIONS	1.	2.	3.	4.	5.	6.	7.	8.	9.
HEIGHTS	SHEER	3-3-0	2-10-7	2-7-7	2-6-0	2-5-0	2-5-0	2-6-1	2-8-4	3-0-5
	BUT. 2		1-7-3	0-8-2	0-5-2	0-4-6	0-6-3	0-10-7	2-3-7	
	BUT. 1	1-10-2	0-6-5	0-3-2	0-2-2	0-2-1	0-2-6	0-4-7	0-10-5	2-7-6
	RABBET	0-5-0	0-1-6	0-0-7	0-0-5	0-0-5	0-0-6	0-1-0	0-1-6	0-5-2
	KEEL BOTTOM	0-3-7	0-1-0	0-0-2	0-0-0	0-0-0	0-0-1	0-0-3	0-1-1	0-3-7
HALF BREADTHS	SHEER	1-5-2	2-3-0	2-10-4	3-2-4	3-3-4	3-1-6	2-9-2	2-1-0	1-1-3
	W.L. 1	1-0-4	2-1-4	2-10-0	3-2-3	3-3-3	3-1-4	2-6-3	1-10-5	0-3-0
	W.L. 2	0-10-2	1-11-3	2-8-8	3-1-3	3-2-4	3-0-4	2-6-3	1-7-3	0-6-2
	W.L. 3	0-6-6	1-7-2	2-4-7	2-10-4	2-11-7	2-9-1	2-1-4	1-1-4	0-5-4
	W.L. 4	0-1-6	0-10-6	1-7-7	2-2-2	2-3-6	1-11-2	1-2-5	0-6-0	0-1-1
DIAGS.	DIAG. 1	1-5-1	2-3-5	3-0-0	3-4-3	3-5-3	3-3-4	2-10-4	2-1-3	1-0-6
	DIAG. 2	1-1-7	2-2-3	2-10-4	3-5-0	3-4-1	3-2-0	2-8-3	1-11-0	0-10-6
	DIAG. 3	1-0-1	1-10-2	2-4-0	2-7-0	2-7-5	2-5-6	2-1-5	1-6-3	0-8-4
	DIAG. 4	0-9-4	1-3-6	1-8-3	1-7-2	1-7-4	1-6-6	1-4-7	1-1-2	0-6-5

All Dimensions Given in Feet, Inches, & Eighths To Outside of Planking.
All Heights Given above Base Line.

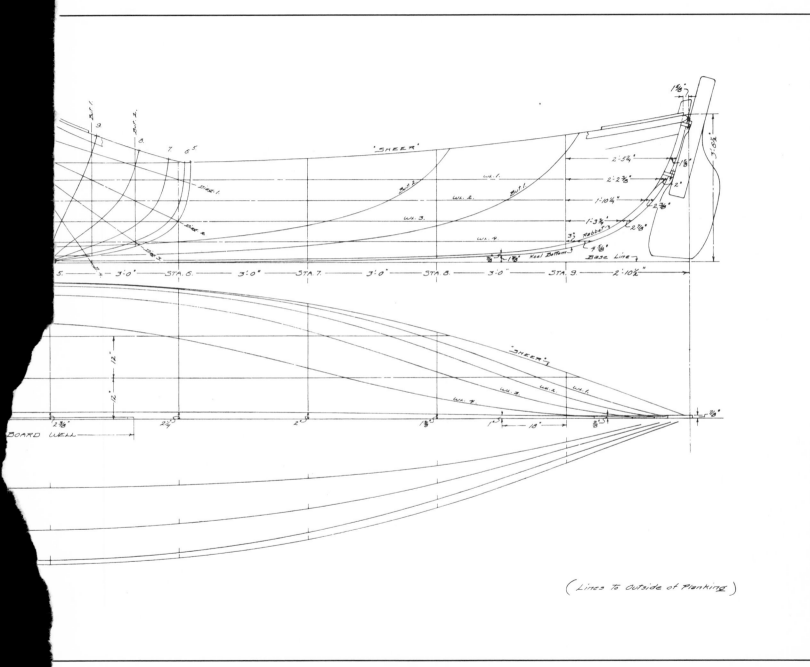

(Lines To Outside of Planking)

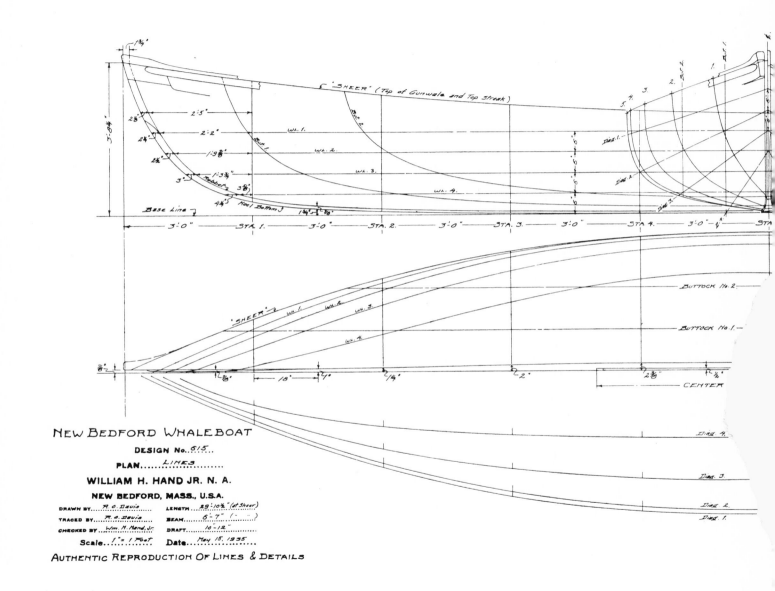

NEW BEDFORD WHALEBOAT

DESIGN No. 615

PLAN LINES

WILLIAM H. HAND JR. N. A.

NEW BEDFORD, MASS., U.S.A.

DRAWN BY R. C. Davis	LENGTH 29'-10¾" (at Sheer)
TRACED BY R. C. Davis	BEAM 6'-7"
CHECKED BY Wm. H. Hand, Jr.	DRAFT 10-12"

Scale 1" = 1 Foot   **Date** May 15, 1935

AUTHENTIC REPRODUCTION OF LINES & DETAILS

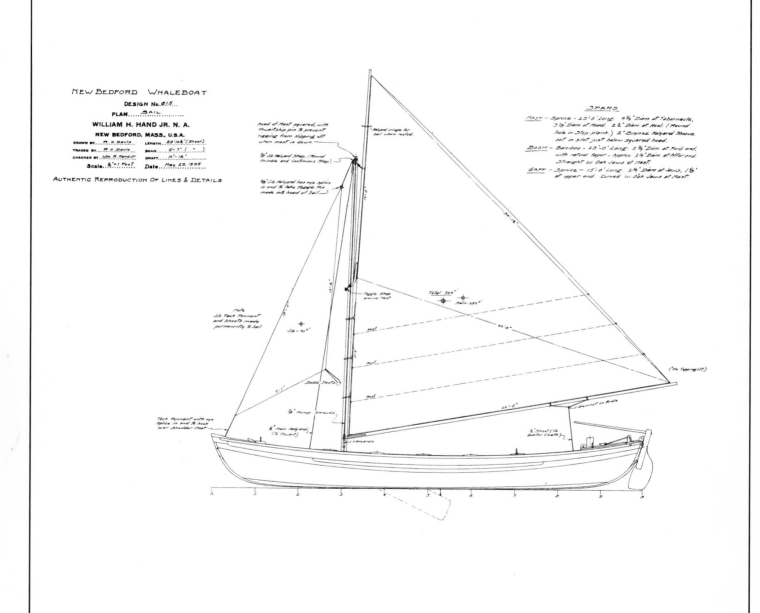

New Bedford Whaleboat

DESIGN No. 915

PLAN...... Sail

WILLIAM H. HAND JR. N. A.

NEW BEDFORD, MASS., U.S.A.

DRAWN BY: M. O. Davis   LENGTH: 23'-10½" (Sheer)
TRACED BY: M. O. Davis   BEAM: 6'-7" (")
CHECKED BY: Wm. H. Hand Jr.   DRAFT: 10"-12"

Scale: ¾" = 1 Foot   Date: May 23, 1935

AUTHENTIC REPRODUCTION OF LINES & DETAILS

SPARS

MAST – Spruce – 23'-6" Long. 4¾" Diam at Tabernacle, 3⅛" Diam at Head. 2¾" Diam at Heel. (Round hole in Step plank.) 2" Bronze Halyard Sheave set in slot just below squared head.

BOOM – Bamboo – 23'-0" Long. 2¾" Diam at Ford end, with natural taper – Approx. 2¼" Diam at After end. Straight W. Oak Jaws at Mast.

GAFF – Spruce – 15'-0" Long. 2¼" Diam at Jaws, 1⅜" at upper end. Curved W. Oak Jaws at Mast.

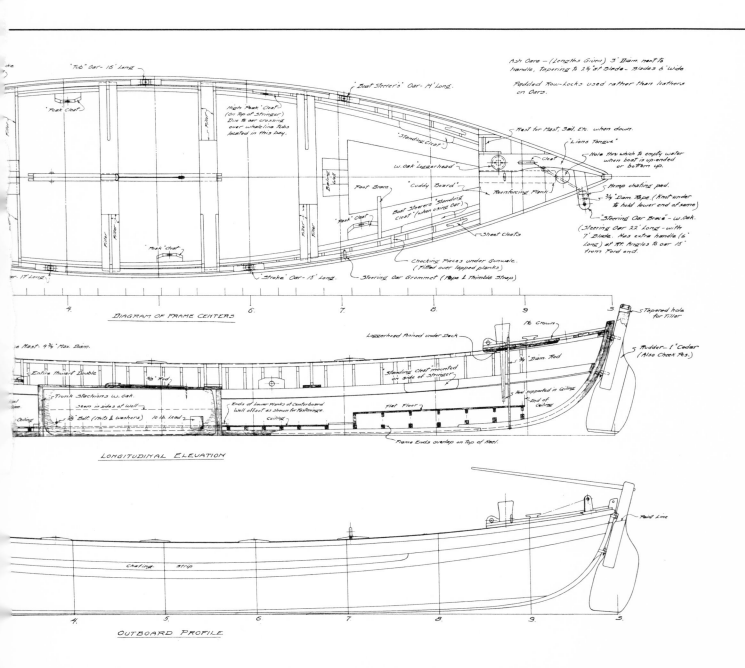

Ash Oars — (Lengths Given) 3" Diam. next to
handle, Tapering to 2¼" at Blade. Blades 6" Wide

Padded Row-Locks used rather than leathers
on Oars.

"Tub" Oar - 15' Long

"Peak Cleat"

"Boat Steerer's" Oar - 14' Long

"High Peak Cleat"
(On Top of Stringer)
Due to oar crossing
over whaleline Tubs
located in this Bay.

"Standing Cleat"

W. Oak Loggerhead

"Cuddy Board"

Foot Brace

"Peak Cleat"

Boat Steerers "Standing
Cleat" (when using Oar)

"Sheet Cleats"

"Peak Cleat"

Rest for Mast, Sail, Etc. when down.

"Lions Tongue"

Cleat

Hole thru which to empty water
when boat is up-ended
or bottom up.

Hemp chafing pad.

¾" Diam. Rope (Knot under
to hold lower end of same)

"Steering Oar Brace" - W. Oak.

(Steering Oar 22' Long - with
7' Blade. Has extra handle (6'
Long) at Rt. Angles to oar 15'
from Ford end.

Checking Pieces under Gunwale.
(Fitted over lapped planks)

Oar - 17' Long

"Stroke" Oar - 15' Long.

Steering Oar Grommet (Rope & Thimble Strap)

DIAGRAM OF FRAME CENTERS

4   6   7   8   9   S

Mast - 4¾" Max. Diam.

Entire Thwart Double

⅜" Rod

Trunk 3 fathoms W. Oak.

Seam in sides of Well

⅜" Bolt. (Nuts & Washers) 10 lb. Lead

Ends of Lower Planks at Centerboard
Well offset as shown for Fastenings.

Ceiling

Loggerhead Pinned under Deck

No Crown

Standing Cleat mounted
on side of Stringer

¾" Diam. Rod

Flat Floor

Keel supported in Ceiling

End of
Ceiling

Frame Ends overlap on Top of Keel.

Tapered hole
for Tiller

Rudder - 1" Cedar
(Also Cheek Pcs.)

LONGITUDINAL ELEVATION

Paint Line

Chafing strip

4   5   6   7   8   9   S

OUTBOARD PROFILE

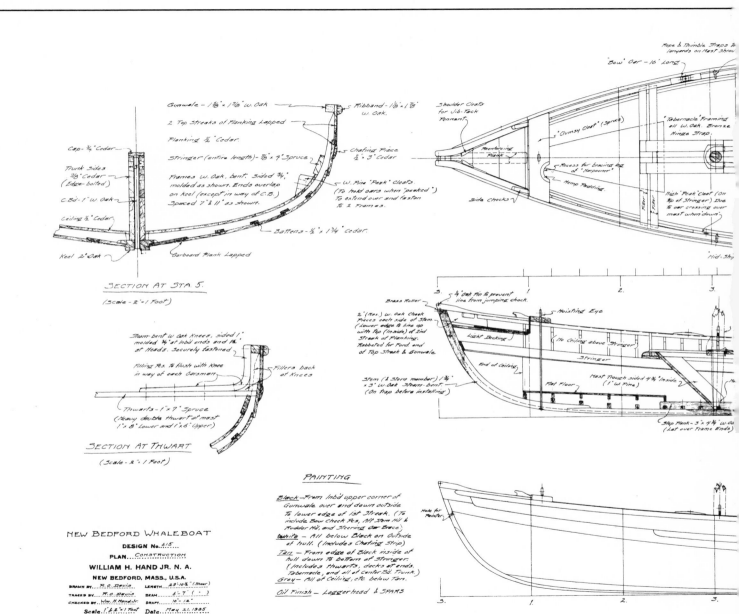

NEW BEDFORD WHALEBOAT

DESIGN No. 415

PLAN... CONSTRUCTION

WILLIAM H. HAND JR. N. A.

NEW BEDFORD, MASS., U.S.A.

DRAWN BY... R.C. Davis	LENGTH... 23'-10¾" (Sheer)
TRACED BY... R.C. Davis	BEAM... 6'-7" (")
CHECKED BY... Wm. H. Hand Jr.	DRAFT... 10"-12"
Scale... 1½ & 2" = 1 Foot	Date... May 21, 1935.

AUTHENTIC REPRODUCTION OF LINES & DETAILS

SECTION AT STA. 5.

(Scale - 2" = 1 Foot)

SECTION AT THWART

(Scale - 2" = 1 Foot)

PAINTING

Bibliography

Aldrich, Herbert Lincoln. *Arctic Alaska and Siberia, or Eight Months with the Arctic Whalemen*. New Bedford: Reynolds Printing, 1937.

Allen, Everett S. *Children of the Light: The Rise and Fall of New Bedford Whaling and the Death of the Arctic Fleet*. Boston: Little, Brown & Co., 1973.

Ansel, Willits, "The *Polaris* Whaleboat," *The Log of Mystic Seaport*, Fall 1982.

Ashley, Clifford W. *The Yankee Whaler*. Garden City: Halcyon House, 1942.

———. *The Ashley Book of Knots*. Garden City: Doubleday, Doran & Co., Inc., 1944.

Baader, Juan. *The Sailing Yacht*. New York: W.W. Norton & Co., Inc., 1965.

Beetle, Charles D. "The Beetle Whaleboat," *The Mariner*, April 1935.

———. "Charles D. Beetle to Build His Last Whaleboat," *New Bedford Standard-Times*, November 22, 1924.

———. "Whaleships in Port and at Sea." Unpublished manuscript.

Beetle, James. "Beetle Whaleboats," *The American Neptune*, October 1943.

Bockstoce, John R. *Whales, Ice, and Men: The History of Whaling in the Western Arctic*. Seattle: University of Washington Press, in association with the New Bedford Whaling Museum, 1986.

Bodfish, Hartson H. *Chasing the Bowhead, As Told by Captain Hartson H. Bodfish and Recorded for Him by Joseph C. Allen*. Cambridge: Harvard University Press, 1936.

Boss, Judith A., and Joseph D. Thomas. *New Bedford: A Pictorial History*. Virginia Beach: Donning Co., 1983.

Bray, Maynard, Benjamin A.G. Fuller, and Peter T. Vermilya. *Mystic Seaport Watercraft*. Mystic: Mystic Seaport, 2001.

Brown, James Templeman. *The Whale Fishery and Its Appliances*. Washington: Government Printing Office, 1883.

Browne, J. Ross. *Etchings of a Whaling Cruise*. 1846; reprint, Cambridge: Belknap Press of Harvard University Press, 1968.

Chapelle, Howard I. *American Small Sailing Craft*. New York: W.W. Norton & Co., Inc., 1951.

——. *The History of the American Sailing Navy*. New York: Bonanza Books, 1949.

——. *The National Watercraft Collection*. Washington: Government Printing Office, 1960.

Chapelle, Howard I., and Edwin Tappan Adney. *The Bark Canoe and Skin Boats of North America*. Washington: Government Printing Office, 1964.

Chapman, Fredrik Henrik. *Architectura Navalis Mercatoria*. 1768; reprint, New York: Praeger Publishers, 1971.

Chatterton, E. Keble. *Whalers and Whaling*. London: T. Fisher Unwin, 1925.

Church, Albert Cook. *Whale Ships and Whaling*. New York: W.W. Norton & Co., Inc., 1938.

Clarke, Robert. "Open Boat Whaling in the Azores," *National Institute of Oceanography, Discovery Reports*, vol. 25, 1954.

Conrad, Joseph. "Christmas Day at Sea," *Last Essays*. Garden City: Doubleday, Page & Co., 1926.

Creighton, Margaret S. *Rites & Passages: The Experience of American Whaling, 1830-1870*. Cambridge: Cambridge University Press, 1995.

Dakin, William John. *Whalemen Adventurers*. Sydney: Sirus Books, 1963.

Davis, William. *Nimrod of the Sea, or The American Whaleman*. 1874; reprint, North Quincy: Christopher Publishing House, 1972.

Dow, George Francis. *Whaleships and Whaling*. Salem: Marine Research Society, 1925.

Dudley, Paul. *An Essay upon the Natural History of Whales*. Philosophical Society of London. Transactions, vol. 3, 1725.

Earle, Capt. J.A.M. "Fighting Sperm Whales," *Yachting*, February 1927.

Edwards, Everett Joshua. *Whale Off*. New York: Coward-McCann Inc., 1956.

Ely, Ben-Ezra Stiles. *"There She Blows": A Narrative of a Whaling Voyage, in the Indian and South Atlantic Oceans*. Middletown: Wesleyan University Press for Mystic Seaport, 1971.

Fenger, Frederick A. *Alone in the Caribbean*. Belmont: Wellington Books, 1958.

Ferguson, Robert. *Harpooner*. Philadelphia: University of Pennsylvania Press, 1936.

Goode, George Brown, ed. *The Fisheries and Fishery Industries of the United States*, Sect. V. Washington: Government Printing Office, 1887.

Goode, George Brown, and J. W. Collins. "The Mackerel Fishery," *The Fisheries and Fishery Industries of the United States*. Washington: Government Printing Office, 1887.

Halabisky, Bruce. "Apprenticing in the Azores: Building the Whaleboat *Bela Vista*," *WoodenBoat*, January/February 1999.

———. "Currents: The flowering of Azorean whaleboats," *WoodenBoat*, November/December 2013.

Haley, Nelson Cole. *Whale Hunt*. Mystic: Mystic Seaport, 1990.

Hall, Henry. *Report on the Shipbuilding Industry of the United States*, Tenth Census, 1880, vol. 8. Washington: Government Printing Office, 1884

Hegarty, Reginald B. *Birth of a Whaleship*. New Bedford: Free Public Library of New Bedford, 1965.

———. *The Rope's End*. Boston: Houghton Mifflin, 1965.

Herreshoff, L. Francis. *The Common Sense of Yacht Design*. New York: Rudder Publishing Co., 1946.

Hichborn, Philip. *Standard Designs for Boats of the United States Navy*. Washington: Government Printing Office. 1900.

Hopkins, William J. *She Blows! And Sparm at That*. Boston and New York: Houghton Mifflin and Co., 1922.

Housby, Trevor. *The Hand of God*. New York: Abelard-Schuman, 1971.

Howland, Llewellyn. *Sou'West and By West of Cape Cod*. Cambridge: Harvard University Press, 1948.

Jackson, Tom. "Currents: Around the Yards," *WoodenBoat*, January/ February 2013, March/April 2013.

———. "Currents: Whaleboats for the *Charles W. Morgan*," *WoodenBoat*, May/June 2012.

———. "One More Whaleboat," *WoodenBoat*, March/April 2003.

Laing, Alexander. *American Ships*. New York: American Heritage Press, 1971.

Leavitt, John F. *The* Charles W. Morgan. Mystic: Mystic Seaport, 1998.

Lee, Lance, and Bruce Halabisky. *Twice Round the Loggerhead: The Culture of Whaling in the Azores*. Stony Creek: Leete's Island Books, 1999.

Lubbock, Basil. *The Arctic Whalers*. Glasgow: Brown, Son and Ferguson, 1937.

"Making Oars for the *Morgan*'s Boats," *The Log of Mystic Seaport*, Winter 1981.

Mattsson, A. Alfred. "Fur Seal Hunting in the South Atlantic," *The American Neptune*, April 1942.

———. "Sealing Boats," *The American Neptune*, October 1943.

Melville, Herman. *Moby-Dick: or, The Whale*. 1851; reprint, New York: Penguin, 2001.

———. *Oomo: A Narrative of Adventures in the South Seas*. 1847; reprint, New York: Penguin, 2007.

Mitman, Carl W., ed. *Catalogue of the Watercraft Collection in the United States National Museum*. Washington: Government Printing Office, 1923.

Murdoch, W.G. Burn. *From Edinburgh to the Antarctic*. London: Longmans, Green and Co., 1894.

Murphy, Robert Cushman. *A Dead Whale or a Stove Boat*. Boston: Houghton Mifflin Co., 1967.

National Whaleboat Project Files, Museum Archives, G.W. Blunt White Library, Mystic Seaport.

Nordhoff, Charles. *Whaling and Fishing*. New York: Dodd, Mead and Co., 1895.

Olmsted, Francis Allyn. *Incidents of a Whaling Voyage*. 1841; reprint, Rutland: Charles E. Tuttle Co., 1969.

Philbrick, Nathaniel. *In the Heart of the Sea: The Tragedy of the Whaleship* Essex. New York: Viking Penguin, 2000.

Purchas, Samuel B.D. *Hakluytus Post Humus, or Purchas His Pilgrimes*. Glasgow: James MacLehose & Son, 1907.

Pyle, Douglas C. *Clean, Sweet Wind: Sailing with the Last Boatmakers of the Caribbean*. New York: International Marine/Ragged Mountain Press, 1998.

Rickard, L.S. *The Whaling Trade in Old New Zealand*. Auckland: Minerva, 1965.

Ronnberg, Erik A.R.,Jr. *To Build a Whaleboat*. New Bedford: Old Dartmouth Historical Society, 1985.

Ross, W. Gilles, ed. *An Arctic Whaling Diary: The Journal of Captain George Comer in Hudson Bay, 1903-1905*. Toronto: University of Toronto Press, 1984.

Rudder, March 1900.

Scammon, Charles M. *The Marine Mammals of the North-western Coast of North America, Described and Illustrated: Together with an Account of the American Whale-Fishery*. 1874; reprint, Berkeley: Heyday Books, 2007.

Schievill, William E. "The Weight of a Whaleboat," *The American Neptune*, January 1960.

Scoresby, William. *An Account of the Arctic Regions, with a History and Description of the Northern Whale-Fishery*. Edinburgh: Archibald Constable and Co., 1820.

Smyth, Herbert Warrington. *Mast and Sail in Europe and Asia*. New York: E.P. Dutton and Co., 1906.

Stackpole, Matthew. "Building Whaleboats for the *Morgan*," *Mystic Seaport Magazine*, Spring/Summer 2013.

Starbuck, Alexander. *History of the American Whale Fishery*, 2 vols. 1878; reprint, New York: Argosy-Antiquarian Ltd., 1964.

Steel, David. *The Elements and Practice of Naval Architecture*. 1805; reprint, n.p.: Sim Comfort associates, 1977.

Tripp, William. *There Goes Flukes*. New Bedford: Reynolds Printing, 1938.

Venables, Bernard. *Baleia! Baleia!* New York: Alfred Knopf, 1969.

Whitman, Nicholas. *A Window Back: Photography in a Whaling Port*. New Bedford: Spinner Publications, 1994.

Glossary

AFTER OAR—The fifth or stroke oar in a whaleboat. The rowlock is on the starboard side.

BATTEN SEAM—A form of carvel planking with a narrow batten behind each seam between the planks. Each plank is fastened to the batten with rivets or clench nails.

BEARER—(1) A long timber set on edge on the boatshop floor that supports the keel during construction. (2) Stanchions between the davits aboard a whaleship against which the boat's gunwale bears. The boat cranes are hinged on the bearers.

BECKET—A short piece of line with an eye at one end and a knot at the other. Often used on the steering-oar brackets in whaleboats.

BOAT CROTCH—An upright fork for holding the two live harpoon irons. It is mounted on the starboard wale just aft of the thigh board.

BOATHEADER—The senior man in a whaleboat, generally a mate. He steers the boat when going on a whale and then goes forward to make the kill.

BOAT SKIDS—A framework over the main deck for stowing spare boats.

BOATSTEERER—The man who pulls the forward most oar and who darts the iron or harpoon. When the whale is fast, he exchanges places with the boatheader and steers the boat, hence the title "boatsteerer." He is responsible for the maintenance of the boat and its gear. In British whaling he is called a harpooner.

BOLT ROPE—Hemp line sewed along the edges of a sail to strengthen it.

BOW BOAT—The boat on the forward davits on the port, or larboard, side.

BOW CLEATS—Large thumb cleats on top of the wales, port and starboard, either just forward of or just aft of the thigh board. Their purpose is to catch the whale line if it jumps out of the chocks and there is no kicking strap. Also used in bowing on.

BOW OAR—The second oar. Its rowlock is on the port side.

BOW ON—To bring a whaleboat up alongside a whale for lancing. The bow oarsman takes the line out of the chocks and brings it back to the port or starboard bow cleat. The boat is then towed parallel, close aboard the whale.

BOX OR WARP BOX—A shallow, lowered portion of the foredeck for coiling the box warp. It is forward of the thigh board.

BOX WARP OR LINE—Three or four fathoms of line coiled in the box. Its purpose is to provide some slack line when the iron is darted.

BRIDLE—A span of line with both ends secure, the hauling power is applied to the middle.

CEILING—The inner planking laid on the frames inside the boat.

CHOCK PIN—A light pin designed to break under strain that prevents the whale line from jumping out of the chocks. It is athwartships through holes in the chocks.

CHOCKS—Heavy pieces of wood on each side of the bow forming a slot between which the whale line runs. A roller or bushing of lead or some other material may be at the bottom of the slot.

CLENCH NAIL—A way of fastening in which nails are driven through the planks to be fastened and bent back into the wood on the backside.

CLUMSY CLEAT—A notch in the thigh board used for bracing the boatsteerer's and boatheader's thigh while darting and lancing.

CRANES—Brackets that swing out from the side of the ship and support the keels of the boats in the davits.

CUDDY BOARD—The short afterdeck of a whaleboat. Various gear is stowed under and the lion's tongue is mounted on top.

DART—The term for heaving the iron or harpoon.

DEADRISE—The angle between the bottom and a horizontal plane in the middle of a boat. The flatter the bottom, the less deadrise.

DEADWOOD—Solid blocking fore and aft in areas where the stem and stern join the keel, built up on the keel.

DIPPING LUGSAIL—A lugsail with tack secured well forward of the mast. The sail is set to leeward of the mast. When going about, the forward end of the gaff has to be dipped to the new lee side.

DRUG OR DROGUE—A heavy wooden block or bucket attached near the end of a whale line. Its purpose is to slow and tire the whale. A different type, called a poke, is made of an inflated sealskin or blackfish bladder.

ENTRANCE—The immersed part of the hull forward of the waist.

FAST—Refers to the harpoon being securely attached to a whale. A fast boat is one with its iron made fast into the whale.

FIRST AND SECOND IRONS—Live irons in the crotch. The first is attached to the end of the whale line and is darted first. The second is attached by the short warp further along the line.

FLARE—Spreading outward of the sides of a boat, as opposed to straight or plumb sides.

FLEMISH COIL—A method of coiling line spirally, layer upon layer, in a line tub.

FOOT BRACE—A curved wooden brace in the stern sheets on the port side under which the man at the steering oar can jam his foot for leverage.

GARBOARD STRAKE—The plank or strake closest to the keel.

GIG TACKLE—Tackle attached to the bow of boats in the davits to secure them as the whaleship pitches.

GRIPES—Two sets of lashings passing around a boat in the davits.

GUNWALE OR WALE—An oak strength member running fore and aft on the inside of the sheer. It stiffens the sheer and is particularly heavy on whaleboats.

HARPOONER—Term and spelling used generally by British for boatsteerer.

HARPOONER OAR—The forward most oar. Its rowlock is on the starboard side. Though American whalemen usually did not use the terms "Harpooner" or "Harpooneer," they referred to this oar as "Harpooner Oar."

HOISTING STRAPS OR BOAT IRONS—Iron rods with eyes fastened at bow and stern for raising and lowering the boats. The eyes are forged at the ends of rods that pass down through the boat.

IRON—The term generally used by Americans for a harpoon.

KICKING STRAP—A line athwartships on the thigh board under which the whale line passes. Its purpose is to prevent the whale line from sweeping aft if it jumps out of the chocks.

LAPSTRAKE OR CLINKER—A form of planking in which the edge of the plank above laps the edge of the plank below. The two are clench-nailed or riveted together.

LARBOARD—Used on whaleships for port side in reference to position aboard the ship; e.g. the larboard boat is the boat on the port quarter.

LION'S TONGUE OR LOGGERHEAD STRIP—A fore and aft curved plank fastened on the cuddy board on the starboard side. The loggerhead's staff passes through a square hole in it.

LIVE IRONS—Irons attached to the whale line, ready for use.

LOGGERHEAD—A bollard in the stern of whaleboats for snubbing the whale line. It is mounted to starboard of the center line.

LOOM—The part of an oar between the blade and the handle.

LOOSE-FOOTED—Refers to a sail whose foot is not laced to a boom.

MIDSHIP OAR—The third or middle oar, the longest one in a whaleboat. Its rowlock is on the starboard side.

MOLDED—A measurement of any timber in a boat from outside to inside, as opposed to sided.

MOLDS—Temporary forms (five to seven) used in whaleboat construction, around which the boat is planked.

NIPPERS—Squares of canvas protecting the hands of a man, usually the after oarsman tending the whale line. They are safer than gloves which might pull the hand into the turns around the loggerhead.

PARREL—A collar or ring holding a running gaff against the mast.

PEAK CLEAT—A block of wood with a hole for the end of the oar. It is mounted on the ceiling or frames opposite the oarlock. The oar is peaked by sliding it inboard and jamming the end in the hole.

RISER OR RISING—Fore and aft stringers or strength members nailed to the inside face of frames. The ends of thwarts lie on them.

172

ROCKER—Fore and aft curvature of the keel.

RUBBING STRIP—A protecting piece of oak running from stem to stern along the outside of the sheer.

RUN—The immersed part of the hull aft of the waist.

SCARF—A joint in planking or wales made by cutting back the ends of the planks at an angle and lapping them. The joint may be fastened with clench nails or rivets.

SHEAVE—A grooved roller over which a line passes.

SHEER STRAKE—The highest plank or strake. Its top edge forms the sheer of the boat.

SIDED—The width of any timber measured on the outside. See molded.

STANDING CLEAT—Blocks of wood, port and starboard, fastened on the risers in the area of the stern sheets. The man steering can stand on these to increase his height of eye.

STANDING LUGSAIL—A lugsail in which the tack secures to the foot of the mast or near it. The gaff is not dipped in tacking.

STERN SHEETS—A short, unpainted section of floorboards aft to provide footing for the man steering.

STOPWATER—A softwood dowel driven across a seam to prevent leaking.

TABERNACLE—In whaleboats, the trough, partners, and hinged block supporting the mast at its base and allowing it to be lowered.

TAIL FEATHERS—Beams projecting over the stern of small whaleships for holding spare whaleboats.

THIGH BOARD—Athwartships plank on top of the wales in the bow with the clumsy cleat cut in it.

THRUM MATTING—Mats made of canvas and rope yard used to prevent chafing. Used on steering-oar bracket and on wales if thole pins are used.

TOPS—In whaleboats the sheer strake, rubbing strip, and wales, which are usually painted a different color from the hull beneath.

TUB OAR—The fourth oar. Its rowlock is on the port side.

WAIF—A flag used in whaleboats for signaling or to mark a dead whale. The end of the staff is pointed and barbed so that it may be stuck upright in the whale.

Index

Willits Ansel is a retired boatbuilder and author who lives in Georgetown, Maine. He worked at the Henry B. duPont Preservation Shipyard at Mystic Seaport for many years, researching and building whaleboats, dories, seine boats, and ships' boats. Willits designed, built, and used many small craft himself, most notably a series of exceptionally beautiful scaled-down eighteen-foot Chesapeake Bay skipjacks. Willits designs boats using the traditional method of sketching first, then carving a model from a block of pine. He enjoys reading classics, hiking, and painting abstracts in oil. Sometimes, boat paint is used in the paintings.

Walt Ansel is a senior shipwright at Mystic Seaport. As a boat/ship rebuilder and restorer he has worked on various projects, including the whaleship *Charles W. Morgan*, steamboat *Sabino*, dragger *Roann*, sandbagger *Annie*, and the Nevins yawl *Pilgrim*. Walt has taught at the WoodenBoat School in Brooklin, Maine, for fifteen years and currently teaches the John Gardner boatbuilding classes at Mystic Seaport.

Evelyn Ansel grew up in and around the water in Mystic, Connecticut. She graduated from Brown University in 2012 with a B.A. in visual arts and the history of art and architecture. Her work in art conservation and maritime heritage preservation has taken her from the Mystic River to the Gulf of Mexico, the Mediterranean, the Pacific Northwest, and back again. She currently lives and works where the Baltic meets Lake Mälaren in Stockholm, Sweden.

Notes

Notes